Export
Profits

Export Profits

A Guide for Small Business

Jack S. Wolf

Upstart Publishing Company, Inc.
The Small Business Publishing Company
Dover, New Hampshire

Publisher's Note: At press time, the telephone numbers and contact names listed in the back of this book were correct. We try to keep the numbers updated, however, please be aware that some may have changed.

Published by Upstart Publishing Company, Inc.
A Division of Dearborn Publishing Group, Inc.
12 Portland Street
Dover, New Hampshire 03820
(800) 235-8866 or (603) 749-5071

Neither the author nor the publisher of this book is engaged in rendering, by the sale of this book, legal, accounting or other professional services. The reader is encouraged to employ the services of a competent professional in such matters.

Library of Congress Cataloging-in-Publication Data

Wolf, Jack S.
    Export profits: a guide for small business/Jack S. Wolf.
    p.   cm.
    Includes index.
    ISBN: 0-936894-18-0 : $19.95
    1. Export marketing—United States—Handbooks, manuals, etc.
2. Small business—United States—Handbooks, manuals, etc.
I. Title.
HF1416.5.W65   1992
658.8'48--dc20
                                      92-41036
                                        CIP

Printed in the United States of America

10 9 8 7 6 5 4 3 2

For a complete catalog of Upstart's small business publications, call (800) 235-8866.

Contents

Foreword

This guide was written to encourage and help small and mid-size American companies develop export sales programs. It is organized around a format that has helped launch many manufacturing firms into new export markets.

Part I, "Think Export," helps answer the question, "Is exporting for me?" Its theme is to encourage you to consider the opportunities for selling abroad. It describes what it takes to be a successful exporter and how commitment in its many forms plays a major part in earning export profits. It introduces export finance early to illustrate the types of export incentive programs being offered by state and federal agencies.

Part II, "Getting Started," discusses the first steps to take. It describes how to identify a foreign market with export potential, how to research that market, including where to find information, and how to test your product in the market in order to minimize the risk of failure.

Part III, "The Export Marketing Plan," presents an action plan for entering and developing a foreign market. The major planning areas discussed are product assessment and adaptation, marketing channels, promotional programs and export pricing.

Part IV, "Sending Your Product Abroad," describes how to find and select a freight forwarder, the role and services of the forwarder, export shipping documents, and international shipping terms.

Part V, "Getting Paid," discusses the various ways to get paid for an export sale as well as how to minimize the risks associated with foreign sales: credit risk, transit risk and foreign exchange risk.

Recommended contacts and sources of information are given throughout. To save you hours of research and contact time, I have included in the Appendixes at the end of the book the names, addresses and telephone, fax and telex numbers of the important sources of help and information.

I accept full responsibility for any errors, faults and omissions this guide may have, and gratefully acknowledge the advice and assistance I have received over the past seven years from many individuals in government offices and in the private sector. Deserving of special mention are Sandy Thorne of the Myers Group, Frank O'Connor of the U.S. Department of Commerce District Office in Boston, Bernie Sweeney in SBA's Springfield office, and UNZ and Company. I also acknowledge the 135 companies who have worked with me over the years. Many of these firms are exporting successfully for the first time. Others are now in foreign markets that they were not in before.

Jack S. Wolf
Amherst, Massachusetts

Part I
Think
Export

Exporting Your Products or Services

You can find profitable foreign markets. The challenge is finding the right market for your firm's goods and services—and that includes overcoming fears you may have. Exporting is tough. No question. But it is no tougher than identifying and profitably serving domestic markets. There are different product specifications, plenty of red tape and jargon to cut through, language and cultural barriers to cross, unknown competition and political and financial risks unfamiliar to most business owners.

U.S. Department of Commerce

Fortunately, there is also plenty of help in jumping these hurdles. The U.S. Department of Commerce is a principal source of information and help to the neophyte exporter. DOC has district offices in major cities across the United States. There, professional trade specialists will

- assess your company's export potential
- provide one-on-one counseling
- use key trade statistics and market research to help you determine your best potential markets
- arrange for customized overseas surveys to zero in on your product's potential market and competition abroad
- provide valuable mailing lists of overseas buyers, agents, and other business contacts
- help you participate in trade events held in markets suitable for your product
- put you in touch with potential foreign buyers and agents
- obtain background data on your potential foreign partners and customers
- make available daily foreign sales leads though an electronic bulletin board
- help you use the office's trade-oriented commercial library.

See Appendix A for a complete listing of the Department of Commerce's International Trade Administration District Offices.

Foreign sales corporation (FSC)

If you decide to export, a 1984 law allows the creation of foreign sales corporations. An FSC is an income-tax saving benefit designed by the federal government to encourage the export of U.S. products. An FSC provides 15 to 32 percent permanent tax savings on income earned from export of American products. When your annual export sales exceed $100,000, you should consider forming an FSC or joining an existing one. There are firms that specialize in organizing FSCs.

An FSC must be headquartered in a qualified foreign country with an IRS-approved tax information exchange agreement, or in a U.S. possession (Virgin Islands, American Samoa, Guam or the Northern Marianas).

There are three types of FSC: a small FSC, with export sales volume of less than $5 million, a regular FSC, with export sales volume of more than $5 million, and the joint or shared FSC.

The joint FSC is the preferred form for small exporters, with export sales of $100,000 to $300,000. It may have up to 25 shareholder companies, who share the cost of opening and maintaining the FSC office. Profits and tax benefits are *not* shared.

Steps to take

Your most difficult task is to decide to enter foreign markets in the first place. Once that decision has been made, the other steps follow in an orderly sequence. They are the steps that form the structure of this export marketing guide:

1. Making the export decision.

2. Determining what information is needed and where to obtain it.

3. Taking advantage of the various export services that are available.

4. Developing an export marketing plan, including selecting foreign "partners."

5. The mechanics of exporting, including getting paid.

Note that you'd follow a similar sequence in approaching any new market. In effect, selling to foreign markets is simply an extension of your present marketing effort. You still have to make sure that the product (or service) will attract enough customers at the right price to ensure a profit.

Conditions are right to look beyond the domestic market and to consider foreign sales opportunities. While it may be easier to sell to customers only three or four hundred miles away, it may not be as profitable as exporting to three or four thousand miles away. For example, your product may be maturing in your domestic market, but be in a growth phase in a foreign market. For instance, India continues to be a good market for 64k microcomputers (and software for these computers) which are considered obsolete in the U.S.

The same principle of finding a need and filling it applies as much to marketing in foreign countries as to the domestic market. A manager with imagination and courage will overcome the barriers of distance and foreign language to find and serve a niche in an international market.

Experiences of Individual Companies

Small businesses make inroads abroad by their ability to develop products quickly and then sell them in well-defined market niches that larger companies bypass or overlook. Interestingly, the markets being attacked are beyond Canada and the countries of western Europe. They extend to Asia, the mid-East countries and to South America as well.

The brief sketches below describe actual export payoffs of some small firms that are now export converts. They are successful small companies profiled in the "Exporting Pays Off" section of *Business America* , the biweekly publication of the International Trade Administration, U. S. Department of Commerce.

LecTec Corporation, Minnetonka, Minnesota

Product: Electrode and medical tape systems (medical products).
Approach: Foreign trade journal advertising.

This 11-year-old company started its export push by placing notices about its product line in overseas trade journals. It located foreign customers and business partners by using the export services of the U.S. Department of Commerce. Company principals worked with personnel in the Minnesota District Office of the International Trade Administration (ITA) and the State of Minnesota Trade Office.

The firm is now exporting to customers in Korea, Taiwan, India, Norway, Denmark, the Netherlands and Italy. Negotiations are underway with distributors in Malaysia, Singapore, Brunei, the Philippines, Saudi Arabia, Kuwait, United Arab Emirates, Oman and Bahrain. LecTec recently entered into an agreement with a large Danish firm, Medicost, to produce diagnostic ECG electrodes to round out the Danish firm's product line. The company is also negotiating with Beirsdorf, a West German firm, to produce medical tapes.

R. L. Drake Company, Miamisburg, Ohio

Product: Devices that enable television sets to pick up signals from satellite dishes.
Approach: Telexing prospects; meeting prospects; advertising in *Commercial News USA*.

Since the firm's receiving devices were easily adapted with only minor modifications to European television sets, executives asked, "Why not Europe?" The sales manager telexed for appointments with potential agents, distributors, and other potential customers in Europe. He visited London and Paris for a total of two weeks and met 25 of those contacted. Five were signed up to market the firm's product. The sales manager notes two lessons learned: you need to let prospective customers see you and know who you are, and developing foreign markets takes a lot of patience.

In two years, exports have grown from zero to 40% of production. Products are sold in 30 countries and in developing markets in the South Pacific. Poland and Yugoslavia have also started to import. The ITA office in Cincinnati helped Drake obtain a validated export license. An advertisement in *Commercial News USA* generated dozens of inquiries from prospective foreign customers.

Thermal Bags by Ingrid, Des Plaines, Illinois

Product: Insulated, non-disposable bags used for catering and food delivery.
Approach: Participating in a domestic and a foreign trade show with a high-quality product.

This $300,000 company had only scattered sales abroad prior to meeting some foreign visitors at the Pizza Exposition in Las Vegas. Visitors to that show from England, Norway, and Australia signed orders worth $8,000. An English visitor suggested staffing a booth at an upcoming trade show in London. The company participated and wrote orders valued at $160,000. Buyers liked the high-quality, nondisposable, and long-life features of the bag. A $40,000 follow-up order was received from the English customer, followed by a $120,000 ocean-container order two months later.

The firm secured export financing assistance for these larger orders from the Illinois Export Authority and the Foreign Credit Insurance Association. Thermal Bags by Ingrid now has new customers lined up in Norway, Sweden, the Netherlands, Spain, France, Mexico, the Middle East, and Panama. Sales volume tripled in 1988.

Fulghum Industries, Wadley, Georgia

Product: Woodyard equipment sold to the pulp and paper industry.
Approach: Assistance from District Office, ITA.

The company decided in mid-1987 to build an export program. In two years the firm went from zero exports to 10% of sales. The Savannah District Office of Commerce's ITA helped in identifying and locating overseas agents and providing country marketing studies. Chile become the first foreign market. Two additional markets, Australia and New Zealand, are the focus of country research.

Production economies were achieved by licensing local manufacturers in these markets to manufacture components for Fulghum equipment. Four new agents have been identified and scheduled for interviewing during an upcoming trip. W. D. Lampp, Director of Marketing, advises, "If your products have value in the United States, chances they will have value in foreign markets too. It is imperative when you start exporting not to be scared away by the complications inherent in exporting. It not as complicated as you think, and it's been very profitable for us."

Quality Control Instruments (QCI), Oak Ridge, Tennessee

Product: Instruments serving the metal-plating and metallurgy industries.
Approach: Journal advertising; trade show involvement; Matchmaker program participation.

Quality Control Instruments is six years old and has four employees. Exports to 26 foreign markets represent one-third of total production. The notoriously difficult Japanese market is the best. The Japanese business was started with an advertisement in a Japanese trade journal. Executives of Nippon Steel met with QCI President Roger Derby at a trade show in Philadelphia in 1986. That meeting led to orders currently running at $5,000 monthly.

The company has sales agents in Hong Kong, South Korea, Singapore, the Philippines and Taiwan. To prepare for the Republic of China market, Derby is studying conversational Chinese.

Export success has led to the development of a new foreign-voltage battery charger used for batteries in QCI's products. The charger is enclosed with shipments of the company's instruments. This merchandising convenience for the firm's foreign customers has created a new market: selling the charger to other U.S. instrument manufacturers to enclose with their overseas shipments.

QCI participated in the Department of Commerce's Matchmaker program in the United Kingdom, the Korea Trade Promotion Corporation (KORTA) U.S. Products Show and Analytical '87 in Mexico City.

Osprey Corporation, Atlanta, Georgia

Product: Air filtration and dust collection equipment for the textile industry.
Approach: A helpful, knowledgeable freight forwarder; customer service.

This 14- year-old company serves a mature and limited industry and is vulnerable to cycles of price competition. They exported only 5% of production in 1980. Exports in 1988 were 50% of production, as a result of a successful customer service program and effective and continuous communication with foreign buyers. Osprey's most helpful connection was a freight forwarder who handled much of the necessary paperwork, language translations, and export regulations.

John Cork, President and Director of Marketing, visits foreign customers frequently. He says, "A small company can often be more attentive to a foreign customer than a larger, more regimented organization. Patience and attention to detail will pay off in future sales. If you treat exporting seriously, it will take your company to a more favorable position, both domestically and internationally."

Small exporters such as these six companies are discovering that they can be competitive abroad. The managements of many small companies have long felt that exporting was only for larger firms. As a greater number of small-company success stories are heard, however, first-time exporters and others who decide to expand into new markets are seeking assistance from stepped-up efforts by the U.S. Department of Commerce, port authorities, trade associations, state agencies and consultants.

What are the Major Benefits?

Here are examples of the major benefits to be gained from exporting:

• *New opportunities for growth.* Aqua Leisure, a manufacturer of fins, snorkels and other water sport products, believed the Mexican market represented a good opportunity to increase sales. An investigation of consumer market segments, channels of distribution, competition, current pricing levels and margins has prompted the firm to develop a comprehensive plan for exporting to Mexico.

• *Fixed costs spread over over a larger sales base.* Asher Benjamin, a small manufacturer of high-quality furniture, identified Japan as an emerging market, reflecting a growing acceptance of exceptionally well-made western style furniture. Additional unit output was estimated to reduce fixed unit costs by more than 20 percent. A favorable study of the market was followed by a new and successful first-time export program.

• *Extending the life of a product.* Totsy Manufacturing Company, a successful producer and marketer of dolls and doll accessories, researched the United Kingdom and discovered that acceptance of fashion dolls in the U. K. lagged the United States. Product and package adaptations were instituted, resulting in a new upswing in sales for one of their key product lines.

• *New and improved product designs.* Product improvements result from a broader customer base and new and diverse customer requirements. WINCO Interior Trim, manufacturers of wooden moldings and trims, discovered that housing and room designs in Japan required many new additions to their basic stock line. These additions found substantial acceptance in parts of the domestic market as well.

• *Improvement in domestic image.* Bunn-O-Matic, Inc., sold four coffeemakers to a West German kitchen-installer who will tranship them to the Soviet Union for use in the new McDonald's fast food outlet. Jack Schleyhahn, Bunn's Export Sales Manager, hopes this installation will lead to additional sales in that country. When Bunn-O-Matic started exporting 15 years ago, foreign sales were negligible. Today, the company has 30 overseas distributors covering 100 countries. A Bunn-O-Matic coffee maker will be seen in Paris, London, Oslo and other major cities in the world, a fact of importance to the firm's U. S. customers.

• *Offset of seasonal sales variations.* Lunt Silversmiths, a quality manufacturer of silver plate, flatware and baby-gift items offset a U. S. seasonal sales pattern by exporting into foreign markets, resulting in less fluctuation in production levels and cash flow.

• *An alternative to intense foreign competition in the United States.* Artmor Plastics Corporation is a major exporter of industrial processing aids such as production tools and dies, rewind caps for tubes and cones and injection moldings used by the textile industry and in the production of paper, rubber, and optical packaging. Although U.S. sales in this industry suffered considerably from import competition during the 1980s, Artmor concentrated on export opportunities and doubled sales during this time. Exports sold directly to industrial customers in Greece, Australia, Canada and other markets now account for 11% of total sales.

What is Required to Succeed?

Following are questions to ask yourself as you ponder the readiness of your firm to launch a successful export effort.

1. Can your firm supply products to *both* domestic and foreign markets on a sustained basis? If it can't now, when will it be able to? What is involved in achieving this capability? If you are operating at 75 or 80 percent of capacity, you enjoy a safety margin that is adequate for expansion into foreign markets.

2. Can you finance export sales? An investment will be required up front to finance an export program, since payment from foreign customers often comes later than domestic payments. How much flexibility do you have on the finance side of the business? There will be additional costs associated with carrying inventory in advance of sales. Additionally, there will be costs associated with preparing catalogs and price sheets, translation services, facsimile transmissions, bank and freight forwarding fees, foreign travel and acquiring market information. Make reasoned estimates for these added costs. Then check them with marketing managers of other firms in your industry who are exporting.

3. Are you willing to take considered risks? The risks associated with exporting include not getting paid promptly, the possibility that your product will be handled poorly, the reliance upon distant intermediaries and questionable distributor or agent actions. These risks can be minimized by thoughtful planning and the follow-through of managerial commitment.

4. What is the level of your firm's commitment to exporting? This is the most critical element. Without commitment, the risk of failure increases substantially. Top management, especially, must be absolutely committed to exporting. A half-hearted effort is likely to fail because program planning, marketing adjustments, financial support and organizational assignments are not high priority. Attention to the domestic market will likely dominate. That translated brochure, the planning for the German trade show booth, or the preparation of that new publicity release for foreign editors will be left undone.

More on Commitment

• Commitment is shown by perseverance and patience over a long time. Foreign market development and the creation and nurturing of solid relationships with foreign buyers is a lengthy process.

• Commitment involves extensive market research. As a serious exporter you must appreciate the importance of seeking out the necessary market information: competition, product/service adaptations, and prospective buyers/users. Market research is a vital and on-going activity. This guide provides specifics on how to find export market research information.

• Commitment extends to a willingness to reorganize your firm. Someone will have to deal with documentation paperwork, inland and international transportation arrangements, foreign correspondence and relations with export intermediaries. A well-organized executive secretary reporting to top management can make a big difference. Sandra Thorne of the Meyers Group, a renowned freight-forwarding and customs house brokerage firm, lists this particular requirement in her short list of the "best pieces of advice to give to the new exporter." In the beginning, many companies rely extensively on third parties.

• Commitment is also expressed by adaptability in two forms: cultural and product.

Cultural adaptability refers to learning how values, norms, superstitions, expectations and business customs vary dramatically between nations. A major lesson to learn early is that many business deals have never materialized because of blunders committed by American managers.

The mistakes of a marketing manager of a mid-size telecommunications component manufacturer who traveled to Saudi Arabia probably cost his company a contract with the Saudi government. He displayed his frustrations regarding the hour or more waits to see those in the appropriate agency. He became annoyed to be told early in the day to return for additional talks. His rush to discuss contract details was the wrong approach completely. His hosts reacted adversely to his aggressive, ill-timed selling tactics. He failed to realize the importance of patience. He did not attempt to build a personal relationship with the agency head and his associates. Just prior to returning home he reviewed his two-week experiences with the commercial officer in the U.S. embassy. It was then he learned too late that he had undoubtedly come across as a rude, arrogant and insensitive American. It is important to learn about a market and its culture before attempting to do business there.

Product adaptability requires fitting products to target markets. This refers not just to the more obvious things such as electric voltage variations and metric measurements, but to less obvious adaptations such as sweetness levels, carburetor adjustment settings for desert climates and brand names that spell trouble when interpreted in a host language. New labels may be required to conform to different-size measurements, fabric content or care instructions. Packages and products may have to be changed because in some countries certain colors have negative connotations.

Examples of actual product adaptations illustrate the importance of product fit:

• Nike, Inc., discovered that in European countries jogging is not accepted to the extent it is in the United States. However, since soccer is a favored sport, the company designed a soccer shoe for export to the European market.

• A large orange juice exporting cooperative had to reformulate the beverage to conform to consumer preference in Taiwan for a sweeter drink.

• A major soup manufacturer attempted to market its condensed soups in the United Kingdom. Sales languished until water was added. Consumers in that market were accustomed to buying canned soup that was similar to others found on store shelves.

• A major refrigerator manufacturer failed to dent the Japanese market until it quieted the motor, which made too much noise through the paper-thin walls of the typical Japanese home.

It is important to grasp the importance of commitment *early*. A successful export venture takes time. Without commitment the necessary investment of time, money and effort to build solid channel relationships and buyer and user awareness will not be made. Failure abroad is not due to a dearth of prospective customers. Successes abroad are realized by taking the time to find the most appropriate markets and then displaying the perseverance and adaptability to earn payoffs from these new customers.

Test Your Readiness

Test yourself and your firm's state of readiness for export by the criteria below. If you answer "yes" to 7 out of 10 criteria you and your firm are prime candidates for marketing abroad. Note: One of the seven "yes" responses *must* be recorded for number 1. An export effort should not be attempted without the chief executive's strong support.

Readiness criteria	*Yes*	*No*
CEO commitment to export	___	___
Quality product	___	___
Cultural adaptability	___	___
Product adaptability	___	___
Personnel reassignment for export	___	___
Market research	___	___
Working capital condition	___	___
Adequate plant capacity	___	___
Foreign competition in U.S. market	___	___
Proprietary product with differentiating design/performance characteristics	___	___

Sources of Funding

There are several programs available to smaller businesses for financing to conduct research, finance production and extend credit to foreign buyers. Many of these programs work through commercial banks. And some banks will apply to an international loan program on an exporter's behalf.

The U. S. Small Business Administration (SBA)

SBA provides export loans and loan guarantees for equipment, facilities, materials and working capital, and for specified market-development activities under SBA's Export Revolving Line of Credit Loan Program (ERLC). Export funding may be used to finance labor and materials, inventory buildup, foreign business travel and trade-show participation.

SBA does not finance a particular small business if it is able to obtain funds from a bank or other private financial institution. The new exporter should explore private sources of funds before requesting SBA help.

In addition to export finance programs, the SBA, through its field offices, offers educational seminars and conferences on exporting. The Service Corps of Retired Executives (SCORE) program offers one-on-one counseling by retired executives with years of international trade experience. SBA's Small Business Development Center (SBDC) program offers professional staff counseling as well as many educational seminars and workshops. SBA's Small Business Institute (SBI) program, offered at more than 400 colleges and universities throughout the country, uses student consultant teams to assist small businesses with planning, problem-solving and market research. An individual SBA program of export assistance can be designed to meet your specific needs through counseling, financial assistance, workshops and training.

Eximbank (Export-Import Bank)

Eximbank is an independent U.S. Government agency providing export financing support for American exporters. It offers guaranteed working capital loans to qualified exporters. It also offers insurance against commercial and political risk through the Foreign Credit Insurance Association (FCIA).

Eximbank and the SBA offer a co-guarantee program to small business exporters. These guarantees cover 85% of loans ranging from $200,000 to $1 million. The funds are to finance labor and materials needed for manufacturing or wholesaling for export and to penetrate foreign markets.

State Export Assistance Programs

Currently twenty-seven states have passed legislation to provide export financing for local firms. Many other state governments are drafting export-assistance legislation to help small business.

A brief description of several state programs illustrates the export assistance approaches being taken by selected state governments.

Washington state's Business Assistance Center has created a computerized information system that allows small and medium-sized businesses to use telephone-computer connections to receive the latest information about trade leads as quickly as possible, while there is still time to make a deal.

Illinois organizes trade missions and participation in trade and catalog shows. Six foreign offices provide businesses with technical assistance and information on export financing, foreign trade zones, overseas agents and distributors, transportation and government regulations.

The Minnesota Trade Office offers statewide seminars and workshops covering the mechanics of exporting, counseling, export financing and the availability of a growing international network of representatives who help Minnesota companies identify profitable foreign market niches.

The Indiana Export Development Authority guarantees small business loans to help finance export sales. The Maritime Opportunity Districts offer tax breaks to Indiana companies that invest in and export from Indiana ports on Lake Michigan and the Ohio River.

In addition to loan guarantee and insurance coverage programs, the California Export Finance Office, drawing from reserves of $4 million, is authorized to guarantee up to 85 percent of a working capital or other pre-export loan from a commercial bank. The Office of Export Development assists both new-to-export companies and established exporters looking to enter new markets with low-cost trade show packages, overseas trade catalog promotions, and trade leads.

Those interested in learning more about state export assistance programs should contact the appropriate state office. See Appendixes, State Export Offices, which lists complete addresses for the export development contact in each state.

Canada and the Common Market

Three recent events will have considerable impact on U.S. exporting:
- The Free Trade Agreement between the U.S. and Canada.
- Europe's move to a single internal market by December 1992.
- The rising spirit of free enterprise in Eastern Europe.

United States-Canada Free Trade Agreement

The FTA (Free Trade Agreement) between the United States and Canada went into effect on January 1, 1989, and will achieve its objectives by 1998. The FTA proposes to phase out all remaining tariffs, quotas and duties between the two countries. It also erases many investment barriers and frees up trade in energy and services. The FTA has important implications for exporters because it will change fundamentally the way companies in the two countries do business with each other. Under FTA, tariffs are scheduled to expire on one of three timetables: immediately (January 1, 1989), over five years (January 1, 1993), over ten years (January 1, 1998). Successes to date have prompted an acceleration of tariff reductions for many product categories.

Canada offers U.S. exporters an unique testing ground. Canadians are familiar with American products. Common language, communication and easily accessible transportation make Canada one of the easiest foreign markets to enter.

To take advantage of market opportunities in the Canadian market and the changes brought forth under FTA, U.S. businesses should proceed as follows:

1. Get familiar with the HS (Harmonized System of Tariff Classification) for your product. HS is the product coding system used by more than 150 countries around the world to classify goods in international trade. Contact the district office of the ITA, Department of Commerce, to obtain your HS number(s).

2. For the tariff removal schedule for your number, more information on the FTA, and to request the "U.S.-Canada Free Trade Agreement Information Kit," contact Office of Canada, Department of Commerce.

3. In addition, get an Office of Canada clarification of FTA definitions for rules of origin and Certificate of Origin. The rules of origin are regulations that determine if the exported good qualifies for tariff treatment under the FTA. The Certificate of Origin is a written declaration completed by the exporter and sent to the importer attesting that the goods being imported meet their specific rule of origin. See Appendixes, Sample Forms, for an example.

The European Community Common Market

The twelve member countries of the EC (European Community)—Ireland, the Netherlands, Belgium, Denmark, West Germany, France, Spain, Portugal, Italy, Luxembourg, Greece and the United Kingdom—have committed themselves to integrating into a single internal market by the end of 1992. This unified European market of 320 million people will be the largest in the world. It will allow goods and services, money and people to move freely across the borders of the twelve countries.

The possibility of the EC expanding from twelve to twenty or more countries is likely. Austria, Norway, Sweden and Turkey have applied for membership, and expect to join in 1996 or soon thereafter. And, at some later date, several East European countries could become candidates as well.

New regulations will eliminate duties and tariffs, harmonize product standards and offer guidelines for mergers and joint ventures. Costly red tape will be reduced because businesses will be able to produce for the market without having to adapt to twelve individual markets with diverse technical standards and health and safety regulations.

What does Europe 1992 mean to U.S. businesses? Will a "Fortress Europe" emerge to protect EC firms from outside competitors? Probably not. EC countries do not represent a monolith. Language, customs and institutions vary significantly among the member countries.

Another reason external tariffs are not likely to be raised is that under the rules of GATT (General Agreement on Tariffs and Trade, subscribed to by 85 governments of countries accounting for 80% of world trade) the elimination of internal barriers do not justify general increases in tariffs for external trading partners. Such increases would have to be accompanied by compensating concessions.

The objective of of the common market is to increase the competitiveness of European industry. If they become more productive at lower costs, they will be more competitive in the common market and in markets in other countries. This is not to say that some protectionism will not arise.

What Should You Do?

Since the bulk of common market directives deal with product standards, testing and certification requirements, how should U.S. business proceed? (See Appendixes for names, addresses and phone numbers.)

1. Stay on top of the rapidly moving EC legislative process. One key document, "Business Initiatives in the EC," may be obtained from the American Chamber of Commerce in Belgium. This chamber is both an information source and an advocate for interested parties who wish to make their views known to the EC.

2. Contact the Department of Commerce for information about the Europe 1992 program to determine if EC-wide regulations cover your product. Check the list of EC 1992 directives available through the Commerce Department's SIMIS

(Single Internal Market Information Service). Another contact for EC information is Europe Now, Department of Commerce.

3. If an EC-wide directive exists covering your product, first obtain copies of the directive from SIMIS, then read it to determine what the technical requirements are for exporting your product there. Also see if any European standards are cited by the directive. If it does, it will give the appropriate reference number, which you can use to obtain a copy of the standard from ANSI (American National Standards Institute).

4. Ask your industry's trade association to provide an assessment of how the EC directive will affect members of your industry. Press the trade association staff to express membership concerns to the EC Commission in Brussels. Other sources in Brussels that can help include branch offices of the larger CPA firms. Also, the Delegation to the European Communities, the EC's Embassy to the U.S., in Washington DC, can provide information on the EC officials who should receive your comments on a directive.

5. Even if no new EC regulations exist for your product, there may still be other European or national regulations that affect it. You may discover them by calling the NIST/NCSCI (National Institute of Standards and Technology, National Center form Standards and Certification Information) at the Department of Commerce.

6. ITA (International Trade Administration) desk officers can also help in obtaining information about any EC country.

7. Another source for EC and European product standards is GATT Inquiry Point/Technical Office, Office of Standards Code and Information, National Bureau of Standards.

8. Trade development industry experts at the Department of Commerce have also been assigned to help U.S. businesses deal with the EC 1992 program.

Eastern Europe

With unbelievable speed, Eastern Europe is toppling its Communist governments. The rest of this century will be spent unifying all Europe. The rescue of the backward economies of Eastern Europe is a daunting challenge, with a staggering cost for debt moratoria, and funds for rebuilding and new investment.

Though it is uncertain what new order and institutional structures will evolve, the West stands to gain new markets. Although some large European and U.S. firms have already made major investments in selected East European countries, it will be a while before the dust settles sufficiently for smaller firms to venture into these countries.

Part II
Getting
Started

Screening and Identifying Market Candidates

Does your product have a market in other countries? For a quick answer, ask yourself how well your product sells in the United States. If it enjoys success in the domestic market, the chances are good that it will sell well abroad in comparable country markets.

Even in the case where a product's sales in the U.S. are losing out to products more technologically advanced, good markets may exist abroad where the level of technology is less. As a general rule, however, a me-too commodity without distinguishing features and consistent high quality will *not* find market acceptance abroad.

For many, the answer to the question above springs from prior business experience. Managers often develop an intuitive sense that identifies market opportunity. In addition to experience, a wealth of information is available to help identify and assess lucrative foreign markets. The new exporter will find many of these sources identified and detailed in this book.

Country markets

How does a small company with no export experience determine what country (or countries) might be worth investigating as a possible export market?

1. Obtain export statistics showing product category exports by country.
2. Narrow your choice to countries with good potential and the fastest market growth rates.
3. To refine your knowledge of these targeted markets further, consult with your District Office and the Washington D.C. country desk specialists of the International Trade Administration (ITA), industry associates, export service providers (e.g., freight forwarders), your state office of international trade, and port authorities. These agencies have research reports, data series and qualitative impressions that will shorten your list.
4. Conduct independent research on the remaining targeted countries. Seek information about
    - recent economic performance
    - lifestyles
    - aspects of the local culture, such as religion, customs, and business practices
    - languages
    - political stability
    - the legal system
    - climate
    - foreign trade barriers (tariff and nontariff).
5. Choose one, two or possibly three countries to research further.

21

6. Research the environmental conditions of the candidate market(s).

7. Test market in the candidate market(s).

Goods classification

Prior to making your first contact with information sources you should *classify your product line*. Many informational sources will need to know your classifications in order to search their data bases. Three classification codes are important.

1. The most common classification for goods and services in the U.S. is the Standard Industrial Classification (SIC).

2. A similar but not identical system is the United Nation's Standard Industrial Trade Classification (SITC). This numerical system is used to classify commodities used in international trade.

3. Another important coding for your product is called the Harmonized System (HS), a ten-digit system that went into effect in the U.S. on January 1, 1989. This system essentially replaces the previously used B and E schedule numbers that were used in compiling U.S. trade statistics. Now the U.S. is in harmony with most of the rest of the world in tracking the international movement of trading nations' commodities.

DOC trade specialists are able to provide you with your SIC, SITC and HS numbers for the products in your line. The HS number is very important because the exporter with a shipment over $2,500 must enter the HS number on the Shipper's Export Declaration (SED), a document prepared for each export shipment. (See Appendix, Sample Documents.)

After you have obtained these classification numbers, you are now ready to begin your information-gathering. An appointment with an ITA trade specialist in the district office of the Department of Commerce (DOC) convenient to you is the place to begin foreign market research effort. The trade specialist will help identify the most viable country markets, provide data to assess market potentials, retrieve data on countries and specific industries and describe DOC services for exporters. Refer to Appendixes, ITA Offices, for the address and telephone number of the district office nearest you.

Resources for Sizing Up Markets

Networking

The emphasis here is the importance of *networking* through individuals associated with the organizations listed below.

• U.S. Departments of Commerce & Agriculture
• Industry-specific trade association(s)
• Customers and suppliers
• State offices of international trade
• International departments of Port Authorities
• Small Business Administration
• Clues from domestic and foreign competitors
• Previous inquiries received from potential buyers
• Contacts made at national and regional trade shows
• Trade press editors (those responsible for media coverage in your industry)

Skillful networking is a time and money saver. Networking is not just necessary at the outset to identify the best markets. It is a continuing process. One should develop an efficient system for logging international contacts. You never know when any one of them will be extremely valuable.

To start, list the key questions that will help you identify the country markets with the best potential:

• the most promising country markets for your product.
• the size of the market for your product category.
• growth trends in that market for the previous three to five years.
• the user segments/industries that are the most promising.
• the major domestic and foreign competitors serving buyers in that market.

Begin with the Department of Commerce and proceed down the resource listing above until your questions are answered. Don't assume that networking contacts will provide you with all the information you seek. In many situations, hard, accurate data are either not available or extremely difficult to find. In many instances the contacts listed above will not be able, or perhaps willing, to provide the precise information in the form you would like.

For those questions not answered directly over the telephone or as follow up to a call, many respondents will likely direct you to sources of governmental and nongovernmental information that can help you rate and evaluate specific country markets. Many useful sources are available directly from governmental agencies and as purchases through the Government Printing Office. (See Appendixes, Agency and Published Sources of Information.)

Asher-Benjamin, a small, high quality furniture manufacturer in New England, began the process of identifying a number of possible country markets for its selective, high-quality line of finished hardwood dining and living room pieces. Informal conversations during a U.S. furniture trade fair brought the U.K., West Germany, and Japan markets to the surface.

A telephone conversation with the executive director of the U.S.-based furniture manufacturers' trade association provided copies of current trade press articles that described how Japanese home builders were planning one or more Western-style rooms in new homes under construction in several major cities in Japan. This building group had noted growing interest in western-style furniture on the part of up-scale Japanese consumers.

The trade specialist of the DOC district office in Boston further reinforced the Japan choice by describing an increasing interest on the part of Japanese furniture dealers in seeking reliable U.S. suppliers of high-quality hardwood furniture. This Japanese retail group had also observed the high-income Japanese interest in Western-style furniture.

It was the commercial desk of the U.S. embassy in Tokyo that passed this market information to the trade specialists in the U.S. district offices of the International Trade Administration. Asher-Benjamin's CEO did not realize that U.S. Embassy personnel would help an individual company in this way.

Through key contacts with informed individuals, Asher-Benjamin management identified and subsequently began to narrow country market options. It was time to research the Japanese furniture market in greater detail.

Selected Government Sources

DOC and SBA sources

Monthly Exports and Imports (Foreign Trade Report 925) is a new publication of the Department of Commerce that provides a commodity by country breakdown of U.S. exports and imports by the SITC product classification code. These data come from one of the best sources of export information available. The statistics will give you a good idea of which countries are buying the largest quantities of your product line.

The SBA's *Export Information Service* (XIS) provides product reports on over 2,700 SITC (the U.N. classification) product categories. If available for your product, the product report identifies the major importing and exporting countries by product as well as aggregate quantities and values involved. The largest 25 markets for a specific product are shown along with a listing of the major exporting nations of that particular product.

Call or write the International Trade Specialist in any regional office of the SBA to determine if your product is listed in the product category (XIS) index and to order the product report. No form need be completed to obtain this information; the request is by telephone. The report will be mailed by the SBA's contracting XIS partner, the Small Business Development Center, University of Georgia. Free.

Commercial Information Management System (CIMS)

CIMS is a computerized database of the U.S. Department of Commerce that provides key market research information. CIMS uses a data base composed of seven-digit SIC numbers. It can also be accessed through a "key word" system. The CIMS network electronically links DOC's International Trade Administration offices worldwide. Industry/country market research information is contained in over 7,000 extracts of completed research reports. Each extract deals with one specific industry in one particular country. An abstract in the database can be obtain in a matter of days.

A typical research extract prepared by U.S. & Foreign Commercial Service personnel contains subheadings such as the following:

Market assessment
Competitive situation
Market access
Profiles of end users
Trade barriers
Trade promotion events and opportunities
Best sales prospects
Statistical data showing total imports, domestic production, exports, total market demand and imports from the U.S.

Some sample abstract titles available in the CIMS database are
  Auto Parts & Accessories: Industry Analysis West Germany
  Biotechnology: Industry Analysis Sweden
  CAD/CAM and Robotics: Industry Analysis Canada
  Computer Demand, Competition and Outlook—Brazil
  Computer Software and Services—West Germany
  Construction Equipment: Industry Analysis Australia
  Food Processing & Packaging Machinery: Industry Analysis Chile

With the advent of CIMS, district offices of the DOC can also access electronically the United Nations and U. S. Bureau of the Census trade information databases. Hard copy reports will answer such questions as:

• Which ten countries were the top importers of my product last year?
• How much did each import?
• Which countries are increasing or decreasing imports of my product, and at what rates?
• Which countries provide my strongest foreign competition in each of the these major foreign markets?

Comparison Shopping Service (CSS)

CSS is a *customized* research service offering you a quick, accurate assessment of how your product will sell in a given market. CSS is available for most standard, off-the-shelf products for 52 countries. (The Commonwealth of Independent States and other emerging markets may be added.) Products manufactured outside the United States will only be considered if they are distributed and sold in the name of a U. S. firm and if their U. S. content is at least 51 percent.

For a modest fee, you get a concise report answering these critical questions:

• Does your product have sales potential in the market?
• Who is supplying a comparable product locally?
• What is the usual sales channel for getting this product into the market?
• What is the going price for a comparable product?
• Are purchasers of such products primarily influenced by price, or by other competitive factors, such as credit, quality, timely delivery, service, promotion, or brand?
• What is the best way to get sales exposure in the market?
• Are there any impediments to selling the product, such as quotas, excessive duties, or local regulations?
• Who might be interested and qualified to represent or purchase your product in this market?
• Who might be an interested, qualified licensing or joint venture partner for your company?

These are the types of questions you would raise during a market visit. Thus, the Comparison Shopping Service is especially valuable for small and first-time exporters with few foreign contacts and limited foreign sales experience.

The answers to these questions are researched by market researchers in the target country who interview importers, distributors, retailers, wholesalers, end-users, and local producers of comparable products. A customized report prepared by the U.S. and Foreign Commercial Service (US&FCS) is available to you in about six weeks. That report should enable you to compare your product to others currently on the market. That type of comparison is basic to assessing export potential.

Example CSS report

What does a typical CSS report look like? The subject captions taken from a report prepared by US&FCS in Bonn are shown below. The research effort focused on solid state electrodes for the West German market for a Minnesota manufacturer of medical products.

Market Overview
    Size of market
    Prices
    Foreign competition
    Market trends
    User markets
    Distribution channels
Market Potential
Local Suppliers in the Market
    Names of firms
    Market shares
Channels of Distribution
Prices
    Competitors' prices
Competitive Factors that Impact Purchases
    Quality
    Role of physicians
    Personal contact
Product Awareness and Exposure
    Recommended trade fairs
    U.S. medical exhibitions
    Direct calls on named cardiologists
Impediments to Marketing
    Import duty
Qualified Representatives
    Agents named
    Distributors named
    Private branders

Mountain Medical Equipment of Denver, Colorado produces oxygen concentrators and other oxygen therapy equipment. Milton Adair, President of the company, attributes

mitment to thorough research of a market before going in. Adair states, "It is important to learn how the industry is set up in a particular country market, who the key people are, how distribution channels are organized, and what options are best for post-sale product servicing. How does the new-to-export firm obtain this type of information? DOC's customized Comparison Shopping Service provides answers to many of these key marketing questions."

Country Consumer Market Research (CCMR)

A considerable amount of country information is offered by the Center for International Research in the U.S. Bureau of the Census in the DOC. The international database is a computerized data bank containing statistical tables of demographic, economic, and social data for all countries of the world. Sources of data include the United Nations and specialized agencies such as UNESCO and the World Health Organization, World Bank, International Monetary Fund and the Organization for Economic Cooperation and Development (OECD).The information in the International Data Base is relevant to the new exporter researching the demographics and social data of a foreign country market. Some of the categories of country data include

• Population and demographics
• Ethnic, Religious and Languages
• Provinces, states and cities
• Literacy and education
• Labor force
• Income
• Gross national product

Publications

Publications produced by the International Trade Administration and other governmental agencies provide specialized country information to assist businesses plan their export programs. The most useful of these that help assess particular country markets are highlighted below. (See also Appendix, Published Sources of Information, for source details.)

Business America. This international trade magazine is published biweekly by the U.S. Department of Commerce, Washington, D. C. Articles discuss a wide variety of international trade subjects, including particular U.S. industry trade opportunities in specific countries, world-wide trade leads, advance notices of planned exhibitions of U.S. products worldwide, sources of market information, and descriptions of particular facets of successful international marketing programs.

Foreign Economic Trends (FETs). These ITA publications are country reports that provide current business and economic data, including the latest economic trends and their impact on U.S. export prospects. FET's are updated annually or semi-annually by country desk specialists and US&FCS embassy personnel for about 100 countries.

Overseas Business Reports (OBRs). An OBR report provides economic and commercial information regarding a particular country. About a dozen of these reports of about 50 pages each are published each year.Considerable marketing information is detailed such as market profiles, channels of distribution, competition, suggested promotional approaches, and international trade regulations.

Background Notes, published by the U.S. Department of State, is another source of sociopolitical and economic information for a particular country, such as history, government, economy and foreign relations.

World Bank Atlas summarizes considerable economic data, such as population, gross domestic product and average growth rates of every country. The World Bank has 151 country members. Its primary focus is on project financing; that is, investment funds designed to improve the economic and social infrastructure in a country. Capital comes from donated funds of many industrialized nations and money borrowed from the international capital markets. The key point here, however, is that the World Bank has collected a substantial amount of economic and social information on individual countries.

The States and Small Business: A Directory of Programs and Activities provides contact information regarding state international assistance offices and, in addition, management, financial and procurement information and assistance as well, all at the state level. State governments are increasing the scope and variety of their services to exporters. In additional to export financing, other state services include export counseling, trade missions and referral lists. Most importantly, a growing number of states are opening up foreign offices to search for export opportunities. Personnel in state offices in foreign countries are on the scene and therefore in a good position to provide useful information about specific country markets where the state has a presence.

Port authorities

The port authorities of Massachusetts, New York/New Jersey, Virginia, Los Angeles, Louisiana and Mississippi's Port of Pascagoula, Washington's Port of Bellingham and Detroit/Wayne County offer various programs to help a new exporter get started. To illustrate, the Trade Development Unit of the Massachusetts Port Authority provides technical and marketing assistance. These efforts include:

• Assessment of a product's export potential
• Evaluation of a company's ability to export
• Marketing research to determine sales opportunities and to analyze competition in a foreign market.
• Development of a marketing plan
• Marketing plan implementation, including trade-show participation, assessment of distributors/agents, introduction to industry experts and to foreign buyers.

Selected Nongovernment Sources

In addition to governmental information, there are a number of nongovernmental sources and contacts that are helpful in researching the relevant environmental conditions of particular country markets.

U.S. trade associations

Every industry has one or more trade groups that represent and advocate the interests of those in the industry. Their staffs are informed about the major trends. They also know which particular member firms are doing exceptionally well in certain international markets. If the members of your industry are exporting abroad, it is very likely the trade association is compiling data on countries, foreign market opportunities, membership experiences and the like.

If you are a member of an industry association, ask your trade group staff to provide you with the foreign market information it is probably collecting. If you do not belong to a trade association, a reference librarian in your university/college or community library can assist you in identifying the appropriate trade association(s) to contact from the *Encyclopedia of Associations*.

Overseas trade associations

Overseas trade associations with offices in the U.S. can be found in the *Encyclopedia of Associations International Organizations*, which lists about 9,000 international membership organizations outside the United States. A second source of 35,000 international trade groups in 176 countries is *World Guide to Trade Associations*, published in Munich, Germany. For Canada, see *Directory of Associations in Canada*. This source lists about 18,000 associations headquartered in Canada. For Great Britain, see *Directory of British Associations*. (See Appendix, Published Sources of Information.)

Customer trade associations

Contacting relevant trade associations abroad may also be helpful in obtaining useful country and industry trend information as well as a fix on their memberships. And, don't forget to consider contacting trade associations whose members represent your major *customers or users*. These trade groups can help you assess that market and identify prospective buyers or users who are players in that market. Equally important, well-informed association staff can provide an overall picture of their members' marketing problems and their product needs.

Trade press editors

Editors of an industry's magazine or newspaper make it their business to keep on top of major trends, including opportunities for export. Issues of such media often contain articles describing foreign market opportunities. The editors themselves are excellent resource persons for information about the export opportunities of a specific country market. They may also know the publishers of comparable print media in your industry *in* that country market.

You will find the name and address of the editor of a particular trade magazine or newspaper in *Business Publications Rates and Data*. If you are a subscriber to a leading publication in your industry, the editor to contact will be named.

Freight forwarders

In addition to shipping and documentation, freight forwarders know the problems associated with exporting to particular markets. They are familiar with conditions in the country of destination, such as port and airport facilities and customs clearance regulations. Ask for recommendations from other area exporters, from your banker or simply check the yellow pages under "Freight Forwarding." A forwarder's helpfulness (or lack of it) at this stage will help you choose your forwarder later.

Chambers of commerce

Chambers in larger metropolitan cities as well as the Chamber of Commerce of the United States in Washington DC have international divisions to help promote international trade and to provide foreign market information to U.S. exporters. Some local chambers publish lists of international marketers in their localities.

The U.S. Chamber's International Trade Division conducts outreach seminars and information dissemination efforts through state and local chambers.

In addition, there are American Chambers of Commerce located in about 57 countries whose memberships consist of American companies, foreign firms and individuals. Their mission of promoting international trade is similar to the 38 countries with Foreign Chambers of Commerce located in one or more cities in the United States. Chambers will usually respond to inquiries received from an American company about market conditions, competition, and trade opportunities. However, their policies vary with regard to detailed and complicated requests. Many will charge a fee to those firms not affiliated with a chamber.

Worldwide Chamber of Commerce, Inc., publishes an annual directory listing U.S., Canadian and Mexican Chambers of Commerce, American Chambers of Commerce Abroad, Foreign Chambers of Commerce and Foreign Chambers of Commerce in the U.S.

(For addresses and phone numbers, see Appendixes, U.S. Chambers of Commerce Abroad and Foreign Chambers of Commerce in the U.S.)

World trade clubs and associations

In every major city and state one will find local and regional chapters of organizations whose mission is to assist members in their international endeavors. They provide a forum for exporters, importers, and service providers (freight forwarders, transportation companies, consultants) to get together at dinner meetings and other program events to discuss mutual interests and information needs. Members of these organizations are valuable sources of information about freight forwarders, packers and banks.

World trade centers

World trade centers serve as the focal point of international trade activities of a particular city and region. A WTC brings together the facilities and services necessary to transact international business. A typical center offers educational facilities, information services and exhibit and showroom space where tenants and visitors can display products and make buyer contact.

The World Trade Centers Association (WTCA) is a nonprofit organization of over 160 world trade center groups in 55 countries. An important service offered by the WTCA is NETWORK, an international electronic trading and communications service that links over 100 World Trade Centers plus 4,000 of their clients and affiliates. NETWORK was created to make international communications quicker and less expensive and to assist companies in finding trade opportunities and partners overseas. The system consists of an electronic mail system, a bulletin board listing offers to buy and sell, and a data base of NETWORK subscribers.

There is local access to NETWORK from 800 cities in 64 countries. All you need is a computer terminal, modem and telephone line. There is a one-time subscription of $250. On-line charges are modest and based on time. You can advertise electronically what you want to buy or sell around the world at low cost. In addition, 70 journals around the world publish the electronic trade leads for a two week period.

Trade development offices

Many major trading partner countries maintain trade promotion offices in the United States. Many are located in New York City. Some nations, such as Japan's External Trade Organization (JETRO), have established additional offices in other cities (San Francisco, Chicago, Los Angeles, Houston, Atlanta, and Denver). These offices are staffed with country and industry-specific experts whose major function is to promote export business from their home countries. However, many countries such as Japan, Korea, and Taiwan, which have sizable trade surpluses with the U.S., are under pressure to help U.S. exporters.

The *Exporter's Encyclopedia* (see below) lists U.S. addresses and telephone numbers of all trade development offices by country.

Publications

For detailed international information about individual *companies,* particular *markets* and specific *industries,* see the directories and indexes listed below. (See Appendix, Published Sources of Information.)

Canadian Key Business Directory contains detailed information on over 20,000 of Canada's most prominent business listings, including name, address, telephone, line of business, number of employees, annual sales, and names and titles of key executives.

Directory of American Firms Operating in Foreign Countries. American corporations with foreign operations, including subsidiaries and affiliates. Volumes II and III are arranged by name of country.

Directory of Foreign Firms Operating in the U.S. 2,200 American-based enterprises owned wholly or in part by more than 1,300 foreign firms. Grouped by country as well as alphabetically.

Europa World Year Book, an authoritative reference for detailed information on the political, economic and commercial sectors of all countries. Volume I contains international organizations and the first part of the alphabetical survey of countries of the world. Volume II contains countries K through Z. Six additional regional volumes have additional information on the geography, history and economy of the Middle East and North Africa, Africa South of the Sahara, the Far East and Australasia, South America, Central America and the Caribbean, Western Europe, and the U.S.A. and Canada.

European Directory of Marketing Information Sources. Official and non-official source material on business and marketing in 17 countries in Europe. A source for the international manager seeking to identify professional contacts or to get acquainted with the social and economic background of individual countries. Includes sources of published information, libraries and information services, leading market research companies, information databases, major business and marketing journals and associations and socioeconomic profiles of each European country.

Exporters Encyclopedia. Detailed information on over 200 world markets. This excellent source book discusses a wide variety of country background topics, such as:

Country profile: population, currency, trading partners, leading banks, country memberships in international agencies, trade authorities.

Communications: descriptions of telephone, direct mail requirements.

Key contacts: commercial offices abroad, domestic business information offices.

Trade regulations: licensing and exchange regulations, import requirements and restrictions, customs tariffs, free trade ports and zones.

Documentation: shipping documents required, *pro forma* invoice, bill of lading, certificates of origin.

Marketing data: agency/distributorship agreement information, government procurement, consumer protection, product standards, safety requirements, labeling regulations, patents and trademarks.

Transportation: entry and warehousing, case markings, principal ports and trade centers.

Business travel: passports and visas, hotels, holidays, health care, telecommunications, and transportation facilities.

Guide to Canadian Manufacturers. Lists the 10,000 top manufacturers, their lines of business, raw materials purchased, capital machinery used in production, products manufactured, number of employees and names and titles of key executives.

International Directory of Corporate Affiliations. Section I is an alphabetical index cross-referencing over 30,000 subsidiaries and affiliates with parent companies. Section II lists foreign parent companies alphabetically. Section III lists U.S. companies with foreign holdings. There is also a geographical index, a SIC index and a trade name index.

International Marketing Handbook. This three-volume source provides *country* information on particular environmental factors such as distribution channels, banking connections, advertising media, transportation systems, consumption patterns, industrial development trends and trade policies.

Japan Trade Directory offers information about Japanese companies and the products they want to import. Good company data as well as more general information such as a guide to the prefectures (governmental jurisdictions and authorities). Part I is an alphabetical import/export index of products and services. Part II provides company and trade and industry association information for direct business contacts.

Major Companies of the Far East. Volume I: South East Asia; Volume II: East Asia. Companies are listed geographically by country and alphabetically within each country. A geographic index and an industry index are also included.

Moody's International Manual. Information about major foreign financial and industrial companies arranged by country with alphabetical, industry/product and location indexes.

Predicasts F&S International Index and *Predicasts F&S Index Europe.* These are companions to the domestic volumes *Predicasts F&S Index.* These indexes annotate company, product and industry information from over 750 business publications and reports. Topics covered include mergers and acquisitions, new products, technological developments, and social and political trends and events affecting business in Europe, Canada, Latin America, Africa, the Middle East, Asia, and the U.S.

Principal International Businesses. Lists 55,000 companies in 133 countries, with addresses, decision-makers, number of employees, lines of business, sales volume, and 4-digit SIC.

U.S. Importers and Exporters Directory. An annual two-volume publication to help identify world markets for over 3,400 products. The alphabetical product index identifies the appropriate Harmonized System (HS) number for each product. The numerical product index lists HS numbers in sequence to facilitate identifying all known U.S. exporters of these products. The company listings by state describes these individual businesses further, including specific export markets. Additional international information included: a listing of foreign consulates and embassies in the United States, U.S. diplomatic offices abroad, international banks in the U.S. offering financial services, and world ports and port authorities grouped by geographical areas.

United Nations Statistical Yearbook contains socioeconomic data for over 200 countries covering population, manufacturing, export/import trade and the like. A
   comprehensive compilation of statistical series. Current volumes include data
   two or more years old.
Worldcasts is an annual series of over 60,000 abstracted forecasts of products for
   150 country markets. The SIC-based data are reported in four country volumes
   and four product volumes.

Researching Environmental Conditions

When initial screening using the networking sources just cited has identified a number of country market choices, it is time to acquire country-specific information that focuses on *market climate and market opportunity*.

In addition to Department of Commerce and other government sources, access to university and urban libraries is also important because of the diversity of country information research sources. Keep in mind that you or someone in your firm will have do some independent research on the most viable countries.

Basic guidelines for narrowing the choices

• Countries with the greatest potential may be the most difficult and expensive to penetrate. (On the other hand, it can be argued that attacking a smaller market can take as much effort and time as a larger one.)

• It is easier to export to countries that are major U.S. trading partners and that have many common characteristics (e.g., Canada and the United Kingdom).

• Previous special knowledge of a country and its environment will make the marketing task that much easier. Although not necessary, attending an appropriate trade fair in a particular market will give you a sense of how your product will be accepted.

Attributes of country selection

Which types of country environment information are the most important to acquire? The important areas and refinements are listed below.

The type of information to be collected depends on what you know about the country, your particular industry and the market served. For example, of you manufacture a consumer good, country data describing the householder market is important. On the other hand, if a business-to-business type of product is to be exported, then data that size up user industry segments is of dominant interest. And the need for acceptable product standards information is more important for consumer electronics than for stainless steel flatware.

Where do you obtain information about these attributes? Both governmental and private sector sources of information are used to acquire the types of information listed above. Keep in mind that the purpose of this country market research effort is to narrow your choice of markets to the best one or two countries that appear to be the most promising ground-floor opportunities.

Economic
Type of economic system
Gross National Product (GNP), per capita GNP
Central banking system, monetary and fiscal policies
International balance of payments, major exports and imports
Labor climate
Inflation
Living standards
Export capability

Demographic
Population characteristics (size, age distribution, geographical distribution)
Urbanization
Social classes
Income distribution
Educational
Literacy
Institutions
Attitudes

Legal/political
Political parties and party strengths
Political stability
Political freedom
Legal system and institutions
Government attitudes toward business and foreign businesses
Enforceability of contracts
Limits on foreign ownership
Intellectual property rights (patents, trademarks, copyrights)
Product liability
Agent/distributor legislation

Cultural
Religions
Beliefs and superstitions
Languages and dialects
Work and achievement ethic
Business customs and practices
Role of the family
Social mobility

Technological
Achievement level
Transfer policies and incentives
Product standards and testing
Infrastructure of the transportation and distribution systems

Banking regulations and restrictions
Currency stability
Foreign currency exchange
Repatriation of profits

Industry specific
Market demand (market size trends)
Competitive intensity
Number, size and location of domestic and foreign competitors
Number, size and location of domestic and foreign suppliers
Number, size and location of buyers/end users
Distribution channels, channel bargaining power of buyers/end users and generally accepted trade terms and margins
Availability of prospective channel partners
Trade regulations, tariff and nontariff barriers (licenses, quotas, taxes, customs clearance delays)

Databases, 800 Hotlines and Software

Databases and telephone hotlines are new links to the world marketplace providing country profiles, key contacts, company data, current trade issues, sources of assistance, market research reports and trade leads. The number is growing rapidly. Most major public and university/college libraries are able to access one or more business databases for a modest retrieval fee.

U.S. databases

Dialog Information Services provides annotated references to books, directories, journal and magazine articles using key words to identify appropriate sources of useful information.

ABI/INFORM, a resource for information on current business conditions and trends. Provides 150-word summaries of articles appearing in nearly 800 professional publications, trade magazines and journals published worldwide.

Compustat and Extel, two of the leading providers of financial data, have teamed up to create GLOBAL Vantage, an international financial database. In addition to company financial data, GLOBAL Vantage provides in-depth pricing and market related information on major companies in 24 countries in Europe, the Pacific Basin, and North America.

The Moody's Investors Service, Inc., database includes business news and financial information on about 4,000 public and private companies in 100 countries. New records are added weekly.

PIERS (Port Import/Export Reporting Service) compiles statistics on U.S. exports compiled from ship manifests. Lists exporters, country of destination, and product data worldwide.

PROMT (Predicasts Overview of Markets and Technology) is a leading multi-industry database covering companies, products and markets. PROMT annotates over 180,000 articles annually from the world's important trade and business press covering all major industries. The SIC system provides the base for PROMT's product indexing. Indexing is also available for type of information, geographical location and over 120,000 specific companies.

European databases

There is a wealth of information about Europe and EC 1992 available in database format. The executive body of the European Community, the EC Commission, is providing for the dissemination of information relating to the EC market. The most recent count indicates that there are about 30 publicly accessible EC databases and databanks. A few examples:

CELEX, the inter-institutional computerized documentation system for community legislation.

COMEXT, a databank on the foreign trade between EC member states and with some 200 non-member countries.

CRONOS, a databank of about one million economic indicators covering every part of the economy of the EC.

EABS, a reference base to all documents published in the framework of the Commission's scientific and technical research.

NTDB, the National Trade Data Bank, includes the best of trade promotion, market studies, and international economic data from fourteen Federal agencies.

SCAD, a bibliographical database of articles published by the Community's institutions or about the Community itself.

800 hotlines

Export Opportunity Hotline (800) 243-7232. This hotline is operated by the non-profit Small Business Foundation of America (SBFA) with the cooperation of a number of trade assistance and small business organizations, government agencies and private companies. Any questions SBFA can answer or information it can provide by phone on the export process, regional events, sources of assistance, EC 1992, etc. is provided at no charge. Only customized services involve modest fees. They include

a) The personalized Country and Market Report, an in-depth analysis tailored to your product or service and a targeted market. $15 each.

b) The Trade Leads Matching Service, a means of putting you in touch with foreign buyers. $40 for a single report.

Export 90's Hotline (800) USA-XPOR. A free service covering country profiles, key contacts, trade environment, current trade issues, country specific bibliographies, and state and federal assistance programs. This is a new program in Massachusetts and, if successful, will be expanded to other states. Responses to questions will be faxed or mailed within three working days.

Trade Information Center. 800-872-8723 (800 USA TRADE). Information on foreign market research, export financing programs, locating overseas buyers, trade missions and fairs, where to find tariff rates and export licensing requirements.

Software

CORE II, is a PC program for a firm's self-assessment of organizational readiness to export. It is a software system that guides one through a series of questions concerning commitment level, products and target markets. Based on the response to these questions, CORE II evaluates a company and products in terms of their degree of readiness for entering the international marketplace. Different courses of action are recommended for companies possessing varying degrees of organizational and product readiness to sell abroad. Contact Kennen International, East Lansing, MI, (517) 351-0500.

Once you have selected a market (or perhaps two) of special interest, the final research step is to test the level of acceptance of your product. There are a number of ways to do this, some quite inexpensively.

Start with the U. S. Department of Commerce. The DOC offers a variety of trade promotion programs that help new exporters test foreign markets and evaluate their export potential. You should contact your US&FCS district office about these services and programs. Ask about fees and prices, since they vary for each event.

Publication

Commercial News USA, a DOC publication, will carry your message around the world. It is an export catalog-magazine carrying descriptions and pictures of U.S. products and is distributed by U.S. Embassies to more than 110,000 screened business readers who are anxious to learn about new products. A listing will test a market's reaction to your product, generate sales leads and locate prospective representatives and customers.

Minimum price for a standard insertion with a photo is $250, a fraction of the cost of commercial advertising. Other insertion options will cost more. A listing in *Commercial News USA* will generate typically 30 to 40 overseas inquiries. Call your nearest Department of Commerce district office for an application form.

Lil' Orbits, Inc., of Minneapolis, with eleven employees, manufacturers high-speed silver-dollar-sized donut making machines. President Ed Anderson placed a standard insertion in Commercial News USA that attracted dozens of inquiries. Lil' Orbits now subcontracts 40% of total production into 26 country markets.

Foreign buyer program (FBP)

This promotional program allows you to show your products to foreign buyers in the United States. Every year FBP supports a number of major domestic trade shows featuring products and services with high export potential in specific U.S. industries. US&FCS officers at U.S. embassies and consulates worldwide recruit qualified foreign buyers to attend these U.S. shows either as individuals or as members of organized trade delegations.

These events, produced by private industry show organizers, are promoted by U.S. embassy newsletters, foreign trade associations, *Commercial News USA*, foreign government agencies, and import agents. At each FBP show the Department of Commerce sponsors a center that provides counseling, interpreters, multilingual brochures and meeting rooms. Contact your nearest district office of the DOC for an upcoming calendar of selected shows.

Matchmaker trade delegations

Manufacturers of products containing 51% or more of U. S. content are eligible for Matchmaker, a program that matches them with potential agents, distributors, and joint venture or licensing partners. US&FCS personnel do complete background work, including evaluating your product's potential, finding and screening contacts, and making arrangements for week-long group trips to major markets in one or two countries.

This program represents an economical means for new exporters to meet face-to-face with prospective clients. Thorough briefings on market requirements and the business climate are also included. For information on how your company can participate in future Matchmaker missions, contact your nearest U.S. Department of Commerce district office.

Suppliers of medical equipment who participated in a Matchmaker trade mission to Germany and Italy were so pleased with the results that many of them joined a similar mission that visited Canada, with stops in Toronto and Montreal. Among the 25 firms on the mission were seven New Jersey firms recruited by the state's international trade office. Two thirds of the members of the mission had never exported to Canada, and most of the remaining members had no previous experience attempting to sell in a foreign market. However, the competitive features of the products and services offered, combined with the creative sales efforts of the American participants, got results from the business appointments arranged for them by the staffs of the US&FCS at the American Consulates in Toronto and Montreal. One American participant was quoted as saying, "I found the quality of the appointments excellent. I hoped for one good contact; now I have choices."

Catalog and video catalog exhibitions

These shows represent a low-cost, low-risk way to generate sales or representation leads for your product. U.S. Embassies worldwide show your catalogs or promotional videos to potential agents, distributors or other buyers of a targeted audience.

A catalog exhibition costs a U.S. firm $100 to $300 to display its product catalogs and sales literature in 10 to 25 overseas markets. Fifty to 500 firms participate.

A video catalog exhibition costs a U.S. firm $1,000 to $1,500 for the development of a video presentation that will be shown in 10 to 50 overseas markets. Participation is limited to 20 U.S. firms.

A private contractor produces a one-hour master video show from audio-visual materials furnished by the participating companies. The presentation is in the language of the countries where exhibitions are scheduled.

In advance of a scheduled exhibition, overseas commercial officers in the US&FCS work with local chambers of commerce, trade associations, and other business organizations to sponsor events at which local prospective agents, distributors and buyers are invited to review the material presented by American companies. All visitors and trade leads are then forwarded to you.

This economical service is still another way to test the level of interest in your product in a particular country market you are unable to visit. Contact your nearest U.S. Department of Commerce district office for fee information and a current schedule of DOC's catalog and video catalog exhibitions.

BIRD-X, a Chicago firm representing bird and rodent control products and dental laboratory supplies, received 120 trade leads as a result of participating in U.S. catalog exhibitions. Mary Kisinger, the firm's International Sales Manager, considers catalog exhibitions a very cost-effective means of showing BIRD-X products overseas.

Foreign trade shows

Trade shows represent one of the best means of testing the acceptance of a product in a country market. A logical way to ascertain market acceptance is to exhibit products in a booth at an international trade fair that showcases one specific, or several related, industries.

DOC organizes a wide variety of special exhibitions each year in many countries around the world. Private show organizers work hand-in-hand with DOC's trade specialists. These events range from solo exhibitions representing U.S. firms exclusively at international trade centers, to U.S. pavilions in the largest international trade fairs. Timed to coincide with overseas buying cycles, the events have become international magnets for agents, distributors and end-users. Local country promotion and turnkey exhibit booth services are provided.

By taking an exhibit booth, a company is announcing its intention to sell internationally. The show catalog usually indicates the company's interest in finding an agent or distributor. Contact the DOC district office for information about the calendar of upcoming trade exhibitions. They will be included in the Export Promotion Calendar published bimonthly by US&FCS' Export Promotion Services, Trade Events Division.

In the past, there was a conspicuous absence of small American firms at Paris' annual SICOB (Salon International d'Informatique Telematique Communication Organisation de Bureau et Bureautique) Trade Show. This year, however, 43 U.S. computer firms displayed their products to nearly 200,000 buyers and distributors from 115 countries. Participation brought some exhibitors immediate paybacks. Patrick Lueben, Vice-President of Sales and Marketing for Computer Anywhere, Inc., of McLean, Virginia, reported orders topping $1 million for multilingual word-processor software. The firms exhibiting at SICOB got a feel for the French market. Many ended up writing sizable sales contracts.

Trade opportunities program (TOP)

Up-to-the-minute leads from around the world can be received daily with the DOC's TOP program. This service provides timely sales leads gathered by U.S. commercial officers worldwide from overseas firms seeking to buy or represent U.S. products and services.

TOP leads are available electronically through DOC's National Technical Information Service (NTIS). NTIS, a government research clearinghouse, is responsible for coordinating publishing TOP leads in many publications, including the *Journal of Commerce*. It also gathers information for the publishing of *Market Share Reports* and *Country Market Surveys*.

Many private sector publishers, trade associations, and other groups subscribe to the system and redistribute the leads in printed or electronic form to their members or clients (e.g., the *Journal of Commerce*). District offices of DOC also receive the leads daily and have them in file for the public.

When Commercial Officers in embassies and consulates overseas identify an exceptional export opportunity, it is designated as a "hot" lead. A "Hot TOP" lead is one with large volume opportunity, a limited time frame, or that fits a product category in an industry in which the U.S. enjoys some differential advantage. These exceptional leads are transmitted to selected district offices who in turn relay them to specific American companies in the region. Hot TOP leads are also distributed through the Economic Bulletin Board along with regular TOP leads.

American Trading Syndicate (ATS) of Escondido, California, markets a wide variety of products, including explosion detectors, surge suppression devices, inflatable signs and telescopes. The firm pursues exporting by targeting specific markets where it is likely to be successful. Key to the company's export success is the effective use of agents who currently operate in 29 countries. These representative are constantly seeking U.S. export opportunities. The company has found Commerce's Trade Opportunities Program (TOP) a valuable source of leads for new customers. Jeff Wohler, President of ATS, claims that their very best customers have been secured as a result of leads from TOP.

Other agencies

The Foreign Agricultural Service (FAS) of the U.S. Department of Agriculture has a worldwide network of attachés. Foreign marketing assistance is provided U.S. companies exporting food and agricultural products through FAS's Agricultural Information and Marketing Service (AIMS). AIMS has an electronic trade lead service similar to Commerce's TOP. Leads are available by computerized direct mail service and through subscription to *Export Briefs*, a weekly listing of FAS trade leads.

Certain non-federal agencies and organizations are also helpful in testing product acceptance in a particular country market, for example, trade missions organized by state offices of international trade and port authorities. Additionally, many state offices and some authorities (Massport in Boston, XPORT in New York/New Jersey, and VEXTRAC in Norfolk, Virginia) staff foreign offices in major trading-partner countries. These on-the-scene representatives will offer suggestions for testing the acceptance of your product (e.g., sending samples to a particular agent to obtain a sense of market receptivity).

Sales test

One reliable means of testing the market is to arrange an actual sale of your product in the country market of interest. This is a realistic test of acceptance.

From the Department of Commerce's district office or from a resource listing provided by your state office of international trade, obtain the names of export trading or management companies that specialize in your product category. These firms are intermediaries between American manufacturers like you and foreign agents/distributors or end-users. Try to arrange a test sale with one of these firms on a *short-term basis* with the express idea of testing market acceptance. (Avoid a contract that would create a long-term, exclusive partnership. It is far too early for that.)

An early sale of this type has several advantages. It will help defray the cost of market research. It will demonstrate that your product is saleable, whether it requires any adaptations and that it is competitive. Finally, you will have made your first export sale! What better way to make the initial step over the international threshold?

An alternative to using a trading or management company is to arrange a "market measurement" sale while participating in one of the organized trade missions discussed above.

Part III
Marketing
Plan

Putting Together Your Plan

Marketing planning is a major management consideration, even before production, because customer preferences and requirements in a new foreign market have tremendous influence on product design and product features. Modest or even substantial product changes may be necessary to sell successfully to customers in the export market.

But keep in mind that marketing also includes *after-sales* support activities as well: warranty protection, credit terms, maintenance, technical training of intermediaries, spare part and repair services, all are important for repeat export business. Even though it is possible to begin exporting as a result of an inquiry by an interested foreign distributor or buying agent, or a chance meeting with a foreign visitor during a U.S. trade show, most export success stories are based on careful planning.

Product assessment/adaptation, selecting a marketing channel, promotion and pricing are the important topics associated with developing a marketing plan.

A successful export strategy involves commitment, long-range marketing planning, and continuity. This is a summary of very similar opinions expressed by a number of business executives interviewed by *Business America*. They suggest that an export marketing plan should cover a two to five year period. They also recommended developing a written draft or outline of the major parts of a plan and a schedule of implementation.

"The marketing plan should be tailored to the foreign market," observes Roberto Rubini, Vice President of Marketing for Cissell Manufacturing, which makes industrial garment-care equipment. "We develop a plan to sell in Denver. We see the Denver plan is not right for Bangkok, so we develop a different plan for Bangkok."

Only a few years ago, IMSL, a scientific and engineering software developer, was a small Houston company. It made no concerted effort to enter the international marketplace. Now, IMSL sees itself as an international corporation with a growing reputation in overseas markets. Income from abroad represents 25% of its annual sales. Company president Walton C. Gregory states, "The company's most important technique for expanding its overseas business is tailoring its approach to individual markets—to their specific problems, standards, and international requirements. For example, we cracked the difficult Japanese market by gaining insights into Japan's protectionism, unique business etiquette, and ways of conducting business."

47

Planning process

Viewing export planning as a *process* involves three major steps:

1. Identifying a country market with export potential. (Part II of this guide describes how to go about doing this.)

2. Establishing export objectives. Specific objectives (goals) will differ from one company to another, but they might include

- An annual export sales volume forecast
- Profit/loss expectations (derived from a one-year export budget)
- Financing upcoming export transactions
- The number and type of channel partnership agreements to be signed
- Planned trade show participations
- Frequency of market visits.

Your company's export goals should be in line with your firm's capabilities, and the opportunities and risks identified during research and test marketing in the targeted country market.

3. Planning the individual elements of the marketing program, which requires answering some key questions:

- How do I prepare my product for export?
- How do I get it to my customers?
- How do I promote it?
- How do I price it?
- How do I provide after-sale service?
- How do I protect it?

Marketing planning will force you to look at realistic options, which in turn answer your key questions and help finalize an export budget.

What does the structure of an export marketing program look like? That is, what are the major decisions? (Note that they are not all that different from a domestic marketing plan.) And for each major decision, what are the *topics* requiring management attention and action?

Major elements of an export plan

Marketing Decision Areas	*Decision Area Topics*
PRODUCT ASSESSMENT/ ADAPTATION	• Product preparation/modification • Foreign government regulations • Post-sales service • Property rights protection
MARKETING CHANNELS	• Indirect channels: Domestic-based intermediaries • Indirect channels: Foreign-based intermediaries • Direct marketing to customers: retailers; end-users • Indirect market entry channels: licensing; franchising; contract manufacturing • Market presence channels: joint ventures; wholly-owned subsidiaries/branches • Finding and choosing channel intermediaries • Drafting agreements
PROMOTION	• Trade leads •Trade shows • Direct mail • Media/Trade Press advertising • Representative/distributor support
PRICING	• Factors that influence entry prices • Calculating ex-factory prices

Product Assessment/Adaptation

Even if your firm has a broad and diverse product line, you should focus on that part of the line that has the best domestic performance. Then determine what alterations are required to assure acceptance in the targeted foreign market.

Product preparation/modification

In many cases there is no need to change the product from that being marketing domestically. Or one of more of a variety of uncontrollable conditions might exist that dictate necessary changes in the product. These range from geographic and climatic conditions to cultural matters such as religious beliefs, difficult or embarrassing language translations, taste preferences, and preferred package dimensions.

A note of caution: Foreign representatives will often ask for product modifications to comply with their perception of the customer's needs. This type of communication is important. However, make sure that requested modifications are realistic and the market is large enough to justify the costs of adaptation.

Examples

- Homemakers in the U.K. are accustomed to preparing ready-to-eat soup. A market entry that required adding water to a condensed preparation failed to sell there.
- An offset duplicating machine had to be modified for a foreign market to accommodate the varying sizes of locally produced paper.
- A large agricultural cooperative marketing a fruit drink to Taiwan had to increase the amount of sweetening to satisfy the taste preferences of that market's consumers.
- A U.S. manufacturer of hardwood office furniture discovered that in Japan most office and institutional furniture is made of metal. But because open offices account for the vast majority of office layouts, a shift was made to export partitions and similar products to fit the open space configuration.
- Fertilizers are exported in varying formulations based on geographical differences in soil.
- Jogging has not developed in Europe as it has in the United States. However, the most popular sport there is "football" (soccer). A U.S. manufacturer accordingly redesigned one of its basic jogging shoes to be appropriate for soccer.
- A U.S. jewelry manufacturer is taking advantage of a trend in Japan where identification with one's school is extraordinarily strong. A new line of college and high school rings has been added for export to that market.
- An electronics firm provides purchasers with switches on its appliances to convert from 110 to 120, 220 or 240 volts, along with a box of adapters that enable

its products to fit varying wall outlets found in different countries. Instruction booklets are planned in several languages. These adaptations will allow this firm to export to a variety of foreign markets.

• A food specialty company with a growing chain of retail shops in Australia exports their entire line of U.S. baked goods with one major alteration. The company added certain fruits, such as sour cherries, to its muffin line because they are indigenous to that country.

Government regulations in the country where you wish to export may require you to modify your product. Tariffs (taxes placed by governments on imports) and other import regulations may be imposed to act as barriers to entry. Nontariff barriers may take the form of health and safety specifications or labeling and packaging requirements. Trade barriers may also take the form of quotas—limitations on the physical volume or value of selected imports.

The marketing of a U.S. made diet soda was held up for over a year by Indonesian authorities because that country's food and drug administration had its own testing standards for synthetic sweetners.

Sources of information

How do you find out about product-related regulations in a particular country market? A starting point might be to check with potential customers who have been identified as a result of your market research or preliminary market testing activities.

Don't forget to ask the International Trade Administration's Country Desk Office and the Industry Specialist about product requirements in your target market.

The freight forwarder who specializes in shipping products to a particular country will most likely have product requirement information for that market.

If yours is an agricultural product, contact the Foreign Agricultural Service, Department of Agriculture. Its Export Product Review Program assists agricultural product exporters by determining if labels, ingredients and packaging comply with the requirements of the country.

For information on foreign standards, testing and certification requirements, contact the National Center for Standards and Certification Information, National Bureau of Standards.

For a fee a standard search will be conducted by the American National Standards Institute (ANSI), the official U.S. repository for all member country product standards.

Underwriters Laboratories assists U.S. exporters in understanding and complying with international standards and certification requirements and procedures. Ask for their TATE (Technical Assistance to Exporters) program. UL will issue a mark showing your product's compliance with certain international standards.

If adaptation to the metric system is a consideration for your product, you can obtain assistance from the U.S. Department of Commerce's Office of Metric Programs.

If you need specific regulation information relative to Europe's common market, you can contact The European Community Information Service.

Department of Commerce's Office of European Community Affairs will also assist you regarding EC regulations.

The European Standards Institute is formed by the combined forces of the European Committee for Standardization (CEN) and the European Committee for Electrotechnical Standardization (CENELEC). These two organizations are the main promoters of using European standards for technical harmonization and in new technologies. American manufacturers and industrial designers should contact CEN/CENELEC to obtain current documentation in their areas of interest.

The ISO 9000 series of quality standards is rapidly becoming the requirement for success in the international marketplace. The series was created in the late 1980s by the International Organization for Standardization. This collective set of five technical standards is designed to offer a uniform way of determining whether manufacturers and service companies implement and document sound quality procedures in design, production, installation, inspection, packaging and marketing. This determination is conducted by a third party auditor. More than fifty countries, including the U.S. and those in the European Community, have endorsed the ISO 9000 series standards. One authoritative source of information and how to register a quality system can be obtained from TimePlace, Inc., Waltham, MA, (800) 544-4023.

One of the most important considerations influencing the long-term success of a company's exporting program is after-sales service. A maintenance, repair and training program must be included as part of product planning.

A U.S. exporter might engage a firm in the target market to service customers, at least until distributors can be trained to provide maintenance and repair. Some firms provide service directly by dispatching service personnel or having technicians stationed permanently in the country.

The expense of providing service directly is usually prohibitive for the new exporter. Therefore, some small exporters arrange a cooperative service effort with other firms that have similar service needs.

Allen Test-Products Division of the Allen Group, Inc., manufactures automotive diagnostic and testing equipment. William Lewis, Vice President-Export, states that the firm's strong post-sales support for its overseas distributors is a key factor in that company's success in foreign markets. This exporter sends out technicians to train foreign distributors' personnel on how to use and service their diagnostic and testing equipment. Lewis states, "The company's goal is to make foreign distributors as knowledgeable and effective as Allen sales and service people in the United States."

Property Rights Protection

Intellectual property is a general term that refers to inventions or other discoveries that have been registered with the federal government. Patents, trademarks, copyrights and mask works (designs of an electrical circuit, the pattern of which is transferred and fixed in a semiconductor chip during the manufacturing process) are considered intellectual property. The U.S. has a long tradition of protecting rights to intellectual property.

Many other countries do not see the need to have such strong protection. Newly industrialized nations in the Pacific Basin and Latin America have lagged behind the protection provided in developed countries. This difference has serious consequences for many commodities in international trade. Piracy and product counterfeiting alone represent a substantial annual loss of revenue for American firms.

GATT negotiations

Intellectual property is one of the more important issues in the current round of multilateral trade negotiations held under the auspices of the General Agreement on Tariffs and Trade (GATT), the Uruguay Round, which began in 1986. GATT's current members account for about 80% of world trade.

Other agreements

The U.S. pressed for GATT negotiations because of the lack of protection offered in other international agreements. Multilateral agreements covering intellectual property rights are the Paris Convention for the Protection of Industrial Property (trademarks and patents) and the Berne Convention for the Protection of Literary and Artistic Works (copyrights).

The Paris Convention,with ninety members, does not establish a minimum term for patent protection and allows country signatories to exclude whole product sectors from protection. Moreover, neither the Berne Convention nor the Paris Convention offer an effective procedure for settling disputes.

For current information on copyright protection through international agreements, contact the United States Copyright Office, Library of Congress.

Computer software

Computer software, a special concern of many U.S. companies, is protected under United States copyright laws. However, copyright protection in foreign countries is provided only if they have extended it to software. At present most do not, although protection is increasing in many countries.

Trademarks

Under provisions of the Paris Convention, filings for trademarks *within six months* of an American filing will date back to the U.S. filing date. Be aware, however, that most international agreements lack the provision that trademarks registered in one signatory nation receive comparable protection in all the others.

Trademark registration

Differences in legal systems affect trademark protection. Common law, the basis of the American legal system, bases ownership of a trademark on usage. In most other countries, however, trademark protection is given to the firm or individual that registers that mark. Some U.S. firms planning to enter a new foreign market have learned that their trademark has already been registered and is owned by someone else. Negotiation with the owner to buy back the mark must follow if the company wishes to enter that market.

Since a company does not need to use a trademark actively in overseas markets to register it (unlike the United States), it is wise to register your mark in those countries that your research has shown to be the best market prospects, even though you may not plan to export there right away. Registration costs are modest, ranging from $150 to $500 per country.

For further information on foreign trademark protection, contact the Foreign Business Practices Division, U.S. Department of Commerce. If you wish to obtain information regarding registered marks in foreign markets, contact the U.S. Patent and Trademark Office.

Patents

Applications for a European patent can be filed in all fields of technology, providing protection in most European countries. For more information contact the European Patent Office in Germany. Patent filing costs can be up to $2,000 or more, not including translation costs where necessary. It is recommended that you consult an attorney for assistance regarding patent filing procedures. The best sources to locate a specialist in international law is your own lawyer, your banker, local bar associations and World Trade Center recommendations.

Problem countries

Although not intended to be complete, the list below identifies countries where it is currently difficult to protect intellectual property.
- Lack of copyright protection: Brazil, India, Korea
- Inadequate copyright protection: Indonesia, Malaysia, Singapore
- Lack of patent protection: Indonesia, Mexico, Thailand
- Inadequate patent protection: Brazil, India, Korea, Philippines, Singapore, Taiwan
- Inadequate protection of trademarks: Brazil, India, Indonesia, Philippines, Thailand
- Product piracy and counterfeiting: Taiwan

Selecting Your Marketing Channels

You must identify and choose the right individuals or intermediary organizations to sell your product. The importance of this cannot be overemphasized. Although specific agencies and organizations will help you with considerable support and assistance, you must invest your own time and initiative in this area.

Who you select as your export partner(s) will be influenced by many factors, such as

- your previous export experience
- your level of experience and success in the U.S. market
- the resources you are willing to commit to an export program
- the size of your firm, which determines the need to delegate export-related responsibilities
- the intensity of your commitment
- conditions, customer expectations, and customs and business practices in the selected overseas market
- the types and capabilities of available channel intermediaries.

Direct or indirect: which is best for you?

Choosing to export directly or indirectly is a fundamental decision. With *direct* exporting, you are responsible for finding and selling to your own customers, shipping to them, collecting payment and servicing your product. (The customs in some countries, e.g., Saudi Arabia, prohibit direct contact with customers unless arranged first by a local intermediary.)

With *indirect* exporting, you establish a relationship with a U.S. or foreign firm or organization who will sell your product abroad. This means that you transfer some of your export marketing activities to a third party. However, even indirect exporting requires management attention and planning on your part.

Direct export: advantages

1. The exporting company has complete control over its export program—markets and strategies are chosen by the firm.
2. Profit margins are usually greater because they are unshared.
3. The exporting firm develops its own network and foreign market contacts along with a closer relationship with foreign buyers and end-users.
4. A direct approach may tend to sharpen your marketing abilities as a result of responding to new foreign customers.

Direct export: disadvantages

1. Internal organizational changes are necessary to support a direct export program. For the small company the need might be satisfied by a single export manager.
2. For the small, new-to-export firm, direct exporting involves more cash outlay, time commitment and risk assumption.
3. Opportunities in direct exporting may be limited to product categories that have a relatively small number of easily identified customers (e.g., commercial aviation and industrial machinery), or foreign firms which use a U.S. product as a component in its product line, or companies who buy a personalized specialty good such as customized packaging machinery.

Indirect export: advantages

1. A way for the small company to enter foreign markets without getting fully involved in the complexities and risks of exporting. An opportunity to begin learning about selling abroad without getting in over your head.
2. An economical means by which the firm with limited resources can penetrate a foreign market. Minimizes cash outlays and internal staffing.
3. Specialized intermediaries with proven international marketing track records who provide a variety of export services along with established networks of foreign market contacts.

Indirect export: disadvantages

1. A new exporter turns considerable control of foreign sales over to another party, which may result in limiting the opportunities to learn by doing.
2. The time and attention of the intermediary are shared with other firms.
3. Profit margins are narrower because they are shared with the intermediary.

Questions to ask yourself

How much control do I want to maintain over foreign sales, customer and product servicing, and customer credit?

Do I have the financial resources for international promotion and considerable foreign travel?

Is a backup foreign-based inventory necessary to support sales abroad?

Do I want to develop my own contacts and network?

Will the time and attention needed for export affect my domestic business?

Export management company (EMC)

An export management company is a private, U.S-based firm that serves as the exporter for several manufacturers, soliciting and transacting export business on behalf of its clients in return for a commission, salary or retainer plus commission. Its primary function is to operate as a manufacturer's export sales department. EMCs vary considerably in size, from individuals to companies employing dozens of marketing and sales specialists.

An EMC typically specializes in a particular product category and/or a specific country, representing manufacturers of complementary products in agreed-upon geographical areas. Measuring the results from an EMC will take time, perhaps a year or more. An agreement with one should not be entered into on a short-term basis.

Well-managed EMCs know the market for your product. They have established networks of market-based intermediaries and end-user customers. They know which trade shows to attend. They understand local shipping, documentation, packaging and product standards requirements.

A manufacturer usually seeks an EMC relationship so that export sales are handled as if it they were domestic transactions. Commissions are paid on sales. However, there are some EMCs that take title to the goods they sell and thus accept foreign customer credit risks. In these situations the EMCs operating margin is greater than when title does not pass. Look for the commission arrangement if you wish to maintain control over prices and customer choice.

"We try to demystify the export process for inexperienced companies," says Leslie Whitney, co-founder of Global Connections International (Globcon) of Poway, California, near San Diego. Globcon, an export management company that specializes in outdoor and sports-related products, works with a manufacturer to develop a basic international market structure that fits into its individual needs. "We help a manufacturer set up his internal organization—the procedures from order entry to delivery," Whitney explains. "We think a company should know who its customers are. Our clients consider us to be their international division. We assist a company with its export paperwork, such as invoices and packing lists. We instruct company officials on banking information and letters of credit, and on where to wire or transfer money. We also set up distribution networks for our clients."

Ninety percent of Globcon's revenues come from a percentage commission on the export sales they handle for a company. Consulting services make up the remaining 10%. This EMC exports for manufacturers in California, Washington, Utah, Colorado, Montana, North Dakota, Massachusetts, Connecticut, New York, Wisconsin and Illinois. The two co-founders travel overseas about half the time. They also rely heavily on the telephone and the fax machine.

Sunnen Products of St. Louis, Missouri, a manufacturer of machine tools and auto-engine reconditioning equipment, is exporting throughout Europe and in parts of Africa and the Middle East. During recent years, Sunnen's Export Management Company has unearthed new markets in Japan, Korea, Taiwan, Singapore, Malaysia, India, New Zealand and China. Robert Sunnen gives much of the credit to the company's EMC partner, whose market awareness and development know-how have produced export sales of 35% of the firm's total production.

Export trading company (ETC)

Manufacturers who do not wish to be directly involved in exporting have an option: they can sell their products outright to an export trading company, which then will resell them overseas.

An export trading company is a private firm, either U.S. or foreign-based, that provides a broad range of export services for manufacturers. The major distinction from an EMC is that the ETC traditionally takes title to the goods it sells abroad. This results in ETCs having a more distant relationship with a supplying manufacturer than does an EMC.

In practice, the operating differences between EMCs and ETCs are not distinct. An EMC may have a contractual arrangement with one manufacturer at the level of joint responsibility, while with another, the same EMC may have an agreement that is simply one of goods purchased and resold.

The Export Trading Company Act of 1982 was designed to stimulate U.S. exports by expanding the formation of export trading companies and export financing by allowing banks to invest in ETCs. Additionally, the legislation gives the ETC immunity from prosecution for activities that heretofore might have been in violation of antitrust laws. Passage of the ETC Act was stimulated by the success of a number of large, bank-related Japanese general trading companies. However, to date the hoped-for results have not materialized. Most U.S. ETCs are relatively small, specializing in either markets or product categories, or both.

Anthony Francis, President of Bartex Corporation of Portland, Oregon, an ETC, explains, "For the manufacturer, our arrangement is just like a domestic sale. It's clean and simple. We take full responsibility; we handle the shipping, the export financing, and other details. For our manufacturing partners, there's no waiting. We buy his products, and he's all done."

Bartex specializes in the export of irrigation and agricultural equipment. Recent annual sales have reached $13 million. The firm sells primarily in the Middle East, but has begun to focus on the Far East, Latin America and Europe.

Paper Machinery Corporation (PMC) was at a crossroads in the early 1970s when it saw limits on U.S. market growth for its machinery for making paper cups and containers. Its exports were small since the firm had made no concentrated effort to build foreign sales.

In 1975 three Japanese printing and packaging firms ordered 30 cup machines. John Baumgartner, Vice President, recalls that company officials believed that then their machinery might have good potential in the export market. The company's managers developed a ten-year export development plan. An important part of that plan included signing up a major Japanese trading company, Kanemapsu Gosho (KG), to sell its products in Japan and other Asian countries. PMC executives go to to Japan at least twice a year to consult with KG and to call on customers. KG officials frequently visit the PMC plant in Milwaukee. Baumgartner is so high on PMC's relationship with KG that he recommends that other U.S. firms explore similar arrangements as a way to crack foreign markets.

Advantages/disadvantages of EMC or ETC

Advantages
• a faster means to enter a new market
• a less costly way to get into export markets
• a way to begin learning how to sell abroad
• a means of selling overseas without getting fully involved

Disadvantages
• loss of control of one's international marketing effort
• sharing of time and effort with other firms' products
• lower profit margin

Buying office

A buying office is a domestic-based organization representing one or more large overseas retailers. The emphasis, therefore, is on consumer goods. These offices often plan domestic trade fairs that may present good export opportunities for testing new consumer items. Contact the district office of the Department of Commerce to obtain a listing of these international buying offices.

Piggyback marketing

Piggyback marketing is an opportunity to export your product as a supplemental product-line to complement the international sales of a larger U.S.company. Sometimes the established firm has organized its own export trading company and needs complementary, noncompetitive products. This channel arrangement is one of the fastest ways to sell overseas through an existing marketing structure. Latching on to a "piggyback" company probably occurs more by accident than by design. A chance conversation while attending a trade show might produce a piggyback marketing opportunity.

ETC cooperative

An ETC cooperative consists of U.S. export-minded firms producing comparable products. They join together to realize economies of scale and the benefits of being part of a group selling overseas. ETC co-ops are more common in agricultural product sectors, although they are also being organized in industry.

Distributor

A distributor is a foreign-based company that takes title to the goods it buys for resale to retailers or end-users. The margins customarily allowed are higher than the commission percentages of representatives, since distributors carry inventories and extend credit to their customers. Sales of the exporter's product are based on the marketing abilities of the distributor, who contacts the marketplace with its own sales force. A distributor is usually assigned a specific territory, country or region, usually on an exclusive basis. This channel is effective when nearby inventories, spare parts and product servicing are important to customers. Several countries also have stringent laws that protect distributors from unwarranted termination.

To sum up, a distributor
- buys your goods outright
- controls selling price to users and resellers
- assumes the costs of marketing
- usually maintains a field sales force
- delivers products to customers
- provides warranty and post-sales product servicing
- operates independently of manufacturing suppliers
- carries complementary and competing lines
- maintains an extensive product inventory
- offers customer credit
- is difficult to terminate (depending upon the country)

George R. Grumbles is President of Universal Data Systems of Huntsville, Alabama, one of the oldest independent computer modem manufacturers in the U.S. The company exports between 10 and 20 percent of its revenue through 20 overseas distributors. Grumbles states, "An essential early step for a beginning exporter is to build a group of overseas distributors. You have to work through nationals. If you send U.S. folks into a foreign country, you have to expect it will take a couple of years for them to find their way around. Instead, you have to find people who are embedded in the local economy."

The firm's carefully selected distributors market Universal's products to end-users and have helped the company cope with trade barriers, special requirements of highly monopolized postal, telephone, and telegraph companies, and preferences for locally manufactured products.

Racine Federated, Inc., of Racine, Wisconsin, manufacturers flow meters that measure temperatures and pressures in the flow of liquids and gases. John W. Petersen, Director-International for Racine Federated, states, "Flow meters were chosen for export because they are versatile products with widespread industrial applications. Also, flow meters are small and lightweight enough to ship by air. This allows us to ship all foreign orders within a two week period."

The company selects its foreign distributors very deliberately. "We are in no hurry," says Petersen, "because we want the right fit." To reduce the chances of a mistake, the company offers prospective distributors a discount to represent it on a trial basis; it signs a permanent sales agreement only when completely satisfied that its flow meters are appropriate in the foreign distributors overall sales program. Petersen is convinced that taking the time needed to accomplish this will serve the best long-term interests of both parties.

Sales representative

A sales rep is a foreign-based individual or firm, comparable to a U.S. manufacturer's representative, selling one or several complementary product lines. The rep, compensated with commissions payable after the foreign customer has paid, acts as your sales agent in an assigned territory for a specified period of time. The representative may operate on either an exclusive or nonexclusive basis. Upon receiving an order, the exporter is responsible for checking the credit standing of the customer and arranging for payment.

Several European and Latin American countries have stringent laws protecting sales agents and other types of middlemen from termination.

If you use a representative
- he places orders with you on behalf of buyers
- your payment comes upon delivery to buyer
- you set the selling price
- you create and control the marketing effort
- he usually operates in a prescribed territory
- he typically sells only complementary lines
- he arranges warranty and product service functions
- he may operate independently or similar to an employee
- he is usually difficult to terminate.

Learning that 50 to 80 percent of the perishable commodities produced in the developing countries go to waste, executives of the Elliott-Williams Company of Indianapolis, believed that they had a natural export market for their product, prefabricated refrigerated buildings. The company aimed its overseas marketing strategy at developing countries. By using the agent/distributor service of their district office of the Department of Commerce, Jay Lahr, Elliott-Williams Director of International Sales, obtained the names and addresses of several good prospective sales representatives. "Good overseas representation is the key factor in this company's export program," he indicates.

When satisfied that he has several promising candidates, Lahr buys an airplane ticket and arranges interviews with as many as twelve prospective representatives in, perhaps, three cities in the country market. It is this face-to-face contact that helps company executives get a sense of which agents can most effectively sell Elliott-Williams products, says Lahr.

Making the choice

Should you use a representative or a distributor? The answer to this question, for the most part, depends on how the individuals and firms who have been identified as your customers in the foreign market learn about and then buy a product like yours. Your marketing experience in the U.S. is likely to reflect the buying practices of your prospective customers in the overseas market. But there are other factors to consider as well.

If you wish to exercise more control over the marketing program, require a direct and somewhat technical sales presence, and have the human and financial resources to devote to the overseas marketing effort, then choosing a sales representative seems more appropriate.

On the other hand, if you manufacture more off-the-shelf products, require a deep or extensive inventory in close proximity to final customers, wish to delegate most marketing activities, and do not wish to finance sales to final users, choose the distributor channel.

Foreign trade organization (FTO)

A foreign trade organization is a state-controlled organization established to control a nation's imports and its "hard" currency reserves. FTOs are usually set up to represent major industry segments, e.g., scientific instrumentation, construction equipment, and metalworking. To export to one of these countries one must deal with the appropriate FTO. Information passed through the FTO is forwarded to the potential product users. If there is user interest, the exporter will be asked for more detailed information and perhaps be asked to participate in a local trade fair, which is essentially a technical presentation given for potential users.

The FTO buying arrangement is usually not that satisfying for new exporters. It is economical, however, involving only contacting the appropriate FTO and doing a mail campaign to users. Even here obtaining the necessary industry data is often difficult.

Centrally controlled economies and those with soft (nonconvertible) currencies, such as most former Soviet republics, eastern European countries, the People's Republic of China, and some developing countries in Africa, presently use FTOs as buyers of foreign imports. The unbelievable economic and political changes currently sweeping the new Soviet commonwealth and eastern European countries, however, may substantially alter or even eliminate FTO-type organizations there.

For updates on FTO buying practice changes, trade fair and exhibition schedules and industry marketing information, contact the East-West Trade Information Center, U. S. Department of Commerce.

The *Directory of Foreign Trade Organizations in Eastern Europe,* edited by Vance T. Petrunoff, is the first major compilation of export/import companies in eastern Europe. The directory lists more than 1,800 FTOs in Bulgaria, Czechoslovakia, East Germany, Hungary, Poland, Romania and the new Commonwealth of Independent States (former Soviet Union). This publication will help you research local markets, locate clients and establish direct contact with appropriate buying organizations, many of which may still be in place.

Curtis Instruments, Inc. of Mount Kisco, N.Y., manufactures instruments and controls for electric-power industrial vehicles. The firm exports to France, the United Kingdom and Germany.

The company began negotiations with an FTO and associated state-owned manufacturers in Bulgaria well before the recent political and economic changes in eastern Europe. One company, Balkancar, the world's largest manufacturer of forklifts and other material-handling vehicles, is the chief source of such equipment for the Soviet and eastern European markets. Curtis' product line was chosen over western European and Asian suppliers because its equipment can be used with rechargeable battery systems.

The company's earlier export program has now matured into a joint venture agreement, the first to be established under a Bulgarian decree liberalizing the nation's economic system. Curtis Instruments owns shares in Curtis/Balkan, the name of the new joint venture company.

End users and retailers

A direct international marketing channel goes from the exporter right to retailers or to the end-users of a product. In some situations this is more appropriate than establishing a distributor or representative network.

If, for example, you are supplying a component for the product line of a foreign manufacturer or manufacturing a customized or specially designed piece of equipment, you could ship directly to the customer. These are unique products which means that customers are usually limited and easily identified.

From the retail side, there are those instances when an exporter meets retail dealers at a foreign or domestic trade show, follows up wih personal visits, and then proceeds to export directly to these specialty retailers.

This is how Ed Kostiner, President of Kostiner Photographic Products of Leeds, Massachusetts, developed his export program to Europe. The one-time movie cinematographer sells high-quality photographic equipment direct to selective retail dealers in Belgium, France, Holland and other European countries.

For those interested in exporting to retailers directly, *Stores of the World Directory* lists department stores as well as the larger specialty retailers, by country. Data listed includes size, buying headquarters, branch locations, and names of executives and buyers.

Direct marketing is a more challenging and difficult method of distribution for small, new-to-export companies. It involves more management time and start-up money. Over a longer term, direct export also involves establishing your own in-house capabilities to manage exports. But this has its advantages because it will enhance your expertise and control of the export program.

Market entry channels

Licensing, franchising, and contract manufacturing are other, indirect ways to achieve a presence in a foreign market.

Licensing is allowing a company in a foreign country to use your trademarks, patents and manufacturing process to manufacture and market your products. Licensing is viewed as an indirect method of market entry because your product ends up in a foreign country without your actually shipping it there.

This market entry option is often chosen where country legislation prohibits importation. Still, U.S. government approval is usually required. This is especially true in those instances when transfer of sensitive technology is involved.

Licensing permits easy, quick entry into a foreign market without large capital outlays, and the risks associated with exporting are greatly reduced. There is a trade-off, however, because licensing is one of the least profitable ways of exporting. The exporting licensor is compensated with royalties based on a fixed amount and/or on sales. Most countries also impose taxes on the royalty revenue.

Licensing is a complicated process. Success hinges on mutual trust between the parties. Every licensee is a potential competitor. Although many U.S. firms have found licensing to be very profitable, there is the risk of losing control of your product and its manufacturing process. Before any negotiations are started, research the licensing regulations of the country in question.

If you pursue a licensing strategy, you must develop a comprehensive contractual arrangement, which includes product coverage, rights sublicensing, territorial coverage, tenure of the agreement, extension and renewal clauses, merchandising and management assistance, quality control, reporting and auditing requirements, and terms and conditions of payment.

Franchising is a form of technology licensing used mainly by service industries. A franchisor permits a franchisee to employ its trademark or service mark in a contractually specified manner for the marketing of goods and services. The franchisor provides continuing support services and in many instances the products used in the franchisee's operation.

Franchises in the U.S. currently account for over $600 billion or about 20% of our Gross National Product. They include outlets in fast food, day care centers, hospitals, dentists, automobile maintenance, temporary-help agencies, real estate, home furnishings and more. The phenomenal growth in the U.S. market is being matched by trends in the European Community and in Asia, and U.S. franchise companies are expanding into these foreign markets.

Studying an overseas market is vital. A bath-products retail franchisor who has had phenomenal success in the U.S. failed in Japan. Bathrooms aren't the fashionable rooms in Japan they are in the U.S. They are very small and not viewed as a room for decoration.

Robert Le Lamer operated a successful bakery in New York City called Le Croisssant Shop, furnished to recreate the ambiance of a Parisian bakery. The specialty: adapting French-style croissants to a variety of fruit and other fillings. The New York store flourished, which prompted Le Lamer to franchise eight additional outlets in New Jersey and Philadelphia. Soon thereafter came the opportunity to franchise abroad.

"We were not really looking to go overseas, it came to us. One of our regular customers was returning home to Israel and was unhappily looking forward to the day when his favorite croissants would no longer be available," says Jacques Pelletier, vice president of

franchising. That started the expansion abroad. A franchise was sold to Tel Aviv's Ramcor Ltd. Le Croissant Shop became Le Croissant Shop International.

Franchises followed in Japan. Discussions are currently taking place with parties in South Korea and Taiwan. "We are very small," Mr. Pelletier states, "yet when people talk with us they realize that we are very serious and that we can back up what we say with support. Consequently we have good relations abroad, and it is more like a family business than a multinational company."

Contract manufacturing is an arrangement with a foreign manufacturer to produce your product in a country to which you would otherwise have exported. The major incentive for a U.S. firm to contract for foreign manufacturing is to gain a foothold in an overseas market through competitive prices. The problem of marketing the foreign firm's output in the local market remains. Some type of distribution channel network must be established. Contract manufacturing may be the first step over a longer term in setting up a wholly-owned production and sales subsidiary.

Market presence channels

Some experienced, well-financed manufacturing exporters are motivated to give their firms a pronounced presence in an overseas market area. There are two channel options that augment market presence: a joint business venture and a wholly-owned subsidiary, or branch.

Joint business ventures are two or more companies who commit resources jointly to pursue a common business objective. Each partner will make a significant contribution in the form of capital, technical skill, raw material resources, or business and political contacts. International joint ventures are frequently formed in conjunction with the licensing of technology by the U.S. firm to the joint venture.

In addition, a nation's government policies may promote the creation of joint ventures—when a government prohibits 100% foreign ownership, desires to reduce foreign import competition faced by its domestic industry, or hopes to benefit from the transfer of technology.

Unique business practices in a country may promote the joint venture option as the best (perhaps even only) way to penetrate a market. Japan, for example, is notorious in this respect. Many U.S. firms have done well in that market only when they establish a joint venture with a Japanese company who understands how to work through the very complicated layer-upon-layer distribution network that exists there.

Sometimes a joint venture grows out of a licensing arrangement when a licensor accepts equity ownership in return for patent rights.

Joint ventures require careful consideration and planning. Organization, tax and anti-trust aspects are complex legal issues calling for consulting advice before entering into a joint-venture agreement. Large accounting firms, international law offices and other specialialized firms offer joint-venture counseling and assistance. For recommendations, ask exporters in your local international association, the district office of the Department of Commerce, your state office of international trade and the international department of the chamber of commerce.

Wholly owned subsidiary or branch is an extension of a U.S. firm in a foreign market by the acquisition of an existing facility or construction of a new one, requiring a relatively substantial investment. Ownership allows sole control over production and marketing, subject to local regulations. This is not a viable option for the new exporter.

Finding and Choosing Intermediaries

After you have assessed and, if necessary, adapted your product to the foreign market you plan to enter, and chosen the type of marketing channel that is most appropriate for your situation, the next task in developing your firm's export program is to locate and choose your partner and customer.

We have indicated above that there is a clear distinction between representatives (agents) and distributors (also referred to as wholesalers, jobbers or dealers). However, since the methods for locating and choosing them are similar, they will be discussed together. Finding and selecting retailers and end users will be treated separately.

There are many ways to find U.S. and foreign representatives and distributors. The first step is to use the services of the Department of Commerce. The ones described here will assist you in locating foreign-based representatives. Contact your nearest district office.

Agent/distributor service (ADS)

If your firm is small and new to export, with limited resources that preclude overseas travel, the custom-tailored ADS service can be of great help. The service includes an assessment of product marketability by local US&FCS specialists who will then contact potential agents or distributors. To start the search, provide the district office with several sets of product literature and a general letter to potential agents and distributors. The turnaround time is 60—90 days from the time you submit your literature. Each country search costs $125.

The district office sends your company's product information to the commercial officer of the U.S. embassy in the country targeted by you. He sends the information to known agents or distributors in the relevant industry, and follows up with a phone call or visit to the agent. Each is evaluated in terms of interest, capability, credibility and financial stability.

The commercial officer compiles a list of at least six of the best qualified and most interested contacts and sends it back to you via the district office. The listings include a brief description of each representative, including history and experience with the product.

You must make the final choice, most likely after traveling to the country and meeting with the best candidates. Ideally, for maximum use of your time and trip expense, try to schedule your market visit to coincide with a trade show.

Numerous firms have reported successful outcomes to their ADS searches. They represent first-time exporters, experienced exporters dissatisfied with their current representatives, export management companies researching new product markets, and entrepreneurs.

Caroline Biological Supply Company in Burlington, North Carolina, manufactures and buys for resale science educational supplies, such as preserved small animals and live insects. According to J. Claude Harmon, export manager, in certain countries where business practices are very different or where the government, rather than companies, buys educational supplies, Caroline Biological finds it necessary to use representatives. Harmon has found that the DOC agent/distributor service has saved his firm time and money by screening inexperienced representatives. "It is not unusual," says Harmon, "when looking for agents on your own, to find very inexperienced product representatives among those interested in your product. Some of them do not even officially have companies."

Export contact list service (ECLS)

The Department of Commerce maintains an ECLS database consisting of thousands of foreign companies interested in doing business with U.S. firms. These contacts have been accumulated over a period of years at trade promotion activities arranged by U.S. embassies. The listing profile includes name, product or service interest, telephone, telex, key individuals, year established and number of employees. These profiles are updated in Commerce's Commercial Information Management System (CIMS). The listing includes potential agents, distributors, licensing partners and retailers who buy industrial and retail products as well as services. The minimum fee for the ECLS service is $10 (25¢ per name or mailing label).

Trade opportunities program (TOP)

Recall that the TOP program provides export leads on a daily basis. These leads come from a variety of organizations and include representation offers and licensing and joint-venture requests. The leads list the products or services of interest, SIC codes, and product specifications. Names and contact information are included so you can respond directly to the overseas inquiry. The TOP program is quick and affordable: $25 plus an on-line fee for the USDOC Economic Bulletin Board.

Other DOC services

Other U.S. Department of Commerce services can be used to identify market contacts and/or generate leads.

Commercial News USA: This publication, published ten times annually, promotes individual products in an advertising format. It is distributed by American embassies and consulates to more than 110,000 representatives and buyers.

Foreign buyer program: Selected U.S. based industry-specific trade shows which Commerce encourages foreign buyers to attend. DOC trade specialists also attend and match U.S. firms with overseas visitors. These visitors include highly qualified agents and distributors seeking product lines to represent.

Matchmaker trade delegations: These events, organized in overseas markets, bring U.S. exporters and potential agents and distributors (or joint-venture and licensing partners) together. Field trips organized by DOC officials facilitate face-to-face meetings with potential representatives and distributors. The costs of a market visit are shared by the participants.

Overseas trade fairs

By participating in an international trade fair, a new exporter will very likely meet a number of attendees who are seeking to add new product lines to their businesses. A show also provides an opportunity to meet those individuals who have been impersonally identified by other means. Contact in advance, indicating your intention to be present at a particular fair, is another way to make the expense of the market visit that much more worthwhile.

Many show producers provide an agent/distributor service. That is, the show catalog listings indicate a particular company's interest in finding an agent or distributor.

For many international fairs, DOC secures an American presence by obtaining space from the fair organizers. In turn, it rents portions of its exhibition area to American companies. This "American Pavilion" atmosphere minimizes the design and construction cost of a booth. Additionally, a pavilion's representative-find service brings U.S. participants into contact with a variety of potential agents and distributors who have been contacted far in advance of the show by U.S. embassy and consulate personnel.

Help from other organizations

In addition to U.S. DOC services, there are a number of other organizations that will help you identify representatives and distributors.
- State offices of international trade.
- Port Authorities.
- Industry-specific U.S. trade associations (your industry's trade group).
- Trade press editors (of your trade magazines).
- Freight forwarders.
- U.S. chambers of commerce.
- Bi-national chambers of commerce.
- World trade clubs and associations.
- World trade centers.
- Trade development offices, e.g., Japan External Trade Organization (JETRO) or the Korean Trade Promotion Center (KOTRA) in New York City.

KOTRA was of tangible help to Luxtec in Sturbridge, MA, by providing complete information on the most reliable Korean firms that might be interested in handling the company's line of fiber-optical light-source headgear for surgeons.

- Agricultural Information and Marketing Services (AIMS), Foreign Agricultural Service (FSA), U. S. Department of Agriculture. AIMS offers a foreign buyer list of over 13,000 foreign firms from 70 countries, disaggregated to show foreign representatives and buyers by product or foreign representatives and buyers by country for all products (contacts are limited to businesses in food and agriculture).

• World Trade Centers Association (WTCA). The WTC Network service is an on-line computerized database that allows you to access and identify potential representatives and distributors who are users of the system. Listings of representative businesses include information on size, location, type of organization and products. Access to WTCA's Network database is $250 plus a modest charge for time on line.

Publications

Business America. Regularly provides lists of Commerce Department-certified fairs. The December issue lists overseas trade fairs coming up during the following year to help prospective companies plan ahead.

European Trade Fairs: A Guide for American Exporters. Information about exhibiting in trade fairs.

How to Find Information on Foreign Firms. Indicates how and where to research foreign firms with U.S. and international sources.

The Standard Handbook of Industrial Distributors. Lists distributors and representatives of industrial products in more than 90 countries. Two volumes.

(See Appendix, Published Sources of Information, for addresses and phone numbers).

Choosing a Representative or a Distributor

When you receive responses of interest as a result of your efforts to identify representatives or distributors, it will be important for you to make some preliminary judgments to enable you to concentrate on the most promising contacts.

Review any communications or inquiries you have received. Check the quality of letterhead correspondence. What type of office facility is indicated? Post office addresses are likely in South American and Middle-Eastern countries, but less likely in other parts of the world. Were public communication facilities used or does a particular letter or fax come from a business office? Is a business startup date indicated? Is the company incorporated by the initials Ltd., A.G., S.A., etc., depending upon the country? Are affiliates or branch offices listed? Does the logo convey a sense of professionalism?

Respond promptly

Reply quickly via telex, fax or air mail to correspondence you receive. If you receive a letter in a foreign language, seek translation help to compose a response. (A nearby university or college may have a translation center, and there are translation services in most cities that are listed in yellow pages.) Compose a well-written cover letter and include product line brochures plus enclosures that detail the following:
- The history and development of your company
- Your background and that of other company officers
- Your bank references
- Industries and customers served in the U.S. and elsewhere
- Your product's major benefits and advantages
- Average price range for your quality level
- Your policies on warranty, credit terms, customer service and returned goods
- The type of relationship you are seeking

Your return correspondence should avoid slang, and terms that may be ambiguous to a foreigner. Sign all letters; do not use form letters or stamped signatures. Write businesslike prose with a courteous tone.

Ask questions

If you have questions or have items you wish clarified, indicate these in your return mailing. In answering a specific inquiry, ask yourself what you want to know about this prospective representative or distributor. Consider sending a simple questionnaire, asking for such information as
- Why does the firm wish to represent you?
- Who else do they represent?
- Which ones are exclusive?

- What product categories are handled?
- Will they give you bank and client references for follow-up?
- What territory do they cover on a regular basis?
- How many salespeople do they have?
- Where are the firm's office and branch locations?
- How would they describe their warehousing and customer service capabilities?

The quality of the responses you receive will further reduce the number of candidates you follow up. If you fail to hear from one or more that seemed to be prime prospects, contact them again via fax or voice phone.

Visit your prospects

Plan to visit those on your short list. Be reconciled to the fact that choosing a new representative or distributor will cost you time and money. However, the investment in travel is worthwhile. Choosing a long-term distribution partner is a very important part of your export marketing program.

Prior to departure, make an appointment to visit with the commercial officer in the U.S. embassy or consulate to obtain the most recent information they have on those firms you plan to interview. Names and addresses of commercial officers are found in *Key Officers in Foreign Service Posts,* a DOC publication.

Face-to-face counseling is but one embassy or consulate service. You can also obtain letters of introduction and minimal-cost office space for up to five days, which includes telephone service, use of audiovisual equipment, and assistance in making appointments. Secretarial and translation services are also available, at your expense. Make your service needs known when you write or fax to arrange the appointment.

Travel tips

Here are some additional travel tips to keep in mind:

- Passports are obtained from certain local post offices and U.S. district courts (plan on a 4–8 week lead time, depending upon the time of year application is made).
- Visas, if needed, are acquired from the foreign country's embassy or consulate in the U.S. (take your passport with you; plan on a 2–6 week delay, depending upon the country).
- Arrange in advance as many details, such as appointments, as you can.
- Plan a flexible schedule to deal with travel delays and unexpected opportunities. Don't reveal your complete itinerary to those you will interview.
- Check country holiday dates and days and hours of the work week. (In some Middle-Eastern countries, the work week runs from Saturday to Thursday. In other countries the midday break may last two to four hours.) *Business America* publishes a list of observed holidays by country. Ask your DOC district office for a free reprint.
- Arrange for necessary travel documents with your travel agent well in advance of your trip.

• Check on needed or recommended vaccinations, if any (consult your doctor or local health center).

Order a WTDR and take your time

Don't hurry the final evaluation process. Prior to visiting the market, or soon upon your return with what is probably a shorter list of top prospects, screen them with World Traders Data Reports (WTDRs). For $100 per report, the US&FCS will screen your prospects and give you confidential background information that is only one year old or less. The service provides crucial insights about your prospective new representative or distributor in a 2–3 page format that includes

• product lines
• number of employees
• capitalization
•bank and trade references
• sales volume
• reputation
• key officers or managers
• subsidiary or parent relationship, if any
• the firm's U.S. customers
• operational problems
• branch locations
• any recent news about the firm.

To order a WTDR report, contact your nearest DOC district office. Your request should include your company's name, address, telephone number and contact person. You supply the name, address and other identifying information about your potential representative or distributor.

If the firm is included in the Commercial Information Management System (the CIMS database), you will receive the necessary information quickly in a printed report. If it is not listed in CIMS, your request is sent to the U.S. embassy or consulate where the firm is located. The turnaround time then is 45–90 days for most countries—except the former Soviet republics and Eastern European countries.

Sometimes a potential representative or distributor will be able to visit you and your manufacturing facility if it can be timed to occur with a U.S. trade show. A visit can be a definite plus prior to your making a final selection and drafting an agreement.

Choosing Export Management or Export Trading Companies

There are several sources to tap if you decide to use a domestic-based export management company (EMC) or a domestic or foreign-based export trading company (ETC). Many of the same sources that recommend agents and distributors will you help identify these service companies: your state's office of international trade development, port authorities, your industry's trade association, chambers of commerce, exporters in your industry, and the like.

Publications

The following two publications are particularly helpful:

Partners in Export Trade. A listing of export service companies indexed geographically and by products.

Directory of Leading U.S. Export Management Companies. Lists EMCs by state and by product categories.

(See Appendix, Published Sources of Information, for addresses and phone numbers.)

EMCs and ETCs are located throughout the United States, so you may be successful in identifying qualified applicants from ads placed in *The Wall Street Journal* or *The Journal of Commerce*.

Membership associations

United States Council for International Business (USCIB). This organization is the U.S. affiliate of the International Chamber of Commerce(ICC) headquarted in Paris. Council membership is tantamount to ICC membership as well. Export service companies constitute part of the membership of USCIB.

American Association of Exporters and Importers (AAEI). AAEI has members from a cross-section of many U.S. industries as well as many service providers including insurance companies, customs house clearance firms, banks, and EMCs and ETCs.

The Federation of International Trade Associations (FITA). The FITA represents dozens of trade clubs and associations across the country. The Federation will refer you to local groups from which you can obtain EMC and ETC referrals.

National Association of Export Companies (NEXCO). NEXCO's membership consists of EMCs and ETCs throughout the U.S. The Association's directory will identify appropriate export service firms. In addition, NEXCO publishes a membership bulletin that will list and describe your trade opportunity.

Overseas Sales and Marketing Association of America (OSMA). An organization similar to NEXCO with service-firm memberships concentrated in the mid-western states.

Export Managers Association of California (EMAC). A membership organization serving small and mid-size businesses in west-coast states. Ask for the EMAC membership directory.

(See Appendix, Agency Sources of Information, for addresses and phone numbers.)

Questions to ask
- Competitors represented?
- Exclusive or nonexclusive representation?
- Familiar with your products and typical customers?
- Frequency of overseas trips; size of travel budget?
- How important will your product lines be to those of other clients represented?
- Names of clients served and their product lines (for background and reference checks)?
- Other clients' lines compatible with yours?
- Sales volume?
- Staff support?
- Type of agreements signed with other clients?
- What country markets are served?

Questions to answer
Take requests for information about you and your company as complimentary, since an effective, well-managed firm is very selective in whom they wish to represent. The export company will want to know how prepared you are to support its marketing efforts abroad, and your production and delivery capabilities.

Whether you choose an EMC or an ETC gets back to the key differences between the two, although as discussed above, there are many similarities.

Recall that the ETC typically takes title to the goods purchased. They enjoy benefits offered by the Export Trading Company Act of 1982 (bank financing strengths and anti-trust immunities). They are U.S. and/or foreign-based entities. There is a more distant relationship between an ETC and its suppliers. They tend not to carry inventory or provide after-sales service.

The domestic-based EMC operates like a manufacturer's representative, soliciting export business, usually on commission, for more than one manufacturing exporter. They tend to specialize by product category and focus on one or more specific markets.

Drafting International Trade Agreements

After you choose your export partner(s), you must negotiate a signed agreement. The purpose of such a written statement is to formalize the mutual obligations and responsibilities of the partnership arrangement.

Sources of advice

First contact the DOC desk specialist of the country market in question, who will alert you to any special considerations unique to that market. Second, a qualified international law attorney, with knowledge of the relevant laws of the country involved, should prepare or review a draft of the agreement. There are too many nuances of international law to risk going it alone. Your law firm, bank, accountant, local, state and national bar associations, local international trade association members, DOC district office, port authority, or the like, will assist you in finding an attorney.

Guide to Drafting International Distributorship Agreements and *Commercial Agency* provide you with the most important questions, and the answers usually given to them, and the risks both parties most frequently run into. The first concentrates on agreements made with a *distributor*. The second, though similar, was written for agreements with a *representative*.

Foreign Business Practices deals with agency/distributor terminations, and describes the representative-distributor termination laws in the countries likely to be of most interest to you. As suggested previously, the legal aspects of termination are complicated because of the laws of many Latin American, European and Middle-Eastern countries designed to protect their nationals. These laws can typically override contractual provisions if there is a conceptual conflict. "Unjust" terminations in these situations can be costly to an exporter.

(See Appendix, Published Sources of Information.)

Key elements of an agreement

1. *Define the nature of the representation.* There is a distinction between a representative distributor and a representative agent. A distributor buys and takes title to goods, sets price, bears the risk of nonpayment, and earns a profit on the resale price of the merchandise. An agent does not take title to goods shipped to the customer. The exporter assumes the risk of nonpayment and also reserves the right to accept or reject purchase orders forwarded by the agent.

The distinction indicated is important, because many foreign countries treat distributors and agents differently when just-cause terminations or non-renewals are executed by the exporter. A similar distinction exists between sales representatives (agents) and employees. Oral or written communications between the U.S. supplier and the foreign representative may, in the eyes of a foreign court, transform an agency agreement into an employment contract. Foreign labor laws can limit employee dismissals and require substantial advance notice; provisions that apply to agent representatives may be more liberal.

2. *Include a specific expiration date in the agreement.* Stating that the agreement remains in effect until cancelled by either party might create problems the exporter should avoid. Instead, a specific termination date is recommended to avoid compensation obligations mandated by legislation in certain countries. Upon renewal, in fact, the exporter should alter some provisions to give the appearance of a new, altered contract.

3. Provide for a long advance notice for non-renewal and termination of an agreement. A substantial time period enhances the exporter's chances of avoiding substantial compensation obligations, especially when a relationship has existed for a number of years.

A "just-cause" termination provision is recommended, and should be based upon legally permissible grounds for terminating representatives in a particular country. The commercial officer of the U.S. embassy or consulate in the market country is familiar with such legislation and will provide good advice on this point.

4. *Should the appointment be exclusive or non-exclusive?* Some countries prohibit a supplier from appointing more than one distributor or representative in the same territory. Others provide that a sales agent's appointment is presumed to be exclusive unless the agreement specifically states that it is non-exclusive.

Even if there are no legal implications to this question, there are some strategic factors that should be considered. There are pros and cons to exclusivity, a condition that many distributors and representatives request:

• The smaller the requested territory, the more desirable an exclusive territory may be. Can the market be developed adequately by one firm?

• If the distributor or agent is willing to base the exclusive arrangement on mutually agreed upon sales quotas, the exclusive appointment can be measured objectively.

• If the representative has a good track record, is organized effectively, and is recommended by other complementary product suppliers, then the establishment of an exclusive arrangement may make sense.

5. *Check for country legislation that prohibits or restricts territorial limitations on distributors.* For example, the European Community does not allow an exporter to prohibit a distributor from selling in other EC countries. The exporter should be aware of specific country legislation of this type.

Suggested coverage of provisions
• Parties to the agreement
• Effective date and length of term (commonly 2 years) including withdrawal notification procedure
• Description of the product line, including catalog numbers
• Clear description of territory to be covered (whole or part of a country)

- Exclusive versus nonexclusive representation
- Assigned rights not transferable
- Obligations of you, the manufacturer, and the channel partner
  -joint promotional activities
  -sales call and market visit frequencies
  -sales literature responsibility
  -reporting and market communications requirements
  -payment terms
  -supply of samples
  -sales support
  -stocking requirement
  -minimum order size
  -payment currency
  -price change notification
  -discounts
  -competitive lines
  -order priority
  -warranty
  -training materials
  -after-sale service
- Conditions necessary for renewal (e.g., sales volume; sales volume growth percentages, other quantitative measures)
- Causes for termination
- Dispute settlement
- Country law of jurisdiction

Formal agreement not always necessary

In spite of the commentary presented here regarding agreements and the need for care regarding their provisions, many successful small exporters do not have formal contractual agreements with foreign trade partners. If the relationship with an agent, distributor or retail dealer is built on mutual understanding and trust, some business formalities, such as a complex agreement, are not required. A considerable amount of business internationally is conducted on a handshake.

However, attaining this enviable level of understanding and mutual trust calls for proven interpersonal skills plus consistent visits to the overseas market. A relationship of this type doesn't just happen.

Very often an informal business relationship evolves into a warm life-long friendship. When this happens, as it has to Ed Kostinger of Kostinger Photographic Products of Leeds, Massachusetts, with his specialty shop customers in several European countries, an exporter will experience one of the great rewards of selling abroad. Mr. Kostinger states, "I'm treated like a member of the families of my retail dealers in Belgium and France. The same is true for them when they visit my family here."

Model Distribution Agreement

An example of an actual distributorship agreement drawn up by an industrial goods manufacturer is presented below. Its provisions reflect the firm's preference to keep agreements of this sort as brief and uncomplicated as possible.

AGREEMENT

(Seller's name and address)

hereinafter called the "Seller" and

(Buyer's name and address)

hereinafter called the "Distributor," hereby enter into the following agreement for the sale of

(Product)

The Distributor agrees:

1. To act as exclusive distributor for the above (trade name) products in the territory of _____ .

2. To promote the sale of above (trade name) products to all segments of the market, and to keep stocks of such products at all times.

3. To attain the agreed-upon increase of _____ % from (date) through (date). To establish an agreed-upon goal to start in (date) and run through (date). This goal will be prepared by Seller and submitted to Distributor for their mutual agreement.

4. To refrain from selling or offering for sale, directly or indirectly, in said territory any products which are competitive with the above products.

5. To defend and promote the interest of the Seller regarding the above products in the said territory. Distributor agrees specifically to consider the (trade name) trademark and any other registered trademarks of the Seller used in commerce in the said territory to be the exclusive property of the Seller, and to advise the Seller immediately by cable or air mail of any infringement of such trademark as soon as Distributor has knowledge thereof.

The Seller agrees:

1. To refer all orders or inquiries for above (trade name) products received from said territory to the Distributor.

2. To make prompt shipments in accordance with the Distributor's orders, subject to the Seller's ability to supply. It is agreed that the Seller will continue to act as purchaser of the above products on behalf of the Distributor and will be responsible for all payments to the manufacturer.

3. To send the Distributor literature as published from time to time, free of charge. In the event that reproduction of large quantities of such literature in a language other than English is required, the Seller will provide artwork required and the Distributor will be responsible for the translation and printing costs.

4. To allow the Distributor, at all times, the lowest export prices in accordance with published export price lists.

This Agreement remains in effect for two years until (date). It is renewable for (time period), starting with the next calendar year. It will be reviewed by both parties three months prior to its termination date and will be renewed by mutual agreement.

This Agreement may be cancelled by the Seller at any time if payments are not made by Distributor as agreed upon.

This Agreement cancels and supersedes all previous agreements between the Seller and the Distributor.

ACCEPTED:

For the Seller
(name)

Date:_____By:_____

For the Distributor
(name)

Date:_____By:_____

Representative/Distributor Support

If you sign an agreement with a representative or a distributor you must do what you can to make it work successfully. Your marketing responsibility does not end when the product is shipped overseas, any more than it does with a domestic shipment.

Channel support reflects genuine commitment on your part, and helps build a solid working relationship with your overseas channel partner. The benefits you realize are comparable to those achieved in the domestic market. Your foreign distributor(s) or representative(s) deserve equal treatment.

Types of support

What types of marketing support should you be providing? Consider the following as part of your international marketing responsibility:

• The assurance of after-sales product service by appointing a local agent to service your products, training your distributor to provide repair and maintenance, establishing service personnel in the target country, or being prepared to provide it yourself by long distance.

• Sales and advertising aids such as special display and point-of-purchase kits, banners and posters, advertising mats or slicks and copy for trade press use, product catalogs and circulars and salesmen's presentation kits. If these types of aids are considered important, then plan on language translation expenses. Your representatives should help you solve translation problems, for they will know how to translate the industry's technical jargon.

• Training literature for distributor salesmen and technical service personnel. Training support may also consist of periodic, required visits to your manufacturing facility or on-site visits of your personnel to the target country.

• A cooperative trade press advertising program in which the cost of foreign media advertising is shared equally or proportionately.

• A system of continuous communication to coordinate joint effort and avoid conflict. You are obligated to inform your foreign partners of new plans. Equally important is that information flow from intermediary to exporter. The intermediary is obligated to inform you of important changes taking place in the market. The point here is that you must assume the responsibility for designing this two-way information system.

• Helping sell your product through to end-users by making occasional joint sales calls, sending out personal letters and conducting direct mail campaigns.

• Qualifying and passing along sales leads you uncover.

• Designing sales contests and other recognition programs—with the advice and consent of your distributor.

• Offering advice and counsel on such things as inventory control systems, emerging technologies, telemarketing ideas, and approaches to local market research.

Sales leads

If a direct marketing channel has been selected, the promotional responsibility is yours. If an indirect channel has been chosen (e.g., a distributor) you may think that you, the exporter, have no role to play in marketing your product. This is incorrect. You have a continuing role to assist your partner in any way that helps expand the foreign market's customer base. Passing along sales leads to your partner has a definite impact on your long-term relationship.

The same Department of Commerce services you use to locate and evaluate an overseas export partner (export contact list service and trade opportunities, foreign buyer, and matchmaker programs) can also be used to generate leads to increase overseas sales.

In addition to DOC services, your local port authority and state office of international trade are two organizations that should be contacted. A number of these have export assistance programs that include generating sales leads for new exporters.

The NETWORK worldwide electronic bulletin board described earlier offers a trade lead service. Electronic "offers to buy," which include the name and profile of the potential buyer, can be retrieved by a subscriber for 35¢ per message. For more detailed information or to arrange to see a demonstration, contact NETWORK Manager (see Appendix, Agency Sources of Information).

Midwest International, Ltd., of Edgewood, Kentucky, manufactures audio and video broadcasting systems, particularly mobile television production systems and satellite communication vehicles. The company serves a number of markets in Asia, Europe, and Central and South America. Midwest's overseas sales agencies are required to send two people to Kentucky for training in the service and maintenance of the mobile systems. As part of purchasing contracts, overseas customers are furnished with a two-year supply of spare parts. Midwest has agreements with its major parts suppliers that its overseas customers may contact them directly for replacement of spare parts when failure of equipment is under manufacturer's warranty. Spare parts are air-freighted to customers by next day priority service. If an overseas customer has a problem with equipment sold by Midwest, a telephone call to one of its overseas agents will initiate a 24-hour technical service call.

J. L. Holder is President of Heyco, Inc. of Kenilworth, N.J., maker of electric components. The overseas distributor represents "a key ingredient in our success." The firm keeps in continuous communication with its distributors by mail, telex, telefax, telephone, and annual visits. Heyco assists with distributor sales promotions, helps produce foreign-language catalogs, provides sample panels for trade shows, and offers information about its new products, together with photos. There is a continuing dialog about competitors' actions.

R. L. Drake Company of Miamisburg, Ohio, manufactures devices that pick up signals from satellite dishes. Rich Renken, International Sales Manager, spends considerable time on his trips training foreign distributors. "You don't just sell your equipment ... you have to train people how to install it, and how to use it."

Bay Technical Associates, Inc., of Bay Saint Louis, Mississippi, is a manufacturer of high tech computer-related electronic equipment. The 110-employee firm exports to 30 countries. President Charles Ramsey, just returned from an overseas trip, says one of his distributors told him, "You treat us as if we were an American distributor. Some American companies treat us as if we were foreigners." Ramsey is determined to keep relationships with overseas distributors on that basis.

Toll-free 800 numbers

A relatively new phenomenon that can play a useful role in overseas channel and customer support is a toll-free international 800 telephone service. It permits calls from representatives, distributors, customers and other key players in a foreign market right to your office at no cost to the caller. A toll-free international service is an efficient way to support your channel partners and to respond quickly to the technical service needs of your customers. (See Appendix, Agency Sources of Information, AT&T 800 service.)

Genigraphics Corporation, a maker of computer-generated graphics equipment located in Liverpool, New York, is using international 800 service.

"We use it for sales contracts, field service reports, shipping and for parts requests for field service repairs," says Linda Hines, telecommunications specialist at Genigraphics. "The sales staff lets us know daily, weekly and monthly results and projected sales," she says. "People in the field can speak directly to the engineers here at home who design the equipment."

International promotional efforts are communication activities designed to inform, educate, and influence customers in a target market. (Promotion also includes the sales support programs for channel partners already discussed.)

For our purposes here, promotional activities include

- trade shows
- direct mail
- trade press advertising

Translations

In many countries it is possible to use your existing brochure materials. But even in a country such as Canada, the U.S.'s major trading partner, an American exporter should accompany English-language versions with those in French. The importance of language cannot be ignored in product and shipping labels, so neither should it when preparing sales materials.

Use care when translating technical language from English to another language. Simply hiring a national of the country to do the translations can create problems. Instead, ask for recommendations from ITA's district office, your state office of international trade, World Trade Center information services, and your contacts in the local international trade association.

One professional firm, Global Translations, maintains a world-wide database of translation experts skilled in translating the technical information of a particular industry.

Berlitz Translation Services have translators and editors review assigned materials and follow that up with layout and graphic artists to create camera-ready copy of a finished product. This is a common procedure at all Berlitz translation centers.

If you have representatives or distributors in place, ask them for assistance in translating your materials properly. They can also send you direct mail pieces of competitors (and copies of their trade newspaper and magazine advertising).

Trade shows

One of the best ways to realize additional sales overseas is to exhibit your products at an appropriate international trade show. U.S. trade shows are not generally a major marketing activity of American firms. In other parts of the world, especially Europe and Asia, however, they are very important marketing efforts. A considerable amount of business is written during these shows. But more than this, an attendee can view the offerings of competitors and gain insights into market preferences and trends.

What better way to present your line then to show it where large numbers of potential customers will view it? Even if you market indirectly through a representative or distributor, you still have a shared responsibility to exhibit at selected shows abroad.

How do you find the right show for your company?

DOC's US&FCS country desk officers will advise you regarding the shows that may be of particular interest to you that are scheduled over the next 12–24 months. (As indicated earlier, each December issue of *Business America* lists upcoming trade shows by industry and by country for the following year.)

In addition, the *Export Promotion Calendar* lists the dates, fair name, location, type of event, and the contact name and telephone number for all upcoming trade shows throughout the world.

When DOC organizes a special exhibition at a trade show it offers extensive local market promotion, a turnkey exhibit booth, and exhibit transportation support.

In addition, a country's embassy in Washington DC or its trade development office in New York or other city locations will assist you. You should also ask principals of your trade association and other exporters in your industry.

Although trade shows deserve a preferred position in your overall promotional effort, be aware that they are expensive. They are less expensive, of course, if you participate with other firms in a DOC or state-sponsored "pavilion" event. Also, regional shows (as opposed to the largest, very expensive fairs) may be the best way to begin trade-fair participation. Otherwise, depending upon the show, the space occupied and the booth investment, the total cost can range from about $8,000 to $30,000 or more. These are large sums of money. But if you figure in the cost of several sales calls in Europe or major cities in Asia as a trade-off, a trade show is an efficient way to write additional business and to initiate fruitful relationships.

By comparison, company participation in DOC, state or port authority-sponsored trade missions ranges from about $4,000 to $7,500, including travel, while the DOC's more impersonal, less effective catalog and video/catalog exhibitions cost from about $200 to $500. Contact DOC's district office for information and application procedures for trade missions and catalog exhibitions.

Planning your participation in a trade fair requires a lead time of 18–24 months since sponsor deadlines usually average 6–12 months. Once a decision to participate has been made, here are some basic items for planning and following up an international trade fair.

Trade show checklist

• What do you want to achieve from the show? Orders? Test the market? A better handle on competitors? To learn about market trends?

• Prepare a budget that includes travel, samples, booth staffing, booth rental and furnishings, literature translations, preshow direct-mail invitations and foreign-language business cards.

• Arrange for the shipment of samples to display. Check with the show's sponsor, since it often appoints a particular freight forwarder for this purpose.

• Obtain a special customs document called an "ATA carnet," pronounced "karnay." (The initials ATA represent a combination of both French and English words and means "Temporary Admission.")

An ATA carnet is a special customs document designed to simplify customs procedures for businesses who wish to take commercial samples and advertising materials, whether accompanied or not, into participating countries for up to one year. It allows you to take take or ship sample products to the approximately forty countries that are members of the ATA Carnet Agreement. Customs officials in participating countries accept ATA carnets as a guarantee that all custom duties and excise taxes will be paid in the event that any of the items covered by the carnet are not taken out of the country within the time period allowed.

To learn about participating countries and to secure a carnet, you should request an application form from the United States Council for International Business (See Appendix, Agency Sources of Information.) The application form asks for a listing of the goods, payment of a modest issuing fee, and a bond or letter of credit for 40% of the value of the samples to cover foreign duties in the event the items are not re-exported to the U.S.

To avoid penalties and delays upon your return, the carnet document should be validated by U.S. Customs prior to the samples' departure (Contact U.S. Customs at the nearest international airport or port for instructions regarding this validation procedure.)

• Booth furnishings and design must be planned. Do show sponsors have local contract service companies on call to provide booth hardware and other accessories? If not, what local companies are recommended?

• Send out a mailing prior to the event to alert prospects that you will be exhibiting in a particular booth and that you look forward to meeting with them during the show. Send a carefully written letter to those potential customers your secondary source research effort has identified, names provided by the DOC's Export Contact List Service and TOP program, port authority recommendations, etc. Give these recipients a reason for seeking you out.

• Develop a press release (in English and in the appropriate country language) if your presence at the trade show will highlight a new technology, a new market entry, a new partnership or licensing agreement with a local firm. Send your release to editors of the industry's media (the names of which you can obtain from the International Edition of *Standard Rate and Data Service*). Your news might be played up by the industry trade press. Publicity is free, and tends to give you a local endorsement.

• Learn who is organizing concurrent seminars and technical symposiums and when papers will be presented. Offer to present a paper on a technical advancement, a new production process, or a new or modified product addition. These papers are often published in the industry's trade journals and tend to enhance the credibility of the presenter.

• Though you may prefer to quote FOB factory prices, potential buyers may prefer to know how much it will cost to get your product to one of his principal ports. Therefore, with estimates supplied by your freight forwarder prior to your departure, be prepared to quote prices that include transportation and insurance costs from your factory to one or more of a buyer's foreign ports.

• Plan on traveling for two to three days after the trade show. You may meet some contacts who warrant further discussion before you return home.

• Upon your return home, acknowledge having met with selected key prospects. This requires some on-the-spot notations on business cards you receive during the show to help jog your memory. Send a tailored letter and an enclosure to each to remind them of your having met. The point is to reinforce a good impression with an early response.

Credit Care Software, Inc., of Maitland, Florida, built up its export business with an aggressive program of trade-fair activities.

The Timberland Company of Hampton, N.H., got involved in exporting by joining a U.S. Department of Commerce export pavilion at the Dusseldorf Shoe Fair in West Germany.

Since 1980, the American Hardware Manufacturers Association has been promoting exports of members' products. For several years, the Association has sponsored a U.S.A. Hardware Pavilion at the Cologne International Hardware Trade Fair, and for a flat fee it will make all arrangements for U.S. participants.

Altek Industries Corporation of Rochester, New York, a 20-employee manufacturer of electronic calibration instruments for the process control industry, achieved success abroad when it sent managers to foreign trade shows and exhibitions. Buyers attending these shows expressed more than just passing interest in the company's products. Co-owners E. Lee Garelick and James Wurtz followed up on the buyer contacts made. They also began to put together a system of overseas sales representatives. Currently, over 20% of Altek's sales come from exports.

Sandco, Inc., of Tulsa, Oklahoma, markets printing supplies and equipment. Sandco's president, Carolea Wheeler, believed an overseas market existed for the firm's products and started traveling to international trade shows in selected markets to meet dealers. Today, attending trade shows remains one of Sandco's most effective ways of expanding its foreign sales. The firm sells to authorized dealers, who resell the products to end users. Sandco's exports, which represent 40% of sales, go to 70 countries.

Direct mail

Direct mail is an important way for small businesses to influence buyers in United States markets. This is also true for getting established in a new foreign market. Well-drafted cover letters and informative, well-designed product and company brochures can be very effective in getting started in a targeted segment of an overseas market. However, given the cost of foreign mailings, be conscious of balancing brochure quality (i.e., weight) against the cost of postage.

The quality of the mailing list and the quality of the mailing are the principal determinants of a successful direct mail campaign. Whatever the mailing list source, try to use the information provided to screen and qualify firms appearing on the list.

Likely sources of mailing lists

From your DOC district office, ask about the following services:

- Commercial Information Management System (CIMS) Foreign Traders Index (FTI) that lists foreign trade prospects by product category and country. A printout is priced from $10 up depending upon the number of listings.
- Trade Opportunities Program (TOP) that generates trade leads.
- Foreign Buyer Program listings of foreign buyers who have attended U.S. industry trade shows.
- Export Contact List Service (ECLS) database of foreign firms interested in doing business with U.S. companies.

If you know your best customer classes in the domestic market, either by description or by Standard Industrial Classification (SIC) code, then you can easily identify good customer prospects in a foreign trade association membership directory. Those directories are often available to members and to purchasers. Association members are usually indexed by location and type of business, giving you an opportunity to qualify firms to receive your direct mailing.

Many state offices of international trade are compiling valuable contact lists by industry sector. See if your state office is one. If so, those contacts represent firms that should probably receive your direct mailings.

Two other organizations that may have good names and addresses for you are the port authority convenient to you, and the U. S. Chamber of Commerce in the country of your interest.

NETWORK, the computerized service of the World Trade Centers Association, also offers an opportunity to add to your mailing list prospects. NETWORK's 4,000 subscribers worldwide are profiled in the system's database. The profiles include company name, contact information, bank references, products of interest, and type of company. Those profiles can be scanned at no cost to a NETWORK subscriber. Those that appear to be potential buyers of a particular product category can be printed out at a cost of $2 each. Contact the World Trade Center nearest you or the World Trade Center in New York.

Geographically targeted trade magazine and newspaper subscribers represent another source of direct mail list prospects. Like their American counterparts who must keep current, your potential customers in an overseas market subscribe to foreign publications that serve that particular industry. Segmented subscription lists by postal zone, type of company and job title, for example, may be purchased.

The editors of comparable trade press publications serving U.S. interests usually know what publishers abroad are producing similar titles in the language of a particular country. Recent issues of your own subscription will refer you to the individual and telephone number to call.

Business Publications Rates and Data is a monthly directory published by Standard Rate and Data Service (SRDS) that includes the appropriate contact names, addresses and telephone numbers of all editors and publishers. Part III lists international publications. The trade press listings are presented alphabetically within industry classes. In addition to naming editors and publishers, they also indicate frequency of issue, advertising rates, total circulation, and the breakdown of circulation by job function. SRDS also publishes several special international editions listing publications originating in the U.K., Canada, Austria, France, Italy, Mexico, Switzerland and Germany.

Mailing list houses compile and sell segmented mailing lists for those businesses who wish to target a specific audience for a direct mail campaign. *Direct Mail List*, also published by SRDS, gives detailed mailing list sources indexed by subject, list title, and list owner, and for each list, quantity, rental cost, minimum order and how the list may be segmented.

There are some specialized international mailing-list houses from whom you may order target lists. International yellow pages directories are another fruitful source for identifying overseas prospects, listing specialized retailers, distributors and end users. The directory of a particular locale may be purchased from AT&T (see Appendix, Agency Sources of Information). Sometimes, if asked, a commercial desk staff member in a U.S. embassy overseas will copy and send the appropriate pages to you.

Direct mailings overseas have made an important contribution to the export success of Heritage Medical Products of Tucker, Georgia. This 30-employee firm manufactures wound drainage units for use in hospital operating rooms. Faced with stiff domestic market competition from large U.S. companies, D. J. Holy, General Manager of the company, looked overseas. Working with US&FCS personnel, Heritage obtained the names and addresses of foreign firms in the medical equipment industry. Additional contact names were obtained with the assistance of the Georgia Department of Commerce. The company sends a cover letter, a brochure and a product sample to 50 to 100 foreign prospects each week. Adding one country at a time since 1982, Heritage sells 80% of its output in 50 countries.

Menlo Tool Company of Warren, Michigan, manufactures carbide cutting tools. Acquired lists of potential foreign customers are sent direct-mail pieces describing the 54-employee company and its product lines. Once relationships are established, Menlo asks its customers for the names of additional prospective customers to contact by mail.

Trade press publicity

Special, newsworthy events like the introduction of a new product, the appointment of a new dealer or distributor, or the opening of a new display showroom offer you the chance to try for free publicity via news releases you send to editors of trade magazines, who present them in news, commentary or editorial formats.

The benefits of this publicity is that it builds credibility and very often produces high-quality sales leads. Therefore, as you prepare the promotion part of your export plan, consider drafting at least one publicity release. It might be a technical article, a product announcement or your planned attendance, as a new market entry, at an upcoming trade show.

Your news release, translated into the country's language, should be forwarded to editors of the leading publications in your target market. To locate these editors you can refer to *Business Publications Rates and Data* mentioned above. If you have channel partners, ask them for their assistance.

Another alternative is to retain an international public relations consultant on a project cost (hourly) basis. There are a number of small agencies who will compose the release and submit it to the appropriate foreign media. Since public relations consultants usually specialize by industry, they have acquired a certain amount of technical understanding. They also have fostered good relationships with key foreign editors.

Trade press advertising

If you advertise to your U.S. market, consider also advertising to a new overseas market. Including paid-for advertising in trade media in your promotion budget depends on how much you believe ads influence your end buyers. If brand name is relatively unimportant, or if your market is limited and concentrated, then media advertising will probably play a minor role in your promotion efforts.

On the other hand, if potential buyers in the industries you serve consistently read selected trade magazines to keep current, then running ads that key in on the performance benefits of your product could be a good investment.

Many U.S. industrial and technical publications are read regularly by foreign readers. The readership profiles are known well by publishers (e.g., Johnston International Publishing Corp.). They can advise you on ad rates and in which publications to consider placing ads.

Showcase USA, a bimonthly U.S. publication, is a good advertising buy for small U.S. exporters.

If you use a U.S. advertising agency to place your ads in domestic trade journals, it should be able to help you locate an agency operating in your target country. If you don't, contact the International Advertising Association. A local agency is recommended because it is more likely to be familiar with market conditions and the range of print and other media available to you.

If you have appointed intermediaries in the target country, seek their advice on choosing trade publications for advertising, and selecting a local ad agency.

Stanley Skalka is President of Victor Stanley Company of Dunkirk, Maryland, manufacturers of street furniture (benches, tables, waste receptacles). Starting with Canada, the 45-employee company now exports to other countries, including England, Europe, the

Middle East, the Caribbean and Japan. The firm advertises in publications with an international readership—airline in-flight journals and U.S. magazines and trade publications.

Commercial News USA

An example of trade media advertising supported by the federal government is *Commercial News USA*. For only $250, an exporter who has been in business at least three years can buy a standard display ad. One-third, one-half and full page ads may also be purchased. The service is limited to advertising "new" products, defined as those that have been on the market for not more than three years. Individual issues also highlight the products of specific industries, with ad copy due three months earlier. When a particular industry is featured, the "new" requirement is waived.

This catalog-magazine, published ten times per year, is distributed through U.S. embassies to more than 110,000 overseas subscribers in 140 countries. Moreover, many commercial officers overseas select product listings for local language reprints in newspapers, trade journals, and other foreign publications. Many foreign publications reproduce selections from *Commercial News*. DOC reports that 97% of U.S. firms using *Commercial News* have fewer than 500 employees. Many are new exporters. The typical response to a listing is 30 to 40 inquiries and $10,000 in sales. Companies that would like to advertise in *Commercial News* should contact their nearest DOC district office.

Craig B. Clayton, President of Globaltel in Los Angeles, purchased a standard ad in Commercial News. This firm's product is "faxfinder," a voice data switch that allows a single telephone line to be shared by two communications devices. The company has received more than 130 responses from 50 countries. Sales from the one ad equal one-half of what Globaltel sold domestically in eighteen months. "Essentially, this ad has catapulted us from working with the OEM to manufacturing on our own and to doing sub-assemblies for large telecom firms like AT&T," claims Clayton.

In addition to U.S. government advertising support, some state offices of international trade offer low-cost advertising services. Contact the appropriate office in your state to learn if its export assistance program includes a trade advertising support service. California's trade program is a case in point. One state export development project consisted of a team effort to produce a special edition of *Commercial News USA* devoted exclusively to California products. Over 120 California companies participated in this joint federal and state program.

NETWORK, the World Trade Center (WTC) electronic information and message system described earlier, is another option for placing a low-cost ad. For $33 a NETWORK subscriber can run an ad up to 200 characters on the Bulletin Board as an "offer to sell." It will be transmitted electronically to other NETWORK subscribers in 64 countries and will stay in the system for two weeks.

Export Pricing

The four major elements of an international marketing plan are product assessment, channels of distribution, promotion and pricing. All should also be viewed as effective competitive weapons. But the fourth, pricing, is often the most challenging for new exporters to use effectively.

Your export pricing should take into account your customers' perception of value, how your product is differentiated from competition, and the interaction of sales volume and profit, as well as costs. Since costs vary over time and fluctuate with volume, they must be considered in relation to the export objectives of your firm, market demand and competition.

Export program objectives

If your overseas marketing expectations are limited to simply finding another market for surplus production of a mature product, then a relatively low penetration price strategy makes sense. On the other hand, you may be willing to build profitability gradually in order to develop and manage a long-term export presence. This objective suggests a moderate price strategy to meet competition and build market share. Or, perhaps you have developed a unique product that has top quality and performance features. This situation will call for a top-end price strategy that helps position the product properly in a well-developed overseas market.

Market demand and size

Your domestic marketing experience tells you that market demand is a key variable to setting a price. It is therefore important to try to judge what the export market will bear. When you investigated the target country, you should have learned something about current prices and market potential. If the market for your product is large and still growing, then you might enter with a moderately competitive price, expecting to improve your profit margin as your volume increases. A mature-market growth rate, however, may dictate a more competitive entry price.

The makeup of the market's customers is also part of the market demand profile. How important is price to customers in the segment you have selected? Is there a sizeable number of innovators who will pay a premium price to buy a new and unique product entry? Does your market consist of a few large potential buyers who are aggressive negotiators, or many small to mid-size prospects?

Competition

Research you conducted earlier should have identified, and also characterized, other competitors selling in your target market. Both the number of competitors and the intensity of their competition will affect your pricing strategy.

If you are faced with a dominant competitor, then you and others will probably follow that leader in pricing. If the market is splintered with spirited competition from a number of effective rivals, then a moderate, meet-the-competition pricing strategy is called for. Or, if your market entry offers users unique product benefits, then it is likely that a meaningful segment of your market will pay a premium for those features.

Costs

Additional costs are incurred when you sell overseas. These include market research and market testing, trade shows, exhibitions, and trade missions, translation costs, recruitment of representatives or distributors, additional packaging and transportation costs, freight forwarder fees, credit checks, minor or major product modifications, and, if applicable, technical training and post-sales service costs.

The amount of additional outlay will vary, depending on how extensive is your product adaptation, whether you select a direct or indirect channel of distribution, what your market-entry promotion costs are, the extent to which you must modify your packaging and labeling, and how critical are warranty, repair and maintenance services to customers in your market.

Calculating your ex-factory (point of origin) export price

Many new exporters believe that prices in a foreign market must be higher to compensate for the added costs of selling overseas. It is true that there are additional export costs that must be covered, but if costs are allocated logically, it is possible to charge comparable or even lower prices in a foreign market and earn a higher after-tax profit.

You should *not* charge costs against an export sale that are already included in your domestic pricing. Those costs are U.S. general and administrative overhead, fixed factory overhead, and domestic marketing expenses. When these cost classes are included in an export price, it may make the price noncompetitive. This false conclusion tends to keep many small firms from attempting an export effort. Adding your customary domestic market profit margin only to total *relevant* costs gives you a true export price.

Although relatively simple to calculate, a cost-plus export price fails to consider the marketplace. The method ignores your customers' perception of value, how your product is differentiated from competition, and the interaction of sales volume and profit. Since costs vary over time and fluctuate with volume, they must be considered in relation to market demand, competition, and the export objectives of your firm.

Incremental pricing

Incremental pricing recognizes that excess capacity can be profitably sold. The cost of *producing* an additional unit consists of the standard costs of direct materials and labor plus variable factory overhead costs, but does *not* include fixed factory overhead and general and administrative costs, since they will be incurred anyway. You then add *export-related* costs such as product modification/change costs, packaging, promotional expenses, and service costs, plus your planned profit margin, to arrive at your ex-factory price.

To illustrate, assume you are producing 1,000 units from a plant with a capacity of 2,000 units. Assume your direct material cost per unit is $500, your direct labor cost per unit is $200, your variable factory overhead cost per unit is $20, and your export marketing costs are $20. If there is negligible additional fixed factory overhead cost required to supply a new export market, then a break-even price of $740 is the *minimum* ex-factory export price you should be willing to accept.

Ex-Factory Price Components

	Standard	Incremental
Direct materials	$500	$500
Direct labor	200	200
Factory overhead		
Fixed	50	
Variable	20	20
Unit Cost	$770	$720
Domestic marketing, general and overhead costs	50	
Export marketing costs (product changes, packaging, service)		20
Profit Margin (25%)	205	185
Ex-Factory Price	$1,025	$ 925

Once an ex-factory price has been determined, you are ready to begin detailing costs for an export quotation. An export quotation worksheet, such as that shown on page 99, is valuable to you, the exporter, as a checklist to make sure that all costs associated with an export sale are included.

The following items should be considered when calculating your export quotation:

- Ex-factory price per unit (including profit margin as illustrated)
- Foreign representative's commission, if applicable (added before freight and other charges)
- Special export packing costs; if required, add 1.0 to 1.5 percent of ex-factory price
- Special strapping, marking and labeling, if applicable
- Freight to the pier, and unloading charges if not included
- Terminal charges
- Consular documents (only required by certain countries)
- Ocean (or air) port-to-port (airport-to-airport) freight
- Freight forwarder fees
- Export credit insurance (commercial and political risk)
- Cost of credit (the cost of money until payment is expected, 30 to 120 days)

These items, when totaled. will give you what is termed a "Cost and Freight" (C&F) export price quote. This is preferred over an ex-factory quote because your buyer wants to know his price to the port of destination, not from your factory.

If you plan to ship an order by sea freight and expect to add the cost of marine insurance in your quote, you must calculate a "Cost-Insurance-Freight" (C.I.F.) to destination export quote.

(Note: A discussion of international shipping terms—terms of sale—which clearly define the responsibilities and liabilities of the buyer and seller relative to an international shipment, will be found in Part IV, Shipping.)

One additional export pricing consideration is the tariff (tax) levied on imported goods to be paid to the government. Although the buyer is responsible for this payment, the tariff, or duty, affects the competitiveness of your product in a specific country market. Use the Harmonized System (HS) number, discussed earlier, to learn about the tariff levied on your product category by the government in your target country. For your HS number, contact your district office of the Department of Commerce.

Sarah Hodson, General Manager of Sandco, a manufacturer of printing supplies and equipment in Tulsa, Oklahoma, advises beginning exporters to do research to find out how their products compare with those of competitors in a specific market. "It is particularly important for a company to calculate how much duties and freight will add to the foreign price of its product."

Your worksheet calculations can now be converted into a pro forma invoice, which is defined as a price *quotation* in an invoice format. Your invoice for a completed overseas sale will be almost identical.

A quotation lists the products requested, detailed product descriptions, gross and net shipping weights (in metric if applicable), total cubic volume and dimensions (also in metric), delivery point, delivery terms (free on board versus cost-insurance-freight, etc.), price of each product ($US), terms of payment, estimated shipping time to U.S. port, estimated date of shipment arrival, validity period for quotation, and total charges to be paid by the buyer.

Pro forma invoices are binding price quotes. Therefore, specifying an expiration time on your quotation will protect you against changes in transportation or other costs prior to the delivery of your product. A hypothetical example of a pro forma invoice sent in response to an end-user's request for a quotation appears on the next page. A standard, commercial pro forma invoice appears in the Appendix, Sample Forms.

The pro forma invoice assists the buyer in obtaining a local import license, should that be required. It can also be used by the buyer to open a Letter of Credit (establish a line of credit at his bank) if this is the payment method that both parties have agreed upon.

PRO FORMA INVOICE

Arlington International
360 Armory Street
Boston, Massachusetts 02017 U.S.A.
Telephone (617) 493-6210
FAX (617) 492-3794
TELEX 27161 ARLNTNC PT

To: Emile Gorto   Your reference: FAX May 3, 1990
del Almo D'Mato,18   Our reference: Int. Order 5-6490
Milan, Italy   Terms of sale: Letter of credit
May 12, 1990
We hereby quote as follows:

Quantity	Model	Description	Unit	Extension
2	W320	Weighing machine	$4,625	$9,250
4	SW15	Scales	$ 375	$1,500

Total FOB Boston domestic packed   10,750
Export packing, inland freight   310
International airport & forwarder's
handling charges FAS Logan Airport, Boston   11,060
Airfreight and insurance   805
C.I.F. Genoa, Italy $ 11,865

Gross shipping weight: 267 kilo
Cubic volume: 3.1 meters

Note: All prices quoted in U.S. dollars.
Prices quoted for merchandise valid for 90 days from this
date.
Any changes in shipping or insurance charges are for account
of the buyer.
Factory shipment estimated 35 days from receipt of purchase
order and letter of credit issuance.

Part IV
Shipping

Don't be overly concerned about sending your product overseas. Although international shipping is usually more costly and takes longer than does domestic shipping, if the paperwork (documentation) is prepared correctly, you will experience little difficulty.

A freight forwarder will prepare most of the shipping documents required. This is why you should begin early to establish a good relationship with a forwarder who will answer your questions, provide valuable advice and get your product to your customer. Even so, you should also start learning something yourself about international shipping. Your responsibility is to understand packing, labeling, documentation and insurance requirements.

Most exporters use forwarders in one way or another. The extent to which you rely on a forwarding agent will depend upon your international trade experience and the size of your in-house staff. However, even if most shipping and documentation functions are turned over to a forwarder, you should still keep tabs on shipments.

Air versus sea transportation

For small-package shipments (up to about 70 pounds) air express is fast and reasonably economical. A general rule of thumb is that a shipment of less than 300 pounds is more cost-effective to ship by air. A freight forwarder can help you determine the best transportation mode for heavier shipments. However, you should consider the following:

• Ask your customer what mode of transportation is expected for the goods being purchased. Ask this before your price is set. If the customer is to pay for freight charges, he will specify how to ship.

• While shipping by sea may be less expensive, it takes much longer and is not as safe as air. When shipping by sea, allow at least two weeks for the shipment to reach a European port and more than one month to reach the Far East.

• With air, it is possible to reach major European cities overnight. However, be aware that passengers, baggage and U.S. mail have priority over commercial shipments. Your forwarder may have negotiated lower air freight charges, but your particular shipment may sit in a warehouse until space becomes available on a low-cost flight.

• Ask your forwarder if the shipment is being sent direct or will be transferred from one airplane to another. The more goods are off-loaded and on-loaded, the greater the chance of breakage or theft.

Checklist
• Will your delivery terms with the customer allow enough time to ship by sea?
• What are your customer's expectations?
• Is your product durable enough to withstand sea transit?
• Is shipping your product by air more costly than by sea?
• How are other companies in your industry shipping?

The Freight Forwarder

Freight forwarders are middlemen who act as the exporter's agent, authorized to arrange for movement of merchandise from a shipping point in the U.S. to a foreign port or a customer's location overseas. They must be licensed and certified by the Federal Maritime Commission.

Freight forwarders have no vested interest in the products for which they arrange transportation. They are *facilitators* who provide services to make it easier for the exporter to ship goods abroad. These services include selecting economical routes and carriers, consolidating shipments of several shippers to lower transportation charges, and preparing many of the shipping documents required when goods move from one country to another.

Some well-managed forwarders are actively involved in international marketing. For example, since they are familiar with the import regulations of foreign countries, they will alert you to unusual problems in a target country. Some will even help you generate sales leads. Some forwarders specialize in ocean freight; others in air freight shipments Most handle both. Still others concentrate on certain regions and countries. The larger firms have subsidiary offices in dozens of countries.

Your freight forwarder becomes involved after you have received a request for a quotation. You ask your forwarder to calculate the cost of transportation if your quoted price is to include those charges. In addition, the forwarder can advise you regarding packing, port charges, consular fees (if any), and costs of documentation and insurance. Moreover, when the shipment is ready to go, your forwarder will review all the documentation to ensure that it is correct.

Services of the freight forwarder

- Helps you determine which mode of transportation best suits your particular needs.
- Seeks the most economical rates (often using computers) and books space for your shipment (on airplane or ship).
- Alerts you regarding special regulations and conditions in the country of destination.
- Determines if an export license is required and assists in getting it.
- Arranges for inland freight.
- Provides warehouse and storage space if your merchandise is to be held at pier terminals awaiting consolidation.
- Arranges for special packing if needed.
- Consolidates your shipment with those of other exporters and loads them into one standard container, usually 20, 30 or 40 feet.

- Books space on the carrier.
- Prepares, examines and distributes necessary documents, e.g., shipper's export declaration, dock receipt, bill of lading, certificate of insurance, and certificate of origin.
- Provides transit insurance under a master policy.
- Prepares the appropriate documents for presentation to the bank for collection.
- Alerts your buyer that the shipment is on its way.
- Forwards all documents directly to your customer or your customer's paying bank.
- Tracks your shipment to its destination.
- Prepares transportation claims with the carrier (if necessary).

What do these services cost?

Your freight forwarder's fees are minimal when you consider the service he provides. Fees you pay the forwarder are in addition to the commissions he earns from carriers. Some forwarding companies buy a large volume of space from airlines and shipping companies at a low cost, and then resell that space to exporters.

The fee for finding you the best shipping rates averages $80. This fee includes investigating other possible charges (such as terminal handling costs for off-loading from truck into the warehouse), the best mode of shipment and the completion of certain documents, including an export declaration form, ocean bill of lading, dock receipt and consular invoice.

In addition, there may be direct, out-of-pocket costs such as communication fees and courier costs that are incurred for you. Additionally, when space is booked, there is a surcharge for making the up-front payment. This might be a flat fee, as low as $10, or a percentage of the money paid. If you delegate the preparation of bank documents to your forwarder, there are fixed fees for performing this service as well.

A conscientious forwarding agent will provide valuable information and perform many no-cost services. Thus, try to develop not only a solid business relationship with a forwarding company, but a close personal tie with one individual in that company in particular.

Typical freight forwarder fee schedule

Basic fee	$80.00
Communications	$15.00
Freight advance/surcharge	2% of amount advanced
Courier	cost
Inland freight	cost
Preparing letter of credit	$37.50
or	
Preparing sight draft	$15.00

Finding and Selecting a Forwarder

The freight forwarder's role can vary from complete documentation and shipment of an export sale to simply arranging the transportation of your goods. Forwarders usually operate better in some areas of the world than others, so consider where you will be exporting when making your selection. In addition, forwarders may specialize in ocean or air freight.

How do you locate a forwarder? Good sources for recommendations include other exporters you meet at international trade association meetings, individuals in the international departments of commercial banks, port authority export assistance offices, your state office of international trade, and so on.

Factors to consider

Affiliate offices. When a forwarder operates in many U.S. and foreign affiliated offices, you get the advantage of the most economical freight rates and documentation-pouch delivery. Moreover, your shipments can be traced more effectively with on-the-scene representation.

Location. Is the forwarder (or an affiliate) located next to an airport or seaport? Is it located near your business? A nearby office will save time and money since you may have to hand-deliver documents and merchandise on occasion.

Services. A full-service forwarder keeps your costs to a minimum. Does the forwarder's services include air and ocean freight? Look for forwarders who perform such extra services as
• emergency air-shipment deliveries to your customers.
• freight delivery directly to your customer's facility.
• consolidation of cargo with shipments of other exporters to lower freight costs.
• preparing needed documents.
• presenting documents to your bank for customer collection and payment.

Expertise in product areas. Does the forwarder specialize in certain product categories, or is the company a general forwarder?

Country specialization. Which countries does the forwarder serve?

Personal interest. Does the forwarder appear to take a personal interest in his clients? Did a representative come to your office or invite you to see their operation?

Credit terms. Forwarders usually pay carriers within seven to ten days from the time they book space. Therefore, they expect you to pay for their invoices within that period. Credit terms should be discussed at the beginning of an exporter-forwarder relationship.

Operating hours. Since many air shipments depart the U.S. at night, a forwarder should provide service at such times to handle problems that may arise.

References. Ask for references from client firms exporting a dollar volume approximately the same as you expect to do. Interview the references provided.

Your selection of a forwarder should also be based on a good reputation for responsiveness and attention to detail.

Be deliberate in selecting a forwarder. The role that agent assumes on your behalf is important to your export success.

Information the forwarder needs from you

- The name of your banker, your account number, and credit references.
- Permission to sign certain legal documents on your behalf through a limited power of attorney, required by the U.S. government. (See Appendix, Sample Forms.)
- Your Internal Revenue Service reporting number (the tax ID number you use on your tax returns). This number will appear on certain documents such as the Shipper's Declaration Form discussed below.
- A supply of your company letterhead paper, invoices, and packing list forms to save time when changes in shipping documentation are required.

The forms described here (and shown in the Appendix, Sample Forms) are the documents you will use most often for export shipments. While you don't have to become a documentation expert, you should understand why they are needed, and how they are completed and used.

Some documents represent U.S. and foreign government legal requirements; others are required by the importer or its bank; still others are transportation documents required by those involved in the shipping process.

Shipping your product abroad requires considerable attention to detail. The documentation involved must be completed properly. Initially it may sound complex, tending to discourage a new exporter. Rely on your forwarder, who deals with shipping documentation every day. Over time you will pick up the jargon as well as the basic procedures.

Export license

All U.S. exports (except for certain products sold to Canada) must have an export license. There are two types of export licenses, *general* and *validated*. The type you need depends on the product you are shipping and where. Most U.S products are shipped under a general license; their export is not regulated. Since the general license is a broad grant of authority by the government to all exporters, no paperwork is required. There are 20 or more general license categories, so ask your forwarder which applies to you. The correct designation is important because it will entered on your Shipper's Export Declaration.

Validated export license

Some commodities are controlled for national security, economic or political reasons. If you are exporting a controlled commodity, you must obtain a validated license. This license is a grant of authority to a particular exporter to ship a specific commodity in a specified quantity only to an identified end-user. Controlled commodities are listed on the Commodity Control List, on file at your DOC district office. Many computer and electronic or high tech products require a validated license for export.

To receive a validated license, you must submit an application to DOC's Bureau of Export Administration (BXA). There is a useful guide called *The Export License: How to Fill Out the Application*, available from BXA.

BXA has improved validated export licensing procedures recently by introducing two services. One, called the Export License Application and Information Network (ELAIN), can be used to transmit an application by computer. After review, the license will be issued electronically. The second service, System for Tracking Export License Applications (STELA), provides a means for an exporter with a touchtone telephone to find out the status of its validated license application.

If you expect to make multiple shipments to the same destination(s), apply for a multiple-transaction validated license. These are used by exporters selling controlled products through a distribution network in certain territories, and by those marketing approved spare parts and components to service providers in approved markets.

In addition to the Shipper's Export Declaration, a Destination Control Statement (DCS) is required for validated license exports. This statement indicates that the shipment will not be sent to an unauthorized destination. If you are a first-time exporter of a controlled product, ask BXA's export assistance staff for guidance on the proper wording of the DCS.

Shipper's export declaration (SED)

The SED is a document required by the Department of Commerce. It is prepared by your forwarder from information you supply. All international shipments valued in excess of $2,500 require a SED. All shipments in excess of $1,000 require one if sent parcel post or if a validated export license is required. (No SED is required for a Canadian export when the U.S.-Canada Free Trade Certificate of Origin is applicable.) This document is used to control exports and to compile aggregate export data. Ask your forwarder for a copy, and ask your district DOC office for a copy of the booklet *Correct Way to Fill Out the Shipper's Export Declaration.*

The one-page form has 24 sections. You must fill out sections l, 4–7 and 14–24. Most sections are self-explanatory and the information requested will be readily available. There are three sections which you may need to investigate more closely:

Section 17: Schedule B Number, the Harmonized System Commodity Number. If you are not sure which HS number your product falls under, seek assistance from your freight forwarder or your local DOC district office.

Section 21: Validated License Number/General License Symbol. If your product does not need a validated license, you need only to indicate the general license symbol. Most products fall under G-DEST. However, since there are 20 or so different general license codes, check with your freight forwarder for the correct one. If your shipment requires a validated license, the number to enter is the one issued by the Bureau of Export Administration.

Section 22: ECCN (Export Commodity Control Number). This entry is necessary only when you have a validated license shipment. Your local DOC district office will provide you with this number.

Shipper's letter of instructions

The letter of instructions is a written statement to your forwarder on how to handle your shipment. For example, if you want your forwarder to combine your merchandise with other exporter shipments, you would say "consolidate" as a special instruction.

Your forwarder will provide you with this multi-part form, the first carbon copy of which can serve as your SED. Thus, although it is your instruction, your forwarder may complete it for you.

Commercial invoice

The commercial invoice is a bill of sale you prepare for the buyer. It closely resembles the pro forma (quotation) invoice. (You may use your commercial invoice as a pro forma if you type that designation in the heading. Your buyer can then use it to obtain an import license, if required, and to apply for a letter of credit, if needed.)

The commercial invoice is often used by foreign customs officials to determine the value of goods for assessing customs duties. Some countries require a consular's invoice form in order to control and identify imports. Your forwarder will advise you on the completion of this invoice, including the insertion of your validated license number and the Destination Control Statement, if required.

Packing list

This document, which you prepare, facilitates the clearance of your goods through customs. Your packing list serves as a checklist to determine that the correct cargo has been received. It also helps the buyer inventory the shipment.

The packing list is essentially a commercial invoice without prices. Information on packing lists should include
- the number of packages in the shipment
- how the packages are numbered
- the gross and net weights of the packages (in both English and metric)
- package dimensions (English and metric)
- quantity of goods in each package
- contents of the shipment
- order number
- place and date of shipment.

You should match the commercial invoice against the packing list to make sure the shipment is complete. The packing list should be attached in a waterproof envelope marked "Packing List" or included in the shipment.

Dock receipt

The dock receipt is prepared by your forwarder. It is used to transfer accountability for the cargo between domestic and international carriers at the pier or warehouse.The ocean carrier signs and returns it to the delivering inland carrier and to your forwarder, thus acknowledging receipt of the cargo.

Bills of lading

A bill of lading is a receipt for the cargo as well as a contract for transportation between an exporter (shipper) and the ocean carrier. It may also be used as a negotiable instrument of ownership which can be bought, sold or traded while the goods are in transit. To be used in this manner, it must be a negotiable "to order" bill of lading, as opposed to a "straight," non-negotiable bill of lading.

An *air waybill of lading* is essentially a through bill of lading which covers both domestic and international flights transporting goods to a specified destination. It is non-negotiable, however, and serves only as a receipt for the shipper, indicating that the airline has accepted the goods and obligates itself to deliver the shipment to the airport of destination.

An *ocean bill of lading* is your only proof that the cargo has been loaded on board the vessel. It is a very important shipping document.

Your freight forwarder will prepare the ocean bill of lading or air waybill bill of lading.

A *through bill of lading* is a single bill of lading covering both the domestic and international carriage of an export shipment. For an ocean shipment two documents are required, an inland bill of lading for the domestic segment, and an ocean bill of lading for the international segment of the shipment.

A *clean bill of lading* is issued when the shipment is received in good order. If damage or a shortage is noted, a clean bill of lading will not be issued.

An *on-board bill of lading* certifies that the cargo has been placed aboard the named vessel and is signed by the master of the vessel or his designee. For a letter of credit transaction, an on-board bill of lading is usually necessary for the shipper to obtain payment from the bank.

An *inland bill of lading*, also known as a waybill in railway transportation or the pro forma bill of lading in trucking, is used to document the transportation of the shipment between the port and the point of origin or destination. It should include information such as marks, numbers, and steamship line to match that entered on a dock receipt. This is the first receipt for your cargo leaving your warehouse or place of shipment. It will be signed and dated by the truck driver at the time goods are picked up. It is an important document, but not negotiable except on shipments by rail or truck to Central America or Canada.

Certificate of insurance

This document assures your customer that insurance coverage is provided to cover loss or damage to the cargo while in transit. It is required when the terms of sale are C.I.F. (cost-insurance-freight). Insurance coverage and the certificate are provided by your forwarder under its master policy.

Certificate of origin

A document usually prepared by your forwarder that is required by some countries to certify precisely in which country the goods were produced. The form must be notarized and signed by the local Chamber of Commerce. Your forwarder will advise you which countries require this certificate and whether it must be visaed (legalized) by the resident consul.

Packing and Marking

Ocean vessel movements can be especially hard on packed cargo. So does loading by means of a sling, net or conveyor equipment. Therefore, pack your boxes or cases tightly. Brace or fill spaces to prevent movement.

Your shipment should be protected from moisture. It may be loaded in the rain or left uncovered for a period of time in a yard. Waterproof packing materials will prevent water and condensation damage.

You (and your warehouse supervisor) can obtain advice on packing from your forwarder or carrier—or an export packer, a service firm that specializes in packing international shipments. Your forwarder will recommend one.

An excellent source that describes and illustrates export packaging guidelines is called *Ports of the World*. This booklet includes suggestions to minimize pilferage, theft and storage or water damage. Another country-by-country shipping regulation resource book is the *Export Shipping Manual*. The *Exporters Encyclopedia* also describes the shipping requirements of individual countries.

Marking and Labeling

To minimize theft, do not describe the contents, or use well-known or easily identified marks on the outside of the package. Your customer may have provided you with specific packing and marking requirements to assist in identifying the shipment. The use of universal handling symbols are important as a means of providing necessary instructions and information. Examples of these universal symbols are shown on the next page.

Too often there are oversights and omissions made in labeling. Be aware of the following labeling problems:

1. Include your full name and address as well as that of the importer. Avoid incomplete and misspelled foreign addresses.

2. Letters of credit from some countries (e.g., Korea) require that the letter-of-credit number be marked on the cartons of a shipment. In some situations you will have to include on the invoice the notation that all your cartons have been marked precisely as described in the letter of credit.

3. If your customer has requested that certain markings and symbols be indicated on a shipment's packages, be sure to follow these instructions.

4. Indicate clearly if special care is required when handling your shipment. Use appropriate labels or hand lettering to make your wishes known (Fragile; Keep Chilled; Do Not Tip).

Marks and symbols

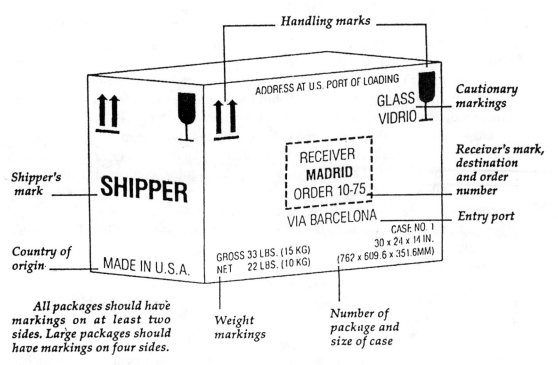

Handling marks

ADDRESS AT U.S. PORT OF LOADING

GLASS
VIDRIO

Cautionary markings

Shipper's mark — SHIPPER

RECEIVER
MADRID
ORDER 10-75

VIA BARCELONA

Receiver's mark, destination and order number

Entry port

CASE NO. 1
30 x 24 x 14 IN.
(762 x 609.6 x 351.6MM)

Country of origin — MADE IN U.S.A.

GROSS 33 LBS. (15 KG)
NET 22 LBS. (10 KG)

All packages should have markings on at least two sides. Large packages should have markings on four sides.

Weight markings

Number of package and size of case

FRAGILE — Q41-101

HANDLE WITH CARE — Q41-102

KEEP DRY — Q41-103

PROTECT FROM HEAT — Q41-104

KEEP FROZEN — Q41-114

PERISHABLE — Q41-113

Q41-105

USE NO HOOKS — Q41-106

SLING HERE SLING HERE — Q41-107

LIFT CART HERE — Q41-108

DO NOT FREEZE — Q41-116

DO NOT STACK — Q41-109

DO NOT ROLL — Q41-110

DO NOT TUMBLE — Q41-111

FOTO
PHOTOGRAPHIC MATERIALS — Q41-112

REFRIGERATE DO NOT FREEZE — Q41-115

How can your shipment documentation help your overseas customer?

You can assist your customer overseas clear customs faster by paying particular attention to certain shipping details. The following is recommended to shippers by F. W. Myers & Company, nationwide forwarders located in major ports in the U.S. and throughout the world.

• Prepare your invoices carefully. Type them clearly and allow sufficient space between items, keeping the data in columns. Make sure your invoices contain all information that will be shown on all well-prepared packing lists.

• Observe closely all instructions with respect to invoicing, packaging, marketing, labeling, etc., sent to you by your customer. As he usually knows the laws governing the import of your product into his country, complying with his instructions will help the shipment to clear quickly.

• On your invoice, show a detailed description of each item with unit price and extended amount, as packed. If multiple cartons are used, the line item should also indicate the carton number. Do not randomly number cartons.

• Mark your goods legibly and conspicuously with the name or pictorial symbol of the consignee and country of origin.

• Mark and number each package so it can be easily identified, with corresponding marks and numbers appearing on your invoice.

• Comply with the provisions or any special legislation and regulation of the U.S., the importing country, and carriers which may apply to your goods, such as those relating to labeling and packing food, drugs, cosmetics, radioactive and other hazardous materials.

If you market hazardous products and substances, you are experienced in dealing with unusual domestic transport requirements. Nonetheless, consult your forwarder about international requirements, including the United Nations recommendations for labeling hazardous materials. *Governments and carriers take the movement of hazardous cargo very seriously.*

Trade terms, shipping terms and terms of sale are phrases used to define the responsibilities and liabilities of both buyer and seller in an international transaction. Trade terms are negotiated at the time of sale, and are included on the commercial invoice and any other contract documents. The International Chamber of Commerce (ICC) introduced and defined terms, called *incoterms*, in 1936. For more than 50 years, incoterms and their definitions have been the most widely used, and widely accepted, standard for trade terms.

Incoterms define which party will assume shipping costs, and the conditions under which title to the goods is transferred from seller to buyer. They also define which party is responsible if the goods are damaged or lost during the shipment. When you and your buyer specify delivery according to incoterms, there need be no dispute arising from that aspect of your transaction.

Incoterms 1990 is the first revision in ten years. *The Guide to Incoterms*, available as a companion volume, will give you a detailed description of each term.

Common incoterms

Ex works (or ex factory, ex warehouse) is a price applied to goods at their point of origin. Your buyer is responsible for the cost of bringing the goods from that point to a foreign destination. This term is of minimum value to a foreign buyer, who is not in a good position to calculate the cost of transportation and insurance to a convenient foreign port.

Free Carrier (named port) is based on FOB, Free On Board (named port). This shipping term indicates that the title to the shipment transfers when it is loaded aboard ship at a named port. By using this term you are responsible, and pay the costs necessary, for placing the goods aboard a ship in the port of the named city. You are responsible for the cost of inland freight, containerization (or other types of packing), and loading charges. You are obligated to provide your customer with a clean bill of lading.

FOB Airport means that you are responsible for delivering the shipment to the airline at the airport of departure, at which time title passes to the buyer.

Free Along Ship (FAS) indicates that you pay all costs to deliver the shipment alongside the carrier's vessel at a named port of export. The buyer is responsible for clearing the goods for export and loading them aboard ship.

Cost and Freight (name of port/airport) means the seller is responsible for the merchandise cost plus freight to bring the shipment to the named (usually an overseas) port (or airport) of destination. However, under C&F, your customer assumes the risk of loss when the goods are delivered to a named carrier at the port (or airport) of shipment.

Cost, Insurance and Freight (named port of destination) is probably the most commonly used shipping term. C.I.F. includes all C&F costs plus the cost of the shipment's insurance. As in a C&F quote, title passes when the shipment is delivered to a named carrier at the port (or airport) of embarkation. If you provide your forwarder with information on your product and its weight and cubic measurement when packed, he will compute a C.I.F. price.

C.I.F. is preferred by foreign customers. Insurance coverage minimizes the risk to them. It also minimizes the risk to a buyer's bank in a letter-of-credit transaction when that bank substitutes its credit for that of the buyer.

Which Incoterm is best for you?

Think of shipping terms in a marketing context as well as the basis for your quoted price. You are new to a target country market. You want to be competitive and to be considered a good source for your product category. An "F.O.B. Dayton, Ohio," price doesn't give a foreign buyer what it costs to get your product to a port in or near the customer's location.

If at all possible, quote your price in U.S. dollars. This eliminates the risk of currency fluctuations. Again, from a marketing perspective, you may wish also to quote your price in your customer's currency. Customer attitudes toward quoting in another currency depend on the strength of the U.S. dollar in relation to other currencies, such as the Japanese Yen or the German Deutschemark. Your objective is to sell your product at a fair price. At times this means that you may have to accept payment in another currency.

Export shipping terms

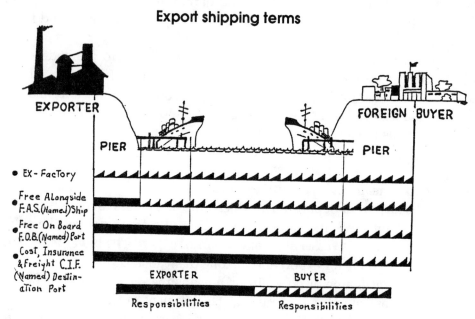

Part V
Getting
Paid

Finding a Banker

The payoff from your exporting efforts is at hand. For the purpose, a capable and experienced banker is another key resource person for the new exporter. Your bank can help you minimize your export credit risks. Therefore, your export planning effort should include informing your banker about the market you plan to enter, the overseas sales you estimate over a specific time period, and the additional financing requirments you forsee. Your objective is to sell the loan officer on an incremental increase in your line of credit based on your repayment history, the collateral you can provide, and a schedule of your repayment program.

What is described here is easier said than done. There are 14,000 banks in the United States. However, the typical commercial bank does not have an international department. Fewer than 300 banks have full-service international departments and foreign branches. The rest have "correspondent" relations with these larger banks, which enable them to conduct international banking business for their customers. You should be aware of this when you have a conversation with a loan officer at your bank, who may have limited experience in international trade financing. You will probably be directed to deal with a key person in a major correspondent bank that can provide the international service you need.

However, if at your bank you run into inexperience and what appears to be a lack of interest and support regarding your export needs, then perhaps you should find another. Contact exporters you meet at your monthly international trade association meetings, other bankers in your city or region, the local chamber of commerce, and your state office of international trade to learn of those banks who service customers in the area of international trade finance. Your freight forwarder will also be able to recommend the more knowledgeable and service-oriented bankers they deal with on a daily basis.

The reason a banker is an important resource is that the better banks provide more than just financial services. A close relationship with a trade finance person in the international department of a major bank can help you

- arrange guaranteed federal or state government export assistance loans
- process collection documents
- obtain creditworthiness information
- reduce foreign currency exchange risks
- research country import regulations.

Export Payment Terms

Which payment terms do you offer foreign buyers? These terms will have considerable impact on your firm's success in penetrating a new country market. When you researched environmental conditions, you learned the usual and customary terms offered to foreign buyers in your industry. But you also want to minimize the risk of nonpayment and receive prompt payment. *The key in offering payment terms to your buyers is to balance your need to minimize risk with the expectations of your foreign customers.*

In addition to the competitive (i.e., marketing) implications, there are other questions you should consider when choosing a method of payment for a shipment.

- What is the credit standing of your customer?
- Has your buyer requested a specific payment method? What happens to the sale if you don't offer what is requested?
- Are you in a buyer's or a seller's market?
- Have you calculated the "cost of delayed payment" in your quoted price? (An imputed interest-rate charge based on the current cost of money should be included in your pricing calculations.)
- Can you withstand a delayed payment, or will you have to borrow against foreign receivables? (Some payment methods, such as documentary collection, will provide you with a prompt, discounted payment. This is discussed under trade financing below.)
- Is the size of this order of such a magnitude that a delayed payment would affect your available working capital?
- What is the country/industry custom? Successful companies in Germany will be insulted if you insist on a letter of credit, for example. In Asian countries, however, this method is considered appropriate.

Common terms of sale

There are five common terms of sale for export payment. These are, in order of least-to-most risk for the exporter:

1. Cash in advance
2. Letter of credit
3. Documentary collection
4. Open account
5. Consignment

Cash in advance

Cash in advance offers you the best protection, but the usual payment terms of your competitors make this a difficult term to quote. It is estimated that only about 10% of international transactions are paid with cash in advance. Most buyers refuse to pay until the shipment is received. Though cash in advance is essentially risk-free, the exporter demanding it will not become a factor in the market. There are some few exceptions, as in the the case where the product is manufactured to buyer specifications or if the product is unique, giving the importing buyer a differentiated advantage.

The sequence of a cash-in-advance payment is

1. You send a price quotation (pro forma invoice) to the buyer, requesting payment prior to shipment.
2. Buyer pays his bank.
3. Buyer's bank pays your bank.
4. Your bank pays you.
5. You ship to buyer.

Letter of credit

This payment method accounts for about 25% of international trade transactions. For centuries the letter of credit has allowed businesses throughout the world to bridge national differences in language, custom and credit practices. It is the preferred method for facilitating foreign trade transactions.

Using a letter of credit substitutes the credit of a bank for the buyer's credit. A letter of credit offers protection to both buyer and seller. You, the seller, are assured of receiving payment. The import buyer is assured that payment will be made only after all the terms and conditions of the letter of credit are met. It is the payment term a new exporter selling to a new market will usually quote.

Exporting goods under a letter of credit involves your company as the "beneficiary," your bank as the "advising" and/or "confirming" bank, your overseas customer, and your customer's "issuing" bank. When a sale is agreed to, the buyer contacts his issuing bank and opens a letter of credit in your favor. The issuing bank's credit is now substituted for that of the buyer.

Your customer's bank issues the credit and forwards it to your bank. Your bank verifies that the instrument is authentic. Your bank forwards it to you to review to make sure it conforms to the agreed-to terms of sale. If your customer's issuing bank requests it, your advising bank will "confirm" the credit and attach its promise to pay. (This saves transmittal time to the issuing bank.) Your bank obtains payment for you through a process referred to as "negotiation." Your bank pays you when the funds are transferred from the foreign bank.

From the time you ship the goods until you receive payment, your bank should keep you informed of the status of the transaction.

It is important that you comply *precisely* with all terms and conditions of the letter of credit (for example, the exact shipping terms as quoted, correct quantities and dollar amounts, proper accompanying documents as required, no misspellings that might create discrepancies, and so on).

Sequence for a letter-of-credit payment
- Based on your quotation, you and your buyer agree on terms and conditions of the sale.
- Buyer asks his issuing bank to open a letter of credit.
- The buyer's bank prepares and issues the letter of credit in your favor.
- The letter of credit is forwarded by the issuing bank to your advising bank.
- Your bank verifies the authenticity of the letter of credit and forwards it to you, the beneficiary.
- You review the letter of credit carefully to make sure you can comply with the terms. (You make shipment only when you are able to comply.) You or your bank contacts your freight forwarder to book transportation. A copy of the letter of credit is given to your forwarder. Your forwarder completes other required documentation as specified in the letter of credit. The goods are shipped.
- You (or your forwarder) deliver the documents, as specified in the letter of credit, for examination to your advising bank.
- When your bank finds the documents conform to the letter of credit, it will follow the payment instructions in the letter of credit and, if named the paying bank, will remit funds to you.
- Your advising bank sends the documents to the buyer's issuing bank for examination. If they are in order, the issuing bank will send the documents to the buyer, charge the buyer's account, and reimburse the advising (paying) bank.
- Your buyer takes the documents and picks up the goods from the carrier.

A bank will charge for a commercial letter of credit between 1/4% and 1% of the amount of payment as handling charges. Additional amendment and confirmation fees related to letters of credit make it a high-cost instrument for export shipments less than $10,000 in value.

Who pays which bank charges can be made clear in the letter of credit instructions you provide your customer.

Variations of letters of credit
- An irrevocable letter of credit cannot be changed without the consent of all parties involved—the foreign banker must pay you, even if the buyer defaults.
- A revocable letter of credit is not advisable since it may be altered or revoked without your permission.
- A confirmed letter of credit is one that has been validated by a U.S. bank. You are still paid even if the buyer's foreign bank defaults. You need not worry about the foreign bank's credit rating.
- With an unconfirmed letter of credit your bank will wait until it receives payment from the issuing foreign bank before it remits payment to you.

The safest option for you when selling to new, unknown buyers is the confirmed, irrevocable letter of credit. With an unconfirmed, irrevocable letter of credit, you rely only on the buyer's bank for payment. Avoid an unconfirmed letter of credit if the buyer's bank is questionable or if the buyer's government is politically or economically unstable.

It is important that you communicate to your customer the provisions of the letter of credit you require. A *letter of credit instruction form* is an excellent way to achieve this (see Appendix, "Sample Documents").

Documentary collection

Documentary collection is a procedure in which a seller and buyer agree that settlement will be effected when a collection instrument (bill of exchange or draft) and other documents—representing title and interest in the goods—are presented. It is estimated that approximately 15% of international trade transactions are paid by a form of documentary collection.

The other documents accompanying a draft are the bill of lading or air waybill, a commercial invoice, a packing list (plus, depending upon a country's import laws, a consular invoice and a certificate of origin).

The *bill of exchange* is a contract drawn by the seller on the foreign buyer. The contract represents a promise to pay the exporter a sum of money within a stipulated amount of time. The seller has to make the shipment before demanding payment from the buyer, and at the same time he is afforded the protection that the buyer will not get possession of the goods before payment is made or on an agreed-upon future date.

The parties to a collection are the "drawer" (the seller who initiates the procedure), the "drawee" (the buyer to whom the collection is to be presented for payment or acceptance), the "remitting bank" (the bank to whom the drawer/seller delivers the collection for processing), and the "collecting bank" (the bank who receives the collection from the remitting bank for presentation for the drawee/buyer for payment or acceptance).

Although these commercial banks act as intermediaries to process the collection documents, they are not responsible for examining them, except to ascertain that the indicated documents are included and that any negotiable documents are in good form.

Collection documents

A *draft* is an unconditional order in writing signed by one party, the exporter, addressed to another, the buyer, directing the drawee/buyer to pay a specified sum of money.

A *sight* draft provides for payment at presentation. It is equivalent to a domestic C.O.D. transaction. One limitation with a sight draft is the amount of time that may pass before payment is received. It takes time for the draft to pass from you, to your bank, to your bank's correspondent bank, to the buyer's bank. Payment may be delayed several weeks.

The major risk is that an irresponsible buyer could refuse to accept the shipment for some reason such as price decline, in which case the seller would have to find another buyer, make a compromise settlement with the original buyer or undertake the cost of having the shipment returned.

A *time* draft incorporates a fixed or determinable future payment date, such as "30 days after sight" or "60 days after bill of lading date," or a specified future date. In a time-draft transaction, the documents representing title to the goods are released to the buyer upon acceptance of the draft. The signing constitutes an acknowledgment of the obligation. The accepted draft is then known as a "trade acceptance" and is only as good as the buyer's credit standing.

The major risk is that the buyer, once in possession of the goods, could refuse payment. As an exporter, you are dependent on your customer's credit standing and goodwill. A time draft is viewed as the "middle ground" between a letter of credit and an open account transaction.

Sequence for a documentary collection

* You or your freight forwarder presents the collection documents to your remitting bank.
* Your remitting bank forwards a transmittal letter and the collection documents to the buyer's collecting bank.
* Your buyer's collecting bank presents the documents to the buyer.
* Your buyer accepts or pays to the collecting bank. In the case of a sight draft, the overseas bank will deliver the documents against payment. For a time draft, documents will be given to the buyer against his acceptance of the draft.
* The buyer's collecting bank advises your remitting bank of acceptance or remits payment.
* You receive payment or advice of payment from your remitting bank.

The cost you incur for documentary collection processing is less than for a letter of credit because your bank is only an agent to collect payment, not a guarantor of that payment. Bank fees will average about 0.125% of the amount of payment.

The set of accepted rules that apply to documentary collection are found in *Uniform Rules for Collection.*

Direct collection letter

Because of the delayed payment often associated with sight drafts, a relatively new payment instrument, the direct collection letter, is becoming popular. This draft is drawn on your customer's bank. You should ask your freight forwarder about this type of draft even though it is not recommended for a first-time shipment to an unknown buyer. Moreover, some countries do not yet allow its use.

When advisable and permissible, by using a direct collection letter the exporter may be paid within 12 to 15 days from the date the bank-supplied collection letter is completed by the freight forwarder and, along with the other required documentation, is sent by courier directly to the buyer's bank. This is two to three weeks faster than a sight draft. Thus, the major benefit is prompt payment. The importer also benefits since no funds are put up front, as in the case of a letter of credit. A typical charge by the freight forwarder for handling a direct collection letter is about $15.

Open account

Open account provides for payment against an invoice. Open-account terms should state the number of days from a specific date (invoice date, shipping date or receipt-of-goods) when payment is due. Payment by the buyer is usually not sent until the merchandise is received. Thus, transit time can be a factor.

It is estimated that about half of all international trade transactions is conducted on an open-account basis.

Open account is quoted after a good and trusted relationship between the buyer and seller has been established. Open account is the most attractive payment method to the buyer, but it is a risky payment method unless the buyer is well known or has been checked thoroughly for credit worthiness. The transaction is totally unsecured. Banks are not involved since the seller is financing the sale.

Open-account terms are not recommended in those instances when the credit-worthiness of your customer is unknown or difficult to ascertain.

As discussed below, you can minimize your credit risk under open account (and documentary collection terms) by buying foreign credit insurance.

Consignment

In this type of transaction the seller ships goods to the foreign buyer who has assumed the responsibility for selling the merchandise. If and when sales are made, the distributor/dealer/ wholesaler forwards payment to the exporter. Title to the goods remains with the exporter until they are sold by the importer. It is obvious that the reputation and credit-worthiness of the foreign buyer are critical.

When you are considering which payment method to quote, consult your freight forwarder, DOC country desk office, or international banker. They will help you balance your credit risks with your marketing objectives.

An export sale, as do most business transactions, creates certain risks. It is important for the new exporter to be able to manage them. Here is a list of common risks with ways to minimize them.

Credit risk

To reduce credit risk, you must evaluate the creditworthiness of your customer just as you would a new customer in the U.S. market. Credit reports on prospective representatives, distributors and end-user buyers are as important in international trade situations as they are in the domestic market. Even with letters of credit, you need to know if your buyer has the credit standing necessary to initiate one.

How do you get a credit report on a foreign company?

• Ask your customer for U.S. company trade references. Then ask these exporters about the firm. There will be those who are not helpful, but there will be others who will tell you about their credit experiences.

• Your banker will have a network of affiliates who can get the type of information you need. This is also true for forwarders, shipping companies and airlines.

• The largest American reporting company, Dun & Bradstreet, is able to report on companies operating in most foreign countries. They will negotiate a contract or cash arrangement with you to supply detailed credit information about foreign firms.

• Ask the reference desk of a major library for D&B's *World Marketing Directory of Principal International Businesses*. Foreign companies are indexed geographically and by product category.

• The U. S. Department of Commerce's World Traders Data Reports provides confidential background information on potential foreign partners and end-user customers. Each report, prepared by a commercial officer in a U.S. embassy or consulate, assesses a prospective customer's reputation and makes a recommendation on whether to do business with the firm and on what basis. A one to three page analysis costs $100 and includes product lines, number of employees, capitalization, bank and trade references, sales volume, reputation and key officers. Information is current, no older than twelve months. To order a WTDR, contact your nearest district office and request the application form.

• Credit information on foreign companies can also be obtained from the National Association of Credit Management's (NACM) Foreign Credit Interchange Bureau (FCIB) subsidiary. Both members and nonmembers of NACM may use the credit check service. A credit report delivered to you in 2 to

3 days will cost about $200. One delivered in 3 to 5 weeks will cost about $145. The information supplied on a foreign company comes from U.S. and foreign agencies with whom NACM has arranged credit report service contracts.

• The Export-Import Bank of the United States (EXIMBANK), a government-owned corporation, offers loans, credit guarantees and insurance programs to assist U.S. firms. EXIMBANK has an extensive list of foreign firms whose credit standing has been checked. A report on a listed firm will be provided to you at no cost.

EXIMBANK has instituted a toll-free small business hotline: 800-424-5201. A specialized service for smaller exporters needing both general information and problem-solving assistance in conducting business overseas. It provides information on export credit, available assistance from other government agencies and certain private sector sources.

The Foreign Credit Insurance Association (FCIA) is administered and directed by EXIMBANK. In addition to its credit insurance programs, FCIA will also provide credit checks at no cost for its policy holders.

Ask FCIA for their publication called the *Guide to Agencies Providing Foreign Credit Information*. It lists firms offering credit reporting services.

• There are a number of foreign credit information firms. Some have contracts to provide credit reports for U.S. credit reporting organizations. One of these is Graydon America, a European company. Like D&B, Graydon will work with you by contract or cash. An individual credit report on a company in western Europe will cost about $105.

Insurance for export risks

Political risk. War, coup attempts, and political unrest might prevent a buyer from paying you. In addition, countries going through critical economic strains with high interest rates, severe inflation and unmanageable trade deficits pose potential political risks as well. Ask your banker for a current assessment of a country's political risk.

The Foreign Credit Insurance Association is probably your best choice for protecting your firm against buyer non-payment (credit) and country (political) risks. The first step is to contact your banker and ask if it participates in FCIA export credit insurance programs. Most do, since payment is guaranteed through EXIMBANK. Your other approach is to contact FCIA directly. (FCIA also has branch offices in Atlanta, Chicago, Cleveland, Houston, Los Angeles, Milwaukee and Washington DC.)

Your banker will apply to FCIA for coverage of both credit and political risks. Commercial risk coverage protects you when your buyer fails to pay because of insolvency, default or bankruptcy. Political risk coverage protects you against certain events such as war, revolution, destabilizing unrest and currency restrictions.

FCIA's insurance policies are designed to help finance small businesses and to make them more competitive in world markets. Specifically, there are two FCIA insurance policy programs of interest to you:

1. The standard policy for the individual exporting company which insures for commercial and political risk. It is referred to as their Comprehensive Short-term Deductible (CSD) policy. It insures you against commercial and political risk up to 180 days in all markets, with a deductible that varies depending upon size of company, number of export shipment applications, history of losses and countries of destination.

2. Special programs policies. FCIA acts as EXIMBANK's agent for special programs policies. There are two categories. One is the umbrella policy that serves several exporting companies (perhaps grouped by an independent insurance broker or a state agency) at lower-than-standard policy premium rates. Ask FCIA for their listing of independent insurance brokers who specialize in international insurance.

A second special programs policy is for individual companies new to exporting. This policy is designed for small or new exporters with $750,000 or less in annual export sales. It provides 95% of invoice protection for commercial risk and 100% protection for political risk. The premium varies according to terms of sale, but is lower than for the standard policy. For example, the premium rate for terms of 1–60 days is 75¢ per $100 of goods' valuation.

Insuring for transit risk

An overseas shipment must be insured against loss or damage in transit. Regardless of the mode (land, sea or air) of transport, international transit insurance is referred to as *marine insurance*.

Even when a sales agreement calls for your customer to provide insurance coverage, you should still insure the shipment. The rationale is that your customer has little incentive to pay you if the goods are lost or damaged.

The simplest means of transit protection is coverage under your forwarder's blanket policy. As long as your export shipments are somewhat irregular and represent only a modest share of total sales, you do not have to concern yourself with contracting with a private insurance company. You will find the forwarder's premium cost is far more reasonable since the exposure to risk is spread over many shipments.

When your export shipments become more frequent and represent a more substantial part of your total business, you can investigate and negotiate an open or blanket policy to cover all your shipments. When the time comes, your forwarder, DOC district office, port authority or those in your local international trade association can recommend reputable insurance companies.

Foreign exchange risk

If your sale is in a foreign currency, there is a risk that your customer's currency may depreciate against the U.S. dollar before you can get payment and convert it into dollars. There is, obviously, no exchange risk if the shipment is paid for in U.S. dollars.

Transfer risk. The risk if your buyer cannot acquire U.S. dollars to pay for the goods. Soft currencies, such as the Yugoslav dinar, have no market outside their countries. Foreign buyers may be able to acquire hard currencies to pay for their import needs at one time, but changes in foreign exchange regulations might prevent that from happening at other times.

Unless an export shipment is to be paid for in U.S. dollars, there is a currency exchange risk. Of course you can quote prices and require payment in U.S. dollars. Then your buyer assumes the currency exchange risk. The strength or weakness of the U.S. dollar in the international foreign exchange markets may have considerable influence on your customer's payment preference.

In some situations, a foreign buyer will prefer to pay for merchandise in local currency. This is more likely to be an issue in a buyer's market. You are subject to a lower price and reduced profits if the U.S. dollar decreases in value relative to your customer's currency during the production and transit period. Your banker can offer good advice relative to the exchange risks that may be involved in a given transaction. DOC's country desk officers can also advise you about a particular country's foreign exchange controls.

Hedging

In the case of a payment to be made in a foreign currency, your banker may recommend hedging the foreign exchange risk. This is done by your bank asking its foreign branch or affiliate to draw up a contract to "sell forward" at a fixed rate an amount of foreign exchange equal to the value of your transaction. This ensures that you will collect your expected revenue from the sale at a fixed dollar rate. The bank assumes the foreign exchange risk involved in return for a fee based on the value of the transaction.

To illustrate the hedging process, assume you receive an order for US$25,000 from a customer in Paris. Your buyer wishes to pay in French Francs and requests 60-day terms. You agree. You contact your bank immediately to determine the number of francs you must receive at current exchange rates to equal US$25,000. Assume the current rate of exchange is 5 francs to 1 U.S. dollar. Multiply the dollar value of your order by 5 to obtain the equivalent value in francs (125,000). Send a FAX to your buyer requesting a return FAX confirmation.

When your buyer's FAX confirmation is received, immediately execute a foreign exchange contract with your bank, agreeing to sell 125,000 francs in 60 days at the rate of 5 to 1, or US$25,000. To do this, your bank must agree to extend a credit line to you to ensure that you will fulfill this contract at maturity. The credit line is not for the full amount, but perhaps 20 percent of the transaction.

Sixty days later, on the due date, your customer pays 125,000 French francs to your bank's branch or affiliate in Paris. US$25,000 is then deposited into your U.S. bank account. You have preserved your profit margin (minus the bank fee) by eliminating the foreign exchange risk.

Appendixes

Agency Information Sources

Published Information Sources

ITA Offices

ITA Country Desk Officers

State Export Offices

U.S. Port Authorities

U.S. Port Authorities, Overseas Offices

U.S. Chambers of Commerce Abroad

Foreign Chambers of Commerce in the U.S.

U.S. Government Bookstores

Department of Commerce Industry Specialists

Important Contacts for Major Foreign Markets

World Trade Centers

U.S. and Foreign Commercial Service Overseas Posts

Sample Forms

Agency Sources of Information
(including databases, hotlines and software)

ABI/INFORM, Client Services Department, UMI/DATA COURIER, 620 South Third Street, Louisville KY 40202-2475, 800-626-2823.

Agricultural Information and Marketing (AIMS), Room 4649, Department of Agriculture, South Building, Washington DC 20250, 202-447-7103.

Agricultural Service, Foreign, Department of Agriculture, 14th Street and Independence Avenue, S.W., Washington DC 20250, 202-447-7115.

American Association of Exporters and Importers (AAEI), 11 West 42nd Street, New York NY 10036, 212-944-2230.

American Association of Port Authorities, 1010 Duke Street, Alexandria, VA 22314, 703-684-5700.

American National Standards Institute (ANSI), 1430 Broadway, New York NY 10018, 212-354-3300.

AT&T 800 service: call 800-422-0400, extension 1509.

AT&T Export 90's Hotline, 800-USA-XPOR, International Strategies, Inc., 260 Franklin Street, Suite 2210, Boston MA 02110, 617-439-6633.

AT&T international telephone directories. P.O. Box 19901, 2855 N. Franklin Road, Indianapolis IN 46219, 800-538-2665.

Berlitz Translation Services, 437 Boylston Street, Boston MA 02116, 617-266-6858.

Blytman International (for international mailing lists), 195 Dry Creek Road, Healdsburg CA 95448, 707-433-3900.

Bureau of Export Administration (BXA), Export Assistance Staff, Room 1099D, U.S. Department of Commerce, 14th & Constitution Avenue N.W., Washington DC 20230, 202-377-1455.

CEM/CENELEC, 2, rue Brederode Bte 5, 1000 Brussels, Belgium, tel: 32-2-519-6811. Address Evangelos Vardakas for CEM, and Hanns-Karl Tronnier for CENELEC. Current documentation regarding European standards.

Center for International Research (CIR)/Bureau of the Census, U. S. Department of Commerce, Scuderi Building, Room 409, Washington DC 20233, 301-763-4811. Fee: $75 for all available information on one country.

Chamber of Commerce of the United States, 1615 H Street, NW, Washington DC 20062, 202-659-6000. International Trade Division, 202-463-5460.

CIMS (Commercial Information Management System). Contact: District office, ITA/US.&FCS, Department of Commerce. CIMS research abstracts: $10 ($12 if provided on diskette). Other customized reports: approximately $40 plus a computer time charge. Also available through the TOP program and the Economic Bulletin Board.

Copyright Office, Library of Congress, Washington, D. C. 20559, 202-479-0700.

Dialog Information Services, 3460 Hillview Avenue, Palo Alto CA 94304, 800-227-1927.

Dun & Bradstreet, International Division, 190 South Orange Avenue, Livingston NJ 07039, 800-932-0025.

East-West Trade Information Center, International Trade Administration, U.S. Department of Commerce, Washington DC 20230, 202-377-2645.

EC Affairs Office, American Chamber of Commerce, 50 Avenue des Arts, 1040 Brussels, Belgium.

EC information databases, Delegation of the EC Commission, 7th Floor, 2100 M Street N.W., Washington DC 20037, 202-862-9500.

Economic Bulletin Board, National Technical Information Service, U.S. Department of Commerce, 5285 Port Royal Road, Springfield VA 22161, 703-487-4630.

ELAIN, 202-377-4811.

Europe Now, Room 1717, Department of Commerce, Washington DC 20230, 202-377-5276.

European Communities, Delegation of the Commission, 2100 M Street N.W., Washington DC 20037.

European Community Affairs, Office of, Department of Commerce, Room 3036, 14th and Constitution Avenue, N.W., Washington DC 20230, 202-377-5276. Managed by Charles Ludolph, who will also assist you regarding EC regulations.

European Community Information Service, 305 East 47th Street, New York NY 10017, 212-371-3804. Also at 2100 M Street, N.W., Washington DC 20037, 202-862-9500.

European Patent Office, Erhardstrasse, 27, 8000 Munich, Germany.

EXIMBANK (Export-Import Bank of the United States), 811 Vermont Avenue N.W., Washington DC 20571, 800-424-5201. For a free foreign firms credit standing report, contact Frances Turner, EXIMBANK Computer Applications, Room 1050, 811 Vermont Avenue, N.W., Washington DC 20571, 202-566-4690.

Export Managers Association of California (EMAC), 14549 Victory Boulevard, Van Nuys CA 91411, 818-782-3350.

Export Opportunity Hotline, 800-243-7232 (inside Washington, 202-223-1104), Small Business Foundation of America, 1155 15th Street N.W., Washington DC 20005.

Federation of International Trade Associations, 1851 Alexander Bell Drive, Reston VA 22091, 703-391-6108.

Foreign Business Practices Division, Office of International Finance and Investment, Bureau of International Economic Policy, International Trade Administration, U.S. Department of Commerce, 14th and Constitution Avenue, N.W., Washington DC 20230, 212-377-2000.

Foreign Credit Insurance Association (FCIA) Credit Department, 40 Rector Street, New York NY 10006, 212-306-5088/5089/5090.

GATT Inquiry Point/Technical Office, Office of Standards Code and Information, National Institute of Standards and Technology, Administration Building, Room A629, Gaithersburg MD 20899, 301-975-4040.

GLOBAL Vantage, Standard & Poor's Compustat Services Inc., 1221 Avenue of the Americas, New York NY 10020-1001. 800-525-8640.

Global Translations, 8 Agawam Road, Acton, Massachusetts 01720, 508-264-0600. Cost: about $20 per 100 words, depending upon the technical difficulty of the translation and the particular language required.

Graydon America, 71 West 23rd Street, New York NY 10010, 212-633-1434. An individual credit report on a company in western Europe will cost about $105.

International Advertising Association, 475 Fifth Avenue, New York NY 10017, 212-557-1133.

International Trade Administration (ITA) desk officer numbers (all prefixed by 202-377-): Belgium and Luxembourg, 5401; Denmark, 3254; France, 8008; Germany, 2434; Greece, 3945; Ireland, 4104; Italy, 2177; Netherlands, 5401; Portugal, 3945; Spain, 4508; United Kingdom, 3748.

International Trade Facilitation Council (formerly the National Council on International Trade Documentation), 350 Broadway, Suite 205, New York NY 10013, 212-925-1400. Annual membership fees, based on size of firm, $750 and up.

Johnston International Publishing Corporation, 386 Park Avenue South, New York NY 10016, 212-689-0120. Publishes industrial magazines read regularly by foreign readers.

Metric Programs, Office of, U.S. Department of Commerce, 14th Street & Constitution Avenue, N.W., Washington DC 20230, 202-377-3036.

Moody's Investors Service Inc., 99 Church Street, New York NY 10007, 800-342-5647.

National Association of Credit Management (NACM), Foreign Credit Interchange Bureau (FCIB), 520 Eighth Avenue, New York NY 10018, 212-947-5368.

National Association of Export Companies (NEXCO), 71 Murray Street, New York NY 10007, 212-481-1891.

National Association of Export Management Companies, Inc., 200 Madison Avenue, New York NY 10016.

National Center for Standards and Certification Information, National Bureau of Standards, Administration Building A629, Gaithersburg MD 20899, 301-975-2000 or 301-974-4040.

National Customs Brokers and Forwarders Association of America (NCBFAA), One World Trade Center, Suite 1153, New York, NY 10048, 212-432-0050.

National Trade Data Bank (NTDB), is operated by the DOC. Information via a monthly CD-ROM, available from National Technical Information Service. To buy singles ($35), call 703-487-4650; to buy an annual subscription ($360), call 703-487-4630. For information, call 202-377-1986.

NETWORK Manager, One World Trade Center, 63N, New York NY 10048, 212-466-8284.

NIST/NCSCI (National Institute of Standards and Technology, National Center for Standards and Certification Information) at the Department of Commerce, 301-975-4040.

Office of Canada, Room 3033, Department of Commerce, Washington DC 20230, 202-377-3101, FAX 202-377-3718.

Office of European Community Affairs, Room 306, Department of Commerce, Washington DC 20230.

Office of Metric Programs, U.S. Department of Commerce, 14th and Constitution Avenue, N.W., Washington DC 20230, 202-377-3036.

Overseas Sales and Marketing Association of America (OSMA), P.O. Box 37, Lake Bluff IL 60044, 312-234-1760.

Patent and Trademark Office, Crystal Plaza, 2021 Jefferson Davis Highway, Arlington VA 703-557-3158.

PIERS (Port Import/Export Reporting Service), Journal of Commerce, 110 Wall Street, New York NY 10005, 212-208-0363.

Port Authorities, American Association of (AAPA), 1010 Duke Street, Alexandria VA 22314, 703-684-5700.

PROMPT, Predicasts, 11001 Cedar Avenue, Cleveland OH 44106, 800-21-6388.

SBA regional offices:

I. 60 Batterymarch Street, 10th Floor, Boston MA 02110, 617-451-2030.

II. 26 Federal Plaza, Room 3108, New York NY 10278, 212-264-7772.

III. 475 Allendale Road, Suite 201, King of Prussia PA 19406, 215-962-3700.

IV. 1375 Peachtree Street, NE, Suite 502, Atlanta GA 30367, 404-347-2797.

V. 230 South Dearborn Street, Room 510, Chicago IL 60604, 312-353-0359.

VI. 8625 King George Drive, Building C, Dallas TX 75235, 214-767-7643.

VII. 911 Walnut Street, Room 1300, Kansas City MO 64106, 816-426-3605.

VIII. One Denver Place, North Tower, 999 18th Street, Suite 701, Denver CO 80202. 303-294-7149.

IX. 450 Golden Gate Avenue, Room 15307, San Francisco CA 94102. 415-556-7487.

X. 915 2nd Avenue, Room 1792, Seattle WA 98174. 206-442-1420.

SIMIS (Single Internal Market: 1992 Information Service). *See* European Community Affairs.

Small Business Administration, Office of International Trade, 409 Third Street, S.W., Washington DC 20416, 800-827-5722 (800 U ASK SBA) or 202-653-7794.

Small Business Foundation, 1155 15th Street N.W., Washington DC 20005. Hotline for Washigton: 202-223-1104; outside Washington: 800-243-7232.

Standard Rate and Data Service (SRDS), 3004 Glenview Road, Wilmette IL 60091, 800-323-4601.

State Development Agencies, National Association of, membership directory, 444 N. Capitol Street, N.W., Washington DC 20001, 202-624-5411.

STELA, 202-377-2753.

State Development Agencies, National Association of, membership directory, 444 N. Capitol Street, N.W., Washington DC 20001, 202-624-5411.

STELA, 202-377-2753.

The Federation of International Trade Associations (FITA), 1851 Alexander Bell Drive, Reston VA 22091, 703-391-6108.

TOP program, USDOC. A one-year subscription costs $25, plus connect time. Connect time ranges from ten cents per minute during the week to five cents per minute on the weekend and after business hours.

Trade development industry experts at U.S. Department of Commerce, Washington D.C. 20230:

Aerospace, Room 6877, 202-377-8228.

Autos and Consumer Goods, Room 4324, 202-377-2762.

Chemicals, Construction Industry Products, and Basic Industries, Room 4045, 202-377-0614.

Construction Projects and Industrial Machinery, Room 2001B, 202-377-2474.

Information Technology, Instrumentation and Electronics, Room 1001A, 202-377-4466.

Service industries, Room 1128, 202-377-3575

Textiles and apparel, Room 3199, 202-377-2043.

Trade Information Center hotline, 800-872-8723 (800 USA TRADE).

U.S. Council for International Business, 1212 Avenue of the Americas, New York NY 10036, 212-354-4480.

Underwriters Laboratories, Technical Assistance to Exporters Program (TATE), 1285 Walt Whitman Road, Melville NY 11747, 516-271-6200.

United States Council for International Business (USCIB), 1212 Avenue of the Americas, 21st Floor, New York NY 10036, 212-354-4480.

UNZ & Company, 190 Baldwin Avenue, Jersey City NJ 07306, 800-631-3098. In New Jersey, 201-795-5400.

World Trade Centers Association, One World Trade Center, 55th Floor, New York NY 10048, 212-313-4600.

Worldwide Chamber of Commerce, Inc., P.O. Box 1029, Loveland CO 80539, 303-663-3231.

Published Sources of Information

The following publications may be purchased from the sources listed, or obtained at the reference desks of most major libraries.

American Export Register, 1990. Thomas International Publishing Co. Inc., 250 West 34th Street, One Penn Plaza, New York NY 10119, 212-290-7343.

Arthur Young International Business Guide. Charles E. Valentine. FCC Publishing, 156 Fifth Avenue, Suite 820, New York NY 10010, 212-206-1150.

Background Notes. published by the U.S. Department of State. Annual subscription: $50; single country copies: $2.25. Order from the Superintendent of Documents, U.S. Government Printing Office, Washington DC 20402 or contact Public Information Service, Bureau of Public Affairs, Room 4827A, Department of State, Washington DC 20520, 202-647-6575.

Basic Guide to Exporting. Superintendent of Documents, U.S. Government Printing Office, Washington DC 20402. Stock number 003-009-00315-6.

Bringing World Markets Closer to Home: A guide to international trade procedures and documentation. Unz and Company, 190 Baldwin Avenue, Jersey City NJ 07036.

Business America. International Trade Administration, U.S. Department of Commerce. Available from Superintendent of Documents, U.S. Government Printing Office, Washington DC 20402. Single copies, $2.25. Annual subscription, $49. Any district office of the DOC International Trade Administration can assist with subscription orders.

Business Publications Rates and Data. Standard Rate and Data Service (SRDS), 3004 Glenview Road, Wilmette IL 60091, 800-323-4601. Three-part volume, $477 yearly. Part I, U.S. business publications' rates and data. Part II, publications in the healthcare fields. Part III, international publications.

Canadian Key Business Directory. Dun's Marketing Services, 365 Bloor Street East, 14th Floor, Toronto, Ontario M4W 3L4 Canada.

Correct Way to Fill Out the Shippers Export Declaration. U.S. Department of Commerce. Contact your district office.

Direct Mail List. Published by Standard Rate and Data Service, 3004 Glenview Road, Wilmette IL 60091, 800-323-4601. Annual subscription, $287.

Directory of American Firms Operating in Foreign Countries. World Trade Academy Press, 50 East 42nd Street, New York NY 10017, 212-697-4999.

Directory of Associations in Canada, Micro Media, Ltd., 158 Pearl Street, Toronto, Ontario M5H 113, Canada, 416-593-5211 or 800-387-2689.

Directory of British Associations. CBD Research Ltd., 15 Wickham Road, Beckenham, Kent BR3 2JS, England.

Directory of Foreign Firms Operating in the U.S. Uniworld Business Publications, 50 East 42nd Street, New York NY 10017.

Directory of Foreign Trade Organizations in Eastern Europe, edited by Vance T. Petrunoff. International Trade Press, P.O. Box 14101, San Francisco CA 94114, 415-495-4765. $125.

Directory of Leading U.S. Export Management Companies. Bergano Book Company, P.O. Box 190, Fairfield CT 06430, 203-254-2054. $45.

Encyclopedia of Associations and *Encyclopedia of Associations International,* Gale Research, Inc., Book Tower, Detroit MI 48244, 313-961-2242.

Europa World Year Book. Europa Publications, Ltd., 18 Bedford Square, London WC1B 3JN, England.

European Directory of Marketing Information Sources. Euromonitor Publications, Ltd., 87-88 Turnmill Street, London EC1M 5QU, England.

European Markets: A Guide to Company and Information Sources. Washington Researcher's Publishing, 2612 P Street, N.W., Washington DC 20677, 202-333-3533. $275.

European Trade Fairs: A Guide for American Exporters. International Trade Administration. Superintendent of Documents, U.S. Government Printing Office, Washington DC 20402, 202-783-3238. $5.

Eximbank Information Kit. Export-Import Bank of the U.S., 811 Vermont Avenue N.W., Washington DC 20571.

Export Administration Regulations. Superintendent of Documents, U.S. Government Printing Office, Washington DC 20402, 202-783-3238.

Export Credit Insurance: The Competitive Edge. Foreign Credit Insurance Association, One World Trade Center, 9th Floor, New York NY 10048.

Export License: How to Fill Out the Application. Bureau of Export Administration (BXA), Export Assistance Staff, Room 1099D, U. S. Department of Commerce, 14th and Constitution Avenue, N.W., Washington DC 20230, 202-377-1455.

Export Sales and Marketing Manual. John R. Jagoe, Export USA Publications, Minneapolis MN.

Export Shipping Manual. Bureau of National Affairs (BNA), 1231 25th Street, N.W., Washington DC 20037, 202-452-4200. $448/year.

Export Trading Company Guidebook. Superintendent of Documents, U.S. Government Printing Office, Washington DC 20402, 202-783-3238. GPO number: 003-009-00523-0. $8.00.

Exporter's Encyclopedia, Dun's Marketing Services, 3 Sylvan Way, Parsippany NJ 07054, 800-526-0651.

Exporter's Guide to Cargo Insurance. American Institute of Marine Underwriters, 14 Wall Street, New York NY 10005.

Exporter's Guide to Federal Resources for Small Business, Interagency Task Force on International Trade, U.S. Small Business Administration. Superintendent of Documents, U.S. Government Printing Office, Washington DC 20402.

Exporting from Start To Finance. L. Fargo Wells and Karin B. Dulat, Liberty House, Blue Ridge Summit PA.

Exportise. Small Business Foundation of America, Inc., 1155 15th Street N.W., Washington DC 20005, 800-243-7232; in Washington, 202-223-1104.

Financing U.S. Exports. International Department, First National Bank of Chicago, One First National Plaza, Chicago IL 60670.

Foreign Business Practices. Superintendent of Documents, U. S. Government Printing Office, Washington DC 20402.

Foreign Commerce Handbook. Chamber of Commerce of the U.S., 1615 H Street N.W., Washington DC 20062.

Foreign Economic Trends (FETs). Single copies ($1.00) available from the Publications Sales Branch, Room 1617M, Department of Commerce, Washington DC 20230. Subscriptions available from the Superintendent of Documents, U.S. Government Printing Office, Washington DC 20402. Annual subscription, $55.

Going International: How to Make Friends and Deal Effectively in the Global Marketplace. Copeland and Griggs, Random House, Inc., New York NY 10022.

Guide To Financing Exports. U.S. and Foreign Commercial Service, International Trade Administration, Room 1617, U.S. Department of Commerce, Washington DC 20230.

Guide to Canadian Manufacturers, Dun's Marketing Services, 365 Bloor Street East, 14th Floor, Toronto, Ontario M4W 3L4 Canada.

Guide to Checking International Credit, Guide to Selecting the Freight Forwarder, Guide to Understanding Drafts, Guide to Understanding Letters of Credit. International Trade Institute, 5055 N. Main Street, Dayton OH 45415.

Guide to Documentary Credit Operations, Guide to Drafting International Distributorship Agreements, Publication #441, $25, and *Commercial Agency*, Publication # 410, $25. International Chamber of Commerce, ICC Publishing Corporation, 156 Fifth Avenue, New York NY 10010, 202-206-1150.

Guide to International Shipping. International Trade Institute, 5055 North Main Street, Dayton, OH 45415, 800-543-2453 or 513-276-5995. $44.50.

How to Find Information on Foreign Firms, Washington Researchers Publishing, 2612 P Street, N.W., Washington DC 20007, 202-333-3533. $85.

How to Get the Most from Overseas Exhibitions. International Trade Administration, Department of Commerce, Washington DC 20230.

Incoterms 1990 and *The Guide to Incoterms*. ICC Publishing Corporation, 156 Fifth Avenue, Suite 820, New York NY 10010, 212-206-1150.

International Directory of Corporate Affiliations. National Register Publishing Co., 3004 Glenview Road, Wilmette IL 60091, 312-256-6067.

International Marketing Handbook. Gale Research, Inc., Book Tower, Detroit MI 48244, 313-961-2242.

Japan Trade Directory. Japan External Trade Organization (JETRO), Publications Department 2-5, Toranomon 2-chome, Minato-ku, Tokyo 105 Japan. Approximately $200.

Journal of Commerce Export Bulletin, 110 Wall Street, New York NY 10005.

Journal of Commerce Transportation Telephone Tickler. Journal of Commerce, 445 Marshall Street, Phillipsburg NJ 08865, 202-859-1300. 1990 edition: 3,000 pages, four volumes (Volume I: Port of New York. Volumes II, III and IV: all other U.S. ports). $65 per set.

Journal of Commerce. Advertising Office, 10 Wall Street, New York NY 10005, 212-425-1616.

Key Officers in Foreign Service Posts. Department of State (Publication #7877, revised periodically). $10 (including three annual updates). Superintendent of Documents, U.S. Government Printing Office, Washington DC 20402, 202-783-3238.

Licensing Guide for Developing Countries. UNIPUB, 345 Park Avenue South, New York NY 10010. Legal aspects of licensing agreements.

Major Companies of the Far East. Volume I: South East Asia; Volume II: East Asia. Graham and Trotman Publishers, Sterling House, 66 Wilton Road, London SW1V 1DE England.

Monthly Exports and Imports (Foreign Trade Report 925). Superintendent of Documents, U. S. Government Printing Office, Washington DC 20402, 202-783-3238.

NASDA Trade Development Catalog. National Association of State Development Agencies, 444 North Capitol Street N.W., Suite 611, Washington DC 20001.

Overseas Business Reports (OBRs). Single copies ($variable) available from the Publications Sales Branch, Room 1617M, U. S. Department of Commerce, Washington DC 20230. Subscriptions available from the Superintendent of Documents, U.S. Government Printing Office, Washington DC 20402. Annual subscription, $14.

Pacific Shipper Weekly. 562 Mission Street, Suite 601, San Francisco CA 94105, 415-546-3946.

Partners in Export Trade. Department or Commerce. Superintendent of Documents, U.S. Government Printing Office, Washington DC 20402. Publication # 003-009-00512-4. $11.

Ports of the World. Insurance Company of North America (INA), 25 Tower, 1600 Arch Street, Philadelphia PA 19103, 215-523-4000, ext. 3622.

Predicasts F&S International Index and *Predicasts F&S Index Europe.* Predicasts, World Headquarters, 11001 Cedar Avenue, Cleveland, OH 44106, 800-321-6388.

Principal International Businesses. Dun's Marketing Services, 3 Sylvan Way, Parsippany NJ 07054, 800-526-0651.

Profitable Exporting: A Complete Guide to Marketing Your Products Abroad. John S. Gordon and J. R. Arnold. Wiley, New York NY.

Shipping Digest. Gyer-McAllister Publications, 51 Madison Avenue, New York NY 10010, 212-689-4411. $38.00.

Showcase USA. Sell Overseas America, 2500 Artesia Boulevard, Redondo Beach CA 90278, 213-376-8788. A bimonthly, advertising U.S. products abroad.

Standard Handbook of Industrial Distributors. Bergano Book Company, P.O. Box 190, Fairfield CT 06430, 203-254-2054.

Standard Industrial Classification (SIC). Published by the Office of Management and Budget, National Technical Information Service, 5285 Port Royal Road, Springfield VA 22161. Can be purchased from the Superintendent of Documents, Washington DC 20402, 202-783-3238. Ask for GPO number 041-001-00314-2. $24.

Standard Industrial Classification Manual. Superintendent of Documents, U.S. Government Printing Office, Washington DC 20402.

Standard International Trade Classification Manual. United Nations, Room DC2-0853, New York, NY 10017.

Standard Rate and Data Service, International Edition. SRDS, 3004 Glenview Road, Wilmette IL 60091, 800-323-4601.

State Export Program Database, 1990. National Association of State Development Agencies, 444 N. Capitol Street, N.W., Suite 611 Washington, DC 20001. $95.

Statistical Classification of Domestic and Foreign Commodities Exported from the U.S. (The Harmonized System). Superintendent of Documents, U.S. Government Printing Office, Washington, D.C. 20402. $48.

Stores of the World Directory. Newman Books, Ltd., 48 Poland Street, London W1V 4PP, England. Tel: 44-1-439-0335.

The States and Small Business: A Directory of Programs and Activities. Available from the Office of State and Local Affairs, Office of the Chief Counsel for Advocacy, U. S. Small Business Administration, 1441 L Street, N.W., Washington DC 20416, 202-634-7642.

The World is Your Market: An Export Guide for Small Business. 1990. Edited by William A. Delphos. Braddock Communications, Washington DC.

U.S. Importers and Exporters Directory. The Journal of Commerce, 445 Marshall Street, Phillipsburg NJ 08865. $375.

Uniform Customs and Practices for Documentary Credits, Publication 400. ICC Publishing Corporation, 156 Fifth Avenue, New York NY 10010, 212-206-1150.

Uniform Rules for Collection, Publication #322. International Chamber of Commerce, ICC Publishing Corporation, 156 Fifth Avenue, Suite 820, New York NY 10010, 212-206-1150. $6.95.

United Nations Standard Industrial Trade Classification (SITC). Available from the United Nations, Room DC2-0853, New York NY 10017, 212-963-8302. $12.50.

United Nations Statistical Yearbook. United Nations and Information Center, 1889 F Street, N.W., Washington DC 20006.

United States Importers and Exporters Directory. Volumes I and II. Journal of Commerce, 110 Wall Street, New York NY 10005.

UNZ Company Catalog for International and Domestic Shippers. UNZ and Company, 190 Baldwin Avenue, Jersey City NJ 07306, 800-631-3098.

Wall Street Journal. Advertising Services Department, Dow Jones & Company, Inc., 420 Lexington Avenue, New York NY 10170.

World Bank Atlas. Price: $6.50. World Bank Bookstore, 701 18th Street, N.W., Washington DC 20013, 202-473-2941. Ask for a free annual listing of all publications.

World Guide to Trade Associations. Saur Verlag KG, Postfach 711009, 8000 Munich, Germany, Tel: 49-89-798901.

Worldcasts. Predicasts, 11001 Cedar Avenue, Cleveland, OH 44106, 800-321-6388 or 216-795-3000. Single volumes, $450; Complete set, $1,300.

International Trade Administration/ US&FCS District Offices

*Denotes regional office with supervisory responsibilities.
†Denotes trade specialist at a branch office.

ALABAMA
*Birmingham—Rm 302, 2015 2nd Ave North, Berry Building, 35203, 205-731-1331
ALASKA
Anchorage—World Trade Center, 4201Tudor Centre Dr., Suite 319, 99508, 907-271-6237
ARIZONA
Phoenix—Federal Building & U.S. Courthouse, 230 North 1st Ave, Rm 3412, 85025, 602-379-3285
ARKANSAS
Little Rock—Suite 811, Savers Federal Building, 320 West Capitol Ave, 72201, 501-324-5794
CALIFORNIA
Los Angeles—Rm, 9200, 11000 Wilshire Blvd, 90024, 213-209-7104
Santa Ana—116-AW 4th St, Suite 1, 92701, 714-836-2461
San Diego—6363 Greenwich Dr, Suite 145, 92122, 619-557-5395
*San Francisco—250 Montgomery St., 14th floor, 94104, 415-705-2300
COLORADO
*Denver—680 World Trade Center, 1625 Broadway, 80202, 303-844-3246
CONNECTICUT
*Hartford—Rm 610-B, Federal Office Building, 450 Main St, 06103, 203-240-3530
DELAWARE—serviced by Philadelphia District Office
DISTRICT OF COLUMBIA

†Washington, D,C,—(Baltimore, Md, District) Rm, 1066 HCHB, Department of Commerce, 14th St, & Constitution Ave,, N,W, 20230, (202) 377-3181
FLORIDA
Miami—Suite 224, Federal Building, 51 SW First Ave, 33130, 305-536-5267
†Clearwater—128 North Osceola Ave, 34615, 313-461-0011
†Jacksonville—3100 University Blvd South, Suite 200A, 32216, 904-791-2796
*Orlando—College of Business Administration, CEBA 11 Rm 346, University of Central Florida, 32816, 407-648-6235
†Tallahassee—Collins Building, Rm 401, 107 W Gaines St, 32304, 904-488-6469
GEORGIA
Atlanta—Plaza Square N., 4360 Chamblee Dunwoody Rd., 30341, 404-452-9101
Savannah—120 Barnard St A-107, 31401, 912-944-4204
HAWAII
Honolulu —4106 Federal Building, PO Box 50026, 300 Ala Moana Blvd, 96850, 808-541-1782
IDAHO
†Boise (Portland, Ore, District)—Hall of Mirrors Building, 700 W State St, 2nd fl, 83720, 208-334-3857

ILLINOIS

Chicago—Rm 1406, Mid Confinental Plaza Building, 55 East Monroe St, 60603, 312-353-4450

†Wheaton—Illinois Institute of Technology, 201 E. Loop Rd., 60187, 312-353-4332

†Rockford—515 North Court St, PO Box 1747, 61110-0247, 815-987-8123

INDIANA

Indianapolis—One North Capitol Ave, Suite 520, 46204, 317-226-6214

IOWA

Des Moines—817 Federal Building, 210 Walnut St, 50309, 515-284-4222

†Cedar Rapids—424 First Ave., N.E., 52401, 319-362-8418

KANSAS

†Wichita—(Kansas City, Missouri, District), 151 N. Voltusia, 67214-4695, 316-269-6160

KENTUCKY

Louisville—Rm, 636B, Gene Snyder Courthouse and Customhouse Building, 601 W Broadway, 40202, 502-582-5066

LOUISIANA

New Orleans- 432 World Trade Center, No 2 Canal St, 70103, 504-589-6546

MAINE

†Augusta—(Boston, Massachusetts, District) 77 Sewall St, 04330, 207-622-8249

MARYLAND

Baltimore—413 US Customhouse, 40 South Gay and Lombard Sts, 21202, 301-962-3560

Gaithersburg—c/o National Institute of Standards and Technology, Bldg. 411, 20899, 301-962-3560

MASSACHUSETTS

Boston—World Trade Center, Suite 307, Commonwealth Pier Area, 02210, 617-565-8563

MICHIGAN

Detroit—1140 McNamara Bldg,, 477 Michigan Ave, 48226, 313-226-3650

†Grand Rapids-300 Monroe NW, Rm 409, 49503, 616-456-2411

MINNESOTA

Minneapolis—108 Federal Building, 110 S 4th St, 55401, 612-348-1638

MISSISSIPPI

Jackson—328 Jackson Mall office Center, 300 Woodrow Wilson Blvd, 39213, 601-965-4388

MISSOURI

*St, Louis—7911 Forsyth Blvd, Suite 610, 63105, 314-425-3302

Kansas City—Rm 635, 601 East 12th St, 64106, 816-426-3141

MONTANA—Serviced by Portland OR District Office

NEBRASKA

Omaha—11133 "0" St, 68137, 402-221-3664

NEVADA

Reno—1755 E Plumb Ln, No 152, 89502, 702-784-5203

NEW HAMPSHIRE—Serviced by Boston District Office

NEW JERSEY

Trenton—3131 Princeton Pike Building, No 6, Suite 100, 08648, 609-989-2100

NEW MEXICO

Albuquerque (Dallas TX District) 625 Silver SW, 3rd Floor, 87102, 505-766-2070

Santa Fe (Dallas TX District)—c/o Economic Development and Tourism Dept, 1100 St, Francis Drive, 87503, 505-988-6261

NEW YORK

Buffalo-1312 Federal Building, 111 West Huron St, 14202, 716-846-4191

†Rochester—111 East Ave, Suite 220, 14604, 716-263-6480

New York—Federal Office Building, 26 Federal Plaza, Rm 3718, Foley Sq, 10278, 212-264-0600

NORTH CAROLINA

*Greensboro—324 W Market St., Rm 203, PO Box 1950, 27402

NORTH DAKOTA—Serviced by Omaha, Nebraska, District Office

OHIO

*Cincinnati—9504 Federal Office Building, 550 Main St, 45202, 513-684-2944

Cleveland—Rm 600, 668 Euclid Ave, 44114, 216-522-4750

OKLAHOMA

Oklahoma City—6601 Broadway Extension, 73116, 405-231-5302

†Tulsa—440 S Houston St., 74127, 918-581-7650

OREGON

Portland—Suite 242, One World Trade Center, 121 SW Salmon St., 97204, 503-326-3001

PENNSYLVANIA

Philadelphia—475 Allendale Road, Suite 202, King of Prussia PA 19406, 215-962-4980

Pittsburgh—2002 Federal Building, 1000 Liberty Ave, 15222, 412-644-2850

PUERTO RICO

San Juan (Halo Rey)—Rm G-55 Federal Building, 00918, 809-766-5555

RHODE ISLAND

†Providence—(Boston MA District) 7 Jackson Walkway, 02903, 401-528-5104, ext 22

SOUTH CAROLINA

Columbia—Strom Thurmond Federal Building, Suite 172, 1835 Assembly St, 29201, 803-765-5345

†Charleston—JC Long Building, Rm 128, 9 Liberty St, 29424, 803-724-4361

SOUTH DAKOTA—Serviced by Omaha District Office

TENNESSEE

Nashville—Suite 1114, Parkway Towers, 404 James Robertson Parkway, 37219-1505, 615-736-5161

†Knoxville—301 E. Church Ave., 37915, 615-549-9268

†Memphis—The Falls Building, Suite 200, 22 North Front St, 38103, 901-544-4137

TEXAS

*Dallas—Rm 7A5, 1100 Commerce St, 75242-0787, 214-767-0542

†Austin—PO Box 12728, 816 Congress Ave, , Suite 1200, 78711, 512-482-5939

Houston—2625 Federal Courthouse, 515 Rusk St, 77002, 713-229-2578

UTAH

Salt Lake City—Suite 105, 324 South State St, 84111, 801-524-5116

VERMONT—Serviced by Boston District Office

VIRGINIA

Richmond—8010 Federal Building, 400 North 8th St, 23240, 804-771-2246

WASHINGTON

Seattle—3131 Elliott Ave, Suite 290, 98121, 206-553-5615

†Spokane—West 808 Spokane Falls Blvd, Suite 625, 99201, 509-353-2922

WEST VIRGINIA

Charleston—405 Capitol St., Suite 809, 25301, 304-347-5123

WISCONSIN

Milwaukee—Federal Building, US Courthouse, Rm 606, 517 E Wisconsin Ave, 53202, 414-297-3473

WYOMING—Serviced by Denver District Office

New exporters can learn a great deal about export opportunities in a particular country market from ITA country desk officers who are country specialists. Write

> Desk Officer (country name and room number below)
> Department of Commerce
> 14th and Constitution Avenue N.W.
> Washington DC 20230

or call (202) 482-(four-digit number below).

COUNTRY	ROOM	PHONE	COUNTRY	ROOM	PHONE
Afghanistan	2029-B	2954	Costa Rica	3029-A	2527
Albania	3419	2645	Cuba	3029-A	2527
Algeria	2033	4652	Cyprus	3044	3945
Angola	3317	0357	Czechoslovakia	3419	2645
Argentina	3021	5427	Denmark	3413	3254
Australia	310	3646	Dominican Republic	3016	2527
Austria	3411	2434	East Caribbean	3022	2527
Bahamas	3029-A	2527	Equador	3027	4302
Bahrain	2039	5545	Egypt	2033	4652
Bangladesh	2029-B	2954	El Salvador	3029-A	5563
Barbados	3029-A	2527	European Community	3036	5276
Belgium	3415	2920	Finland	3413	3254
Bermuda	3029-A	2527	France	3042	8008
Boliva	3314	4302	Germany	3411	2434
Botswana	3317	5148	Ghana	3317	4564
Brazil	3017	3871	Greece	3044	3945
Brunei	2310	3875	Guatamala	3022	5563
Bulgaria	3419	2645	Guadeloupe	3029-A	2527
Burma	3820	5334	Guinea	3317	4564
Cambodia	2323	4681	Haiti	3029-A	2521
Cameroon	3317	0357	Honduras	3029-A	2527
Canada	3314	3101	Hong Kong	2323	2462
Cape Verde	3317	4564	Hungary	3421	2645
Caymans	3029-A	2527	Iceland	3413	3254
Chile	3027	4302	India	2029-B	2954
Columbia	3027	4302	Indonesia	2032	3875

COUNTRY	ROOM	PHONE	COUNTRY	ROOM	PHONE
Iran	2039	5767	Panama	3029-A	2527
Iraq	2039	5767	Peru	3027	4302
Ireland	3415	2920	Philippines	2310	3875
Israel	2039	4652	Poland	3419	2645
Italy	3045	2177	Portugal	3042	3945
Ivory Coast	3317	4388	Puerto Rico	3029-A	2527
Jamaica	3029-A	2527	Red China	2317	3583
Japan	2318	4527	Romania	3419	2645
Jordan	2038	5767	Saudi Arabia	2039	5767
Kenya	3317	4564	Singapore	2310	3875
Korea	2034	4399	South Africa	3317	5148
Kuwait	2039	5767	Spain	3042	4509
Laos	2325	3583	Sri Lanka	2029-B	2954
Lebanon	2039	5767	St. Martin	3029-A	2527
Liberia	3317	4564	Sudan	3317	4564
Luxembourg	3415	2920	Sweden	3413	4414
Macao	2325	3853	Switzerland	3044	2897
Madagascar	3317	0357	Syria	2039	5767
Malaysia	2310	3875	Taiwan	2034	4957
Malawi	2310	3875	Tanzania	3317	4564
Malta	3415	5401	Thailand	2032	3875
Martinique	3029-A	2527	Tunisia	2039	5737
Mexico	3028	2332	Turkey	3042	2434
Morocco	2039	5737	U.S.S.R.	3414	4655
Mozambique	3317	5148	United Arab Emirates	2039	5545
Namibia	3319	5148	United Kingdom	4212	4104
Nepal	2029-B	2954	Uruguay	3021	5427
Netherlands	3415	5401	Venezuela	3027	4302
Neth. Antilles	3029-A	2527	Vietnam	2323	4681
New Zealand	2310	3647	Virgin Islands (U.S.)	3016	2912
Nicaragua	3029-A	2527	Yugoslavia	3046	5373
Nigeria	3321	4388	Zaire	3317	0357
Norway	3413	4414	Zambia	3317	5148
Pakistan	1029-B	2954	Zimbabwe	3317	5148

State Export Offices

States marked with an asterisk are not members of the National Association of State Development Agencies, 444 N. Capitol Street N.W., Washington DC 20001, 202-624-5411.

ALABAMA
  Fred F. Denton, Director, International Development, 135 South Union Street, Montgomery 36130, 205-263-0048
ALASKA
  Robert G. Poe, Director, Governor's Office of International Trade, 3601 C Street, Suite 798, Anchorage 99503, 907-561-5585
ARIZONA
  Peter Cunningham, Assistant Director, International Trade and Investment, Arizona Department of Commerce, 3800 N. Central, Suite 1400, Phoenix 85012, 602-280-1300
ARKANSAS
  Maria Haley, Director, International Trade Division, 501-682-7678; Charles Sloan, Director, Foreign Investment, 501-682-7690; Arkansas Industrial Development Commission, One Capitol Mall, Room 4C 300, Little Rock 72201
*CALIFORNIA
  George Mignano, Executive Director, California State World Trade Commission, 1121 L Street, Suite 310, Sacramento 95815, 916-324-5511, 916-324-5791 (Fax)
*COLORAD0
  Morgan Smith, Director, International Trade Office, Office of Economic Development, 1625 Broadway, Suite 1710, Denver 80202, 303-892-3840
CONNECTICUT
  Matthew Broder, Director, Business Recruitment and Sales, Department of Economic Development, 865 Brook Street, Rocky Hill 06067-3405, 203-258-4256
DELAWARE
  Donal P. Sullivan, Director, Business Development, 302-736-4271; Lawrence E. Windley, International Trade Specialist, 302-736-4271; Delaware Development Office, 99 Kings Highway, Dover 19903; Claire D. Wilson, International Trade Specialist, Delaware Development Office, World Trade Section, 820 French Street, Wilmington 19801, 302-571-6262
FLORIDA
  Tom Slattery, Bureau Chief, International Trade Division, Florida Department of Commerce, 107 West Gaines Street, Tallahassee 32399-2000, 904-487-1399

GEORGIA

Kevin Langston, Director, International Trade, Georgia Department of Industry, Trade and Tourism, 285 Peachtree Center Avenue N.E., Atlanta 30303-1232, 404-656-3571

HAWAII

Kenneth Kwak, Chief, International Services Branch, Department of Planning and Economic Development, P.O. Box 2359, Honolulu 96804, 808-548-3048

IDAHO

Gary Whitwell, Administrator, Division of Business Development, Idaho Department of Commerce, 700 West State Street, Joe R. Williams Building, Boise 83720, 208-334-2470

ILLINOIS

Nan K. Hendrickson, Manager, International Business Division, Illinois Department of Commerce and Community Affairs, 100 West Randolph Street, Chicago 60601, 312-917-7164; Eric Pitcher, Assistant to Division Manager, Office of Foreign Investment, 312-917-2331, 312-917-6732 (Fax); Robert H. Newtson, Director, Illinois Export Council, 214 State Capitol, Springfield 62706

INDIANA

Philip M. Grebe, Director, International Trade Division, 317-232-8846; Bob Mason, Industrial Development Division, 317-232-8888; Indiana Department of Commerce, One North Capitol, Suite 700, Indianapolis, Indiana 46204-2248

*IOWA

Mike Doyle, Marketing Manager, International Trade Division, Department of Economic Development, 200 East Grand Avenue, Des Moines 50309, 515-281-3138

KANSAS

Harry Falisbury, Director, Trade Development; John Watson, Director, International Development; Kansas Department of Commerce, 400 S.W. 8th Street, Suite 500, Topeka 66603-3957, 913-296-4027

KENTUCKY

Andrew T. Coiner, Executive Director, Office of International Marketing, Cabinet for Economic Development, Capitol Plaza Tower, 24th Floor, Frankfort 40601, 502-564-2170

LOUISIANA

Don Hays, Director; Bill Jackson, Directo;, Ben Ross, Assistant Secretary; Office of International Trade, P.O. Box 94185, Baton Rouge 70804-9185, 504-342-9232

MAINE

Margaret B. Henderson, Assistant Commissioner, International Trade, Department of Economic and Community Development, State House Station 59, Augusta, Maine 04333, 207-289-5700; Daniel Marra, President, Maine World Trade Association, 77 Sewall Street, Augusta 04330-6332, 207-622-0234

MARYLAND
   Eric Feldman, Director, International Division; Marie Torres, Director, Export Finance Program; Andrew Gordon, Director, International Program Development; Harold R. Zassenhaus, Executive Director; Office of International Trade, 401 East Pratt Street, Baltimore 21202, 301-333-4295

MASSACHUSETTS
   Abbie Goodman, Executive Director, Office of International Trade, 100 Cambridge Street, Room 902, Boston 02202, 617-367-1830

MICHIGAN
   Mona Gubow, Director, Community Export Alliance, Department of Commerce, P.O. Box 30225, Lansing 48909, 517-335-2102

MINNESOTA
   Richard Bohr, Executive Director, Minnesota Trade Office, 1000 Minnesota World Trade Center, 30 East 7th Street, St. Paul 55101-4902, 612-297-4657, 612-296-3555 (Fax); Cheryl Bann, Director, Export Outreach and Education, 612-296-1690; Christine De Witt, Office of International Marketing and Investment

MISSISSIPPI
   Liz Cleveland, Manager, Trade and Export Division, 601-359-3444; Bob Fairbank, Associate Director, Foreign Investment, 601-359-3155; Department of Economic Development, P.O. Box 849, Jackson 39205

MISSOURI
   Angie Kenworthy, Senior Trade Specialist, Economic Development Programs, P.O. Box 118, Jefferson City 65102, 314-751-4999

*MONTANA
   John Maloney, International Trade Officer, Montana Department of Commerce, Capitol Station, 1424 9th Avenue, Helena 59620-0410, 406-444-3923

NEBRASKA
   Susan Rouch, International Trade Promotion, 402-471-4668; Robert Burns, Development Consultant, Office of International Trade and Foreign Investment, 402-471-4668; Department of Economic Development, 301 Centennial Mall South, 4th Floor, P.O. Box 94666, Lincoln 68509

NEVADA
   Julie Wilcox, Director, International Program, Commission on Economic Development, 600 East Williams, Suite 203, Carson City 89710, 702-687-4325

*NEW HAMPSHIRE
   William Herman, Programs Information Officer, Department of Resources and Economic Development, 105 Loudon Road, Building 2, Concord 03301, 603-271-2591

NEW JERSEY
   A. Philip Ferzan, Director, 201-648-3518; Diane Burke, Deputy Director of Exporting, 201-648-3518; Paul Struncius, Foreign Investment Specialist, 201-648-3518; Division of International Trade, Department of Commerce and Economic Development, Gateway 4, 100 Mulberry Street, Newark 07102

*NEW MEXICO

Roberto Castillo, Director, Office of International Trade, Economic Development and Tourism Department, 1100 St. Francis Drive, Santa Fe 87503, 505-827-0309

NEW YORK

R. Barry Spaulding, Deputy Commissioner, International Division, Department of Economic Development, 1515 Broadway, 51st Floor, New York 10036, 212-827-6100

NORTH DAKOTA

Jack Minton, International Trade Consultant, North Dakota Economic Development Commission, Liberty Memorial Building, State Capitol Grounds, Bismark 58505, 701-224-2810

OHIO

Dan Waterman, Deputy Director, International Trade Division, Ohio Department of Development, 77 S. High Street, P.O. Box 1001, Columbus 43215, 614-466-5017

OKLAHOMA

Gary H. Miller, Director, International Trade, 405-843-9770, and David G. Wantland, Program Manager, Export Finance Program, 405-841-5129, Department of Commerce, P.O. Box 26980, Oklahoma City 73126-0980

OREGON

Tony Allison, Director, International Trade Division, Oregon Economic Development Department, 121 Southwest Salmon, Suite 300, Portland 97204, 503-229-5625 or 800-452-7813

PENNSYLVANIA

Harvey Embick, Director, Bureau of Foreign Investment, Pennsylvania Department of Commerce, 486 Forum Building, Harrisburg 17120, 717-787-1356

*RHODE ISLAND

Christine Smith, Business Industry Representative, International Trade, Department of Economic Development, 7 Jackson Walkway, Providence 02903, 401-277-2601

SOUTH CAROLINA

Frank Newman, Associate Director, International Business Development, South Carolina State Development Board, P.O. Box 927, Columbia 29202, 803-734-0400

SOUTH DAKOTA

David Brotzman, Director, Export Trade Marketing Division, 711 Wells, Capitol Lake Plaza, Pierre 57501-3335, 605-773-5032

*TENNESSEE

Leigh Wieland, Director, Export Trade Promotion Office, and Bob Parsons, Assistant Commissioner, International & National Marketing, 320 6th Avenue North, Nashville 37219-5308, 615-741-5870

TEXAS
Director, International Trade, Texas Department of Commerce, P.O. Box 12728, Austin, Texas 78711, 512-472-5059

UTAH
J. Andrew Johnson, Director, International Business Development, Utah Department of Community and Economic Development, 6150 State Office Building, Salt Lake City 84114, 801-538-3052

VERMONT
Ron Mackinnon, Commissioner, Department of Economic Development, Pavillion Office Building, Montpelier 05602, 802-828-3221

VIRGINIA
E. W. Davis, Deputy Director, International Marketing, Department of Economic Development, P.O. Box 798, Richmond 23206-0798, 804-371-8201, 804-786-1121 (Fax)

WASHINGTON
Don Lorentz, Director, Domestic and International Division, 206-464-6283, and Harry Berryman, Domestic and International Trade Investment Division, 206-464-6282, Department of Trade and Development, 312 First Avenue North, Seattle 98109

WEST VIRGINIA
Steve Spence, Director and Trade Representative, Governor's Office of Community and Industrial Development, State Capitol, Room M146, Charleston 25305, 304-348-0400

*WISCONSIN
Ralph Graner, Director, Bureau of International Development, Department of Development, P.O. Box 7970, Madison 53707, 608-266-9487

WYOMING
Richard Lindsey, Director, International Trade Division, Economic Development and Stabilization Board, Herschler Building, 3rd Floor, East Wing, Cheyenne 82002, 307-777-6412

U.S. Port Authorities

Additional information, including a directory of U.S. Port Authorities and the services they provide, may be obtained from the American Association of Port Authorities, 1010 Duke Street, Alexandria VA 22314.

ALABAMA
Alabama State Docks Department, P.O. Box 1588, Mobile, AL 36633, Tel: (205) 690-6113, Fax (205) 690-6079, John B. Dutton, Director

ALASKA
Port of Anchorage, 2000 Anchorage Port Road, Anchorage, Alaska 99501, Tel: (907) 272-1531, Fax (907) 235-3140, Capt. H. "Glen" Glenzer, Jr. (USN-, Ret.), Port Director

Port of Cordova, P.O. Box 1210, Cordova, AK 99574, Tel: (907) 4246400, Fax: (907) 4246000, Dale R. Muma, Port Director

Port of Dutch Harbor, P.O. Box 89, Unalaska, AK 99685, Tel: (907) 581-1254, Fax (907) (907) 581-1417, Gary Daily, Port Director

Port of Homer, 491 East Pioneer, Homer, AK 99603-7624, Tel: (907) 235-3160, Fax (907) 235-3140, Bill Toskey, Port Director

Port of Kenai, 210 Fidalgo, Kenai, AK 99611, Tel: (907) 283-7535, Fax (907) 262-1892, Keith Kornelis, Port Director

Port of Kodiak, City of Kodiak, P.O. Box 1397, Kodiak, AK 99615, Tel: (907) 486-5789, Fax (907) 486-4009, G.V. McCorkle, Harbor Master/Port Administrator

Matanuska-Susitna Borough Port, Commission, P.O. Box 1608, Palmer, AK 99645, Tel: (907) 745-9831, Fax (907) 745-0886, Harry A. Utti, Port Specialist

Port of Saint Paul, City of Saint Paul, Saint Paul, AK 99660, Tel: (907) 546-2331, Fax (907) 546-2365, Vern McCorkle, Port director

Port of Seward, City of Seward, P.O. Box 167, Seward, AK 99664, Tel: (907) 2242231, Fax: (907) 224-3248, Foster Singleton, Port Director

Port of Valdez, P.O. Box 307, Valdez, AK 99686, Tel: (907) 835-4313, Fax (907) 835-2992, Tom McAllister, Port, Director

Whittier Port Authority, Commission, P.O. Box 608, Whitticr, AK 99693, Tel: (907) 4742330, Fax (907) 472-2404, Penny Mendenhall, Port Director

AMERICAN SAMOA
Port of Pago Pago, Department of Port Administration, Govermnent of American Samoa, P.O. Box 1539, Pago Pago, American Samoa 96799, Tel: (684) 633-4251, HA. Meredith, Port Director

CALIFORNIA
Port of Hueneme, P.O. Box 608, Port Hueneme, CA 93041, Tel: (805) 488-3677, Fax (805) 488-2620, Anthony J. Taormina, Executive Director

154

Humboldt Bay Harbor District, P.O. Box 1030, Eureka, CA 95502-1030, Tel: (707) 443-0801, Fax. (707) 443-0801, Jack B. Alderson Executive Director

Port of Long Beach, P.O. Box 570, Long Beach, CA 90801, Tel: (213) 437-0041, Fax. (213) 437-3231, Steven R. Dillenbeck, Acting Executive Director

Port of Los Angeles, P.O. Box 151, San Pedro, CA 90733-0151, Tel: (213) 519-3400, Fax (213) 831-0439, Ezunial Burts, Executive Director

Port of Oakland, P.O. Box 2064, Oakland, CA 94604, Tel: (415) 444-3188, Fax (415) 444-2093, Nolan R. Gimpel, Chief Executive Officer

Port of Redwood City, 475 Seaport Boulevard, Redwood City, CA 94063-2794, Tel: (415) 365-1613, Fax: (415) 369-7636, Floyd Shelton, Port Manager

Port of Richmond, P.O. Box 4046, Richmond, CA 94804, Tel: (415) 620-6784, Fax (415) 620-6716, Michael Powers, Port Director

Port of Sacramento, World Trade Center, P.O. Box 815, West Sacramento, CA 95619, Tel: (916) 371-8000, Fax (916) 372-4802, John G. Sulpizio, Acting Port Director

San Diego Unified Port District, P.O. Box 448, San Diego, CA 92112, Tel: (619) 291-3900, Fax (619) 291-0753, Don L. Nay, Port Director

Port of San Francisco, Ferry Building, Room 3100, San Francisco, CA 94111-4163, Tel: (415) 2740400 , Fax (415) 398-1269, Michael J. Huerta, Executive Director

Port of Stockton, P.O. Box 2089, Stockton, CA 95201, Tel: (209) 946-0246, Fax (209) 465-7244, Alexander Krygsman, Port Director

CONNECTICUT
Connecticut Department of Economic Development, Bureau of Waterways, State Pier, New London, CT 06320, Tel: (203) 443-3856, Frances M. McDermott, Director

DELAWARE
Port of Wilmington, P.O. Box 1191, Wilmington, DE 19889, Tel: (302) 571-4600, Fax (302) 571-4646, Kenneth H. Mack, Port Director

FLORIDA
Canaveral Port Authority, P.O. Box 267, Port Canaveral Station, Cape Canaveral, FL 32920, Tel: (407) 783-7831, Fax (407) 784-6223, Charles M. Rowland, Port Manager

Fort Pierce Port Authority, Route 5, Box 168, Fort Pierce, FL 33450, Tel: (305) 461-7899, Curtis King, Director

Jacksonville Port Authority, P.O. Box 3005, Jacksonville, FL 32206, Tel: (904) 630-3000, Fax (904) 353-1611, Paul D. deMariano, Managing Director

Key West Port & Transit Authority, P.O. Box 1078, Key West, FL 33041, Tel: (305) 292-8161, Charles S. Hamilin, Executive, Director

Manatee County Port Authority, Route No. 1, Palmetto, FL 33561, Tel: (813) 722-6621, Fax (813) 729-1463, Claude E. McGavic, Port Director

Port of Miami, 1015 North America Way, Miami, FL 33132, Tel: (305) 371-7678, Fax (305) 372-7918, Carmen J. Lunetta, Port Director

Nassau County Ocean Highway and Port, Authority, P.O. Box 2, Fernandina Beach, FL 32034, Tel: (904) 2610098, E. E. "Gene" Lasserre, Chairman

Port of Palm Beach, P.O. Box 9935, Riviera Beach, FL 33404 , Tel: (407) 842-4201, Fax (407) 8424240, Benson B. Murphy, Executive Director

Panama City Port Authority , P.O. Box 15895 , Panama City, FL 32406, Tel: (904) 763-8471, Fax (904) 769-5673 , H. R. "Rudy" Etheredge, Port Director

Port of Pensacola, P.O. Box 889, Pensacola, FL 32594, Tel: (904) 435-1870, Fax (904) 435-1879, David A. Schaller, Port Director

Port Everglades Authority, 1850 Eller Drive, Fort Lauderdale, FL 33316, Tel: (305) 523-3404, Fax (305) 525-1910, Joel Alesi, Executive Director

Port of St. Petersburg, 107 Eighth Avenue, S.E., St. Petersburg, FL 33701, Tel: (813) 893-7654, Fax (813) 822-4767, D. Tirnothy Travis, Port Director

Tampa Port Authority, P.O. Box 2192, Tampa, FL 33601, Tel: (813) 248-1924, Fax (813) 247-2352, Emmett C. Lee, Jr., Port Director

GEORGIA

Georgia Ports Authority, P.O. Box 2406, Savannah, GA 31402, Tel: (912) 964-3811, Fax (912) 964-3941, George J. Nichols, Executive Director

GUAM

Port Authority of Guam, 1026 Cabras Highway, Suite 201, Piti Guam 96910, Tel: (671) 477-9931, Fax (771) 477-2689, David B. Tydingco, General Manager

HAWAII

Department of Transportation, Harbors Division, 79 So. Nimitz Highway, Honolulu, HI 96813, Tel: (808) 548-2570, Fax (808) 548-6009, David K Higa, Chief of Harbors Division

ILLINOIS

Illinois International Port District, 3600 E. 95th Street, 95th & Lakefront, Chicago, IL 60617, Tel: (312) 646 4400, Fax (312) 646-5606, Anthony Ianello, Acting Executive Director

Waukegan Port District, P.O. Box 620, Waukegan IL 60079, Tel: (312) 244-3133, Fax (312) 244-1348, Donald B. Freeborn, Executive Director

INDIANA

Indiana Port Commission, 150 W. Market St., Suite 603, Indianapolis, IN 46204, Tel: (317) 232-9200, Fax. (317) 232-0137, Frank G. Martin, Jr., Executive Director

LOUISIANA

Greater Baton Rouge Port, Commission, P.O. Box 380, Port Allen, LA 70767, Tel: (504) 387-4207, Fax (504) 387-1534, Gary K. Pruitt, Executive Director

Port of Lake Charles, P.O. Box AAA, Lake Charles, LA 70602, Tel: (318) 439-3661, Fax (318) 493-4923, William T. Duke, Port Director

Port of New Orleans, P.O. Box 60046, New Orleans, LA 70160, Tel: (504) 522-2551, Fax (504) 5244156, J. Ron Brinson, President, & Chief Executive Officer

Plaquemines Port Harbor & Terminal District, Woodlawn Building, Rt. 1, Box 53A, Braithwaite, LA 70040, Tel: (504) 682-0081, Fax (504) 682-0081 ext. 2444, H.R. Benvenutti, Port Manager

St. Bernard Port, Harbor & Terminal, P.O. Box 1331, Chalmette, LA 70044-1331, Tel: (504) 277-8418, Fax (504) 277-8471, Harold C. Felger, President

The Port of South Louisiana, P.O. Box 909, LaPlace, LA 70069-0909, Tel: (504) 652-9278/568-6269, Fax (504) 652-9518, Richard J. Clements, Port Director

MAINE

Department of Transportation, Division of Ports and Marine Transportation, Transportation Building, State House-Station 16, Augusta, ME 04330, Tel: (207) 289-2841, Fax (207) 289-2896, Robert D. Elder, Director

Eastport Port Authority, P.O. Box 278, Eastport, ME 04631, Tel: (207) 853-4614, James C. Doyle, Port Director

City of Portland, 2 Portland Fish Pier, Suite 307, Portland, ME 04101, Tel: (207) 773-1613, Fax (207) 773-0285, Thomas F. Velleau, Director of Transportation & Waterfront Facilities

MARYLAND

Maryland Port Administration, World Trade Center, Baltimore, MD 21202, Tel: (301) 333-4500, Fax (301) 333-1126, Brendan W. O'Malley, Executive Director

MASSACHUSETTS

Massachusetts Port Authority, Maritime Department, Fish Pier East II, Northern Avenue, Boston, MA 02110, Tel: (617) 973-5354, Fax (617) 973-5357, Anne D. Aylward, Maritime Director

Fall River Port Authority, State Pier, Water Street, Fall River, MA 02721, Tel: (508) 674-5707, William Torpey, General Manager

MICHIGAN

Detroit-Wayne County Port Authority, 174 South Clark Street, Detroit, MI 48209, Tel: (313) 841-6700, Fax (313) 841-6705, James H. Kellow, Executive Director

Port of Monroe, Monroe Port Commission, P.O. Box 585, Monroe, MI 48161, Tel: (313) 241 6480, Fax (313) 241-0813

St. Joseph River Board of Harbor Commissioners, County Court House, Room 101, St. Joseph, MI 49805, Tel: (616) 983-7111, Aaron Anthony, Secretary

MINNESOTA

Seaway Port Authority of Duluth, P.O. Box 6877, Duluth, MN 55806, Tel: (218) 727-8525, Fax (218) 727-6888, Davis Helberg, Executive Director

MISSISSIPPI

Mississippi State Port Authority at Gulfport, P.O. Box 40, Gulfport, MS 39502, Tel: (601) 865-4300, Fax (601) 865-4307, William W. Edwards, Executive Director

Port of Pascagoula/Jackson County Port Authority, P.O. Box 70, Pascagoula, MS 39568-0070, Tel: (601) 762-4041, Fax (601) 762-7476, Paul W. Smith, Port Director

NEW HAMPSHIRE
New Hampshire State Port Authority, P.O. Box 506, Portsmouth, NH 03801, Tel: (603) 436-8500, Fax (603) 427-0771, Ernest Connor, Director

NEW JERSEY
Delaware River Port Authority, Bridge Plaza, Camden, NJ 08101, Tel: (609) 963-6420; (215) 925-8780, Fax (609) 964-8106, Eugene J. McCaffrey, Sr., Executive Director

South Jersey Port Commission, P.O. Box 129, Camden, NJ 08104, Tel: (609) 541-8500; (215) 923-6294, Fax (609) 757-1923, Joseph A. Balzano, Executive Director

NEW YORK
Albany Port District Commission, Administration Bldg., Albany, NY 12202, Tel: (518) 463-8763, Frank W. Keane, General Manager

The Port Authority of New York & New Jersey, One World Trade Center, New York, NY 10048, Tel: (212) 466-7000, Fax (212) 839-9261, Lillian C. Liburdi, Director, Ports Department

New York City Department of Ports & Trade, Battery Maritime Bldg., New York, NY 10004, Tel: (212) 806-6700, Fax (212) 805-7903, Patricia Zedalis, Acting Commissioner

Ogdensburg Bridge and Port Authority, Bridge Plaza, Ogdensburg, NY 13669, Tel: (315) 393-4080, Fax (315) 393-7068, Danny L. Duprey, Executive Director

Port of Oswego Authority, P.O. Box 387, Oswego, NY 13126, Tel: (315) 343-4503, Fax (315)343-5498, Jack Fitzgibbons, Executive Director

NORTH CAROLINA
North Carolina State Ports Authority, P.O. Box 9002, Wilmington, NC 28402, Tel: (919) 763-1621, Fax (919) 763 6440, James A. Scott, Jr. Executive Director

OHIO
Ashtabula Port Authority, P.O. Box 889, Ashtabula, OH 44004, Tel: (216) 992-8428, Armando Santilli, Chairman

Port of Cleveland-Cuyahoga County Port Authority, 101 Erieside Avenue, Cleveland, OH 44114, Tel: (216) 241-8004, Fax (216) 241-8016, RAdm Anthony Fugaro, Executive Director

Conneaut Port Authority, P.O. Box 218, Conneaut, OH 44030, Tel: (216) 593-3443, Glenn Dalrymple, Chairman

Fairport Harbor Port Authority, 20 Third Street, Village Hall, Fairport Harbor, OH 44077, Tel: (216) 354-3577, Tom Hill, Chairman

Huron-Joint Port Authority, P.O. Box 468, Huron, OH 44839, Tel: (419) 433-5240, Floren James, Chairman

Lorain Port Authority, Room 511, City Hall, Lorain, OH 44052, Tel: (216) 244-2269, Richard M. Novak, Executive Director

Toledo-Lucas County Port Authority, One Maritime Plaza, Toledo, OH 436041-866, Tel: (419) 243-8251, Fax (419) 243-1835, Gary L. Failor, President & CEO

OREGON

Port of Astoria, 1 Portway, Astoria, OR 97103, Tel: (503) 325-4521, Steve Felkins, Director

Oregon International Port of Coos Bay, Front & Market Streets, Coos Bay, OR 97420, Tel: (503) 267-PORT, Fax (503) 269-1475, Paul W. Vogel, General Manager

Port of Newport, 600 Southeast Bay Boulevard, Newport, OR 97365-4338, Tel: (503) 265-7758, John H. Mohr, Port General Manager

Port of Portland, P.O. Box 3529, Portland, OR 97208, Tel: (503) 231-5000, Fax: (503) 231-5332, Robert L. Woodell, Executive Director

Port of St. Helens, P.O. Box 598, St. Helens, OR 97051, Tel: (503) 397-2888, Peter Williamson, General Manager

PENNSYLVANIA

Philadelphia Port Corporation, 210 West Washington Square, Philadelphia, PA 19106, Tel: (215) 928-9100, Fax (215) 928-1488, John P. LaRue, President

Erie-Western Pennsylvania Port Authority, Room 507, Municipal Building, Erie, PA 16501, Tel: (814) 870-7557, Fax (814) 870-6651, Larry Morosky, Executive Director

PUERTO RICO

Port of Ponce, P.O. Box 125, Playa Station, Ponce, PR 00734-4125, Tel: (809) 842-5064, Pedro Berlingeri, Port Director

Puerto Rico Ports Authority, G.P.O. Box 2829, San Juan, PR 00936, Tel: (809) 723-2260, Fax (908) 722-7867, Jose R. Buitrago, Executive Director

RHODE ISLAND

Port of Providence, Marine Terminal Building, Municipal Wharf, Providence, RI 02905, Tel: (401) 781-4717, Fax: (401) 461-6240, John D'Antuano, Executive Director

Rhode Island Port Authority and Economic Development Corporation, Seven Jackson Walkway, Providence, RI 02903, Tel: (401) 277-2601, Fax (401) 277-2102, Norton L. Berman, Executive Director

SAIPAN

Commonwealth Ports Authority of Saipan, P.O. Box 1055, Saipan, CM 96950, Tel: (670) 234-8315, Fax (670) 234-5962, Carlos A. Shoda, Executive Director

SOUTH CAROLINA

South Carolina State Ports Authority, P.O. Box 817, Charleston, SC 29402, Tel: (803) 723-8651, Fax (803) 577-8616, W. Don Welch, Executive Director

TEXAS

Port of Beaumont, P.O. Drawer 2297, Beaumont, TX 77704, Tel: (409) 835-5367, Fax (409) 835-0512, B. G. Masters, Port Director

Brazos River Harbor Navigation, District P.O. Box 615, Freeport, TX 77541, Tel: (409) 233-2667, Fax (409) 233-5625, Armand J. Reixach, Port Director

Port of Brownsville, P.O. Box 3070, Brownsville, TX 78523-3070, Tel: (512) 831-4592, Fax (512) 831-3181, James Kruse, Port Director

Port of Corpus Christi Authority, P.O. Box 1541, Corpus Christi TX 78403, Tel: (512) 882-5633, Fax (512) 8,82-7110, Harry G. Plomarity, Port Director

Port of Galveston, P.O. Box 328, Galveston, TX 77550, Tel: (409) 765-9321, Fax (409) 766-6107, Douglas J. Marchand, CEO & General Manger

Port of Houston Authority, P.O. Box 2562, Houston, TX 77252, Tel: (713) 226-2100, Fax (713) 226-2134, James D. Pugh, Executive Director

Orange County Navigation Port District, P.O. Box 516, Orange, TX 77631-0516, Tel: (409) 883-4363, Fax (409) 883-5607, Bryan Norwood, Interim Port Director

Port of Port Arthur, P.O. Box 1428, Port Arthur, TX 77640, Tel: (409) 983-2011, Fax (409) 985-9312, Ben M. Goldstein, Port Director

Port Isabel-San Benito Navigation District, P.O. Box 218, Port Isabel, TX 78578-0218, Tel: (512) 943-7826, Fax (512) 943-8922, Robert C. Cornelison, Port Director & General Manager

Port of Point Comfort, P.O. Box 397, Port Lavaca, TX 77978, Tel: (512) 987-2813, Douglas Lynch, Port Director

VIRGIN ISLANDS

Virgin Islands Port Authority, P.O. Box 597, Harry S. Truman Airports, St. Thomas, Vl 00803-1707, Tel: (809) 774-1629, Fax (809) 774-0025, John E. Harding, Executive Director

VIRGINIA

Chesapeake Port Authority, 411 Cedar Road, Chesapeake, VA 23320, Tel: (804) 436-4121, Fax (804) 547-9389, M. Barry Owens, Executive Director

Port of Richmond Commission, 5000 Deepwater Terminal Road, Richmond, VA 23234, Tel: (804) 743-PORT, Fax (804) 271-1524, James McCarville, Port Director

Virginia Port Authority, 600 World Trade Center, Norfolk, VA 23510, Tel: (804) 683-8000, Fax (804) 683-8500, J. Robert Bray, Executive Director

WASHINGTON

Port of Anacortes, P.O. Box 297, Anacortes, WA 98221, Tel: (206) 293-3134, Fax (206) 293-9608, Joseph Baier, General Manager

Port of Bellingham, P.O. Box 1737, Bellingham, WA 98227, Tel: (206) 676-2500, Fax (206) 671-6411, Donald C. Fleming, General Manager

Port of Everett, P.O. Box 538, Everett, WA 9820,6, Tel: (206) 259-3164, Fax (206) 252-7366, Phlilip Bannan, Executive Director

Port of Grays Harbor, P.O. Box 660, Aberdeen, WA 98520, Tel: (206) 533-9528, Fax (206) 533-9505, Clifford C. Muller, General Manager

Port of Kalama, P.O. Box 70, Kalama, WA 98625, Tel: (206) 673-2325, Fax (206) 673-5017, John W. Fratt, Manager

Port of Longview, P.O. Box 1258, Longview, WA 98632, Tel: (206) 425-3305, Fax (206) 425-8650, Kenneth B. O'Hollaren, Manager

Port of Olympia, P.O. Box 827, Olympia, WA 98507, Tel: (206) 586-6150, Fax (206) 586-4653, Douglas P. Edison, Manager

Port of Port Angeles, P.O. Box 1350, Port Angeles, WA 98362, Tel: (206) 457-8527, Fax (206) 452-3959, D. G. Hendricks, Executive Director

Port of Seattle, P.O. Box 1209, Seattle, WA 98111, Tel: (206) 728-3000, Fax (206) 728-3252, Zegar van Asch van Wijck, Executive Director

Port of Tacoma, P.O. Box 1837, Tacoma, WA 98401, Tel: (206) 383-5841, Fax (206) 572-3436, John J. Terpstra, Executive Director

Port of Vancouver WA, P.O. Box 1180, Vancouver, WA 98666, Tel: (206) 693-3611, Fax (503) 285-6991, Byron H. Hanke, Executive Director

WISCONSIN

Port of Green Bay, P.O. Box 1600, Green Bay, WI 54301, Tel: (414) 436-3265, Fax (414) 436-3069, Alan T. Johnson, Port Director

Port of Milwaukee, 500 North Harbor Drive, Milwaukee, WI 53202, Tel: (414) 278-3511, Fax (414) 226-8506, Kenneth I. Szallai, Port Director

Superior Board of Harbor Commissioners, 409 Hammond Avenue, Superior, WI 5488, Tel: (715) 394-0335, Marshall Weems, Director of Planning and Port Development

U.S. Port Authorities, Overseas Offices

DELAWARE RIVER PORT AUTHORITY
Europe
  7 Braderijstraat, Bus 14, Antwerp. Belgium 2000, Phone: 03-234-39-60, Telex: 846-73460, Contact: Rolf D. Ludmann, Regional Manager, Europe
Japan
  1214 World Trade Center Building, Tokyo, 105, Japan, Phone: 436-5581/3, Telex: 781-24876, Contact: Mitsuru Takahashi, Marketing Manager, Japan Office
Hong Kong
  Asia Transportation Limited, Bank of America Tower, 28th Floor, Harcourt Road, Hong Kong, Phone: 5-225133, Telex: 80523 ATL HX, Contact: Albert K. H. Chan, Director and Vice President
Brazil
  Duncan Fox Ltd., Rua Hemique Martins, 644a, CEP 01435 Jardim Paulista, Sao Paulo, Brazil, Phone: (11) 887 8043, Contact: Irinaldo H. Lima, Regional Representative
Australia
  64 Castlereagh St., 8th Floor, Suite 26, Sydney, Australia 2000, Phone: 233-2911, TLX: 790-121086, Contact: Peter B. Horne, Regional Manager

GEORGIA PORTS AUTHORITY
Europe
  Haakon VII's gt. SB, 0161 Oslo l, Norway, Phone: 425926/425935, Telex: 78416 ESOBEN, Contact: Arthur Rondan, Director
Mediterranean/Middle East/Africa
  Vass. Sofias Avenue, No. 33, Athens, Greece, Phone: 7217675/7215623, Telex: 218344 IBS GR, Contact: Basil G. Grekousis, Director
Asia
  United Centre, 18F, 95 Queensway, Hong Kong, Phone: 294338, Telex: 65034 GAPTS HX, Contact: Charles P. K. Leon, Director
Far East
518 Fuji Building, 2-3 Marunouchi, 3-chome, Chiyoda-Ku, Tokyo, Japan, Phone: 214-3851/3852, Contact: Isao Togioka, Director
Korea
  c/o IRC Limited, Jung-ang Building, Suite 605, Yoido-Dong, 44-26, Youngdungpo-ku, Seoul, South Korea, Phone: 783-4754/4755, Contact: Peter E. Bartholomew, Managing Director

HOUSTON PORT AUTHORITY
Venezuela

> Torre KLM, Pent House, Avda. Romulo Gallegos, Santa Eduvigis, Caracas 1071, Venezuela, Phone: 283-2067, 283-1489, Fax: 283-2067, Telex: 25541 27244, Contact: Arturo Gamez, South American Sales Manager

LONG BEACH CA
Australia

> J. F. R. Strang Pty., Ltd., 185-189 O'Riordan Street, Mascot, Sydney, N.S.W. 2000, Australia, Phone: 669-1099, Telex: 790-20198, Fax: (612) 693-2753, Contact: John F. R. Strang

Indonesia

> P.T. Baptista Transportation & Cargo Co., Nisma Bumiputera, 3rd Floor, J1, Jen. Sudirman Kav. 75, Jakarta, 12910 Indonesia, Phone: 578-1428, Telex: 796-44614, Contact: Zoelkornain Ali

Hong Kong

> Asia Transportation Ltd., Bank of America Tower, 28th Floor, Harcourt Road/ G.P.O. 3742, Central Hong Kong, Phone: 5-225133, Telex: 780-80523, Fax: 852-810-5021, Contact: Capt. Eddy Chan

Korea

> Asia Shipping Co., CPO 4159, Marine Center 118, 10th Floor, Namdaemoon-ro, 2-Ka/Choong, Seoul, South Korea, Phone: 7530731/5, Telex: 787-26521, Fax: 82-051-754-3028, Contact: Y. B Yun

Malaysia

> Straits Transportation Pte., Ltd., 6th Floor, UBN Tower, P.O. Box 6140, PUDC 50250, Kuala Lumpur, Malaysia, Contact: Jalan P. Ramlee

Singapore

> Straits Transportation Pte., Ltd., Far Eastern Bank Building, 156 Cecil St., Room 6d-F, 7th Floor, P.O. Box 2572, Singapore 9045, Phone: 2223222, Telex: 786-22140, Fax: 2251190, Contact: Capt. L. Y. Kong

Taiwan

> United Shipping Corp., 126 Nanking East Road, Section 4, World Building, 11th Floor, Taipei, Taiwan, Republic of China, Phone: 2-741-0136, Telex: 785-14152, Fax: 2-773-3509, Contact: Michael K. Wong

LOS ANGELES CA
Japan

> Room 612 TBR Building, 2-10-2 Nagata-Cho, Chiyoda-Ku, Tokyo, Japan, Phone: (03) 580-2697, Telex: 23963-POLATKO, Fax: (03) 592-2014, Contact: Shuji Nomura

Singapore

> c/o Sea Consortium Pte. Ltd., 20 McCallum Street, 14-01, Asia Chambers, Singapore 0106, Phone: 223-9033, Telex: 21105-SLACON, Fax: 225-7496, Contact: Bob Bell

Taiwan
    10-1, Lin Shen South Road, Taipei, Taiwan, Republic of China, Phone: (02) 393-8650, Telex: 23213-UNITEDEX, Fax: (2) 341-0671, Contact: Shin-I Lin
Korea
    Hyopsung Shipping Corp., Kwang Hwa Moon, P.O. Box 236, Seoul, South Korea, Phone: (02) 752-2445, Telex: 24811-SEOUL, Fax: (02) 755-0587, Contact: T. E. Wang
Hong Kong
    WORLDPORT LA, 6/F Bank of Canton Building, 6 Des Voem Road, Central Hong Kong, Phone: (05) 244-558, Telex: 65779-HKBC HX, Fax: (05) 8100-235, Contacts: William Mortson, Paul Mak
New Zealand
    Dundas Martime Services, Ltd., P.O. Box 28046, Wellington, New Zealand, Phone: (04) 726-246 or 729-434, Telex: 31262-UALWN, Fax: (04) 734739, Contact: Richard Dundas
Chile
    Pacific Steam Navigation Co., Moneda 970, 9th Floor, Santiago, Chile, Phone: (02) 698-3013, Telex: 645283 PSNC CT, Fax: (02) 728-869, Contact: Felix Ibanez
Australia
    Thompson Clarke Williamson, Suite 8, Sandbridge Bay Towers, 11 Beach Street 3207, Victoria, Australia, Phone: (03) 646-3155, Telex: 38914-TCWAUS, Fax: (03) 646-3437, Contacts: Malcolm Thompson, Richard Clarke
Brazil
    Wilson Sons S/A Comercio, Industria e Agencia de Navegacao, Avenida Paulista 1776, 8th Floor, CEP 01310, Sao Paul, S.P., Brazil, Phone: (11) 251-4644, Telex: 1122620 WSON BR, Fax: (11) 251-2014, Contact: Ian Ross
England
    Eurolist Limited, 34/35 Leadenhall Street, London EC3 1AR, England, Phone: (01) 488-4567, Telex: 8812360-PARLONG, Contact: Hans Andersen
Denmark
    Eurolist Limited, P.O. Box 2556, 21001 Copenhagen, Denmark, Phone: (01) 269-734, Telex: 21280-LGC DK, Contact: Hans Andersen

MARYLAND PORT ADMINISTRATION
Brussels
    222 Avenue Louise-Bte 1, B-1050, Brussels, Belgium, Phone: (02) 648-93-90, Telex: 26862, Fax: (02) 647-7500, Contacts: Igor O. Weinert, Horst F. Winter
London
    Dingwall Road, Croydon, England CRO 3ET, Phone: (01) 681-1918/19, Telex: 944584, Fax: (01) 681-5645, Contact: Douglas H. Dickerson
Hong Kong
    Bond Center, Room 803, East Tower, 89 Queensway, Hong Kong, Phone: 5-250-131, Telex: 75456, Fax: 5-845-3455, Contact: Donald B. Allison

Japan
>   Yurakucho Building 322, 10-1, Yuraku-cho 1 Chome, Chiyoda-ku, Tokyo 100, Japan, Phone: (03) 212-0901, Telex: J28533, Fax: (03) 213-7260, Contact: Tadanobu Watanabe, Director

MASSACHUSETTS PORT AUTHORITY

Japan
>   New Diamond Building, 4-4 Kasumigaseki l-chome, Chiyoda-ku, Tokyo 100, Japan, Phone: 506-9002, Telex: 222-7310, Fax: 506-9003, Contact: Kinichi Fujino

London
>   87 Jermyn Street, London SWl, England, Phone: 930-7949, Telex: (851) 9178 35, Fax: 930-0751, Contact: Issac Graves

MIAMI FL

Far East
>   Dunning & Associates, Tower I Admiralty Center-Suite 2605, Harcourt Road, Hong Kong, Phone: 011-852-5-276985, Telex: 61416, Contact: Len Dunning

Europe
>   Eurolist Ltd., P.O. Box 256, 2100 Copenhagen, Denmark, Phone: (011) 451 269-734, Contact: Hans Andersen

NEW ORLEANS

Far East
>   Port of New Orleans, P.O. Box 96, World Trade Center Building, Tokyo 105, Japan, Phone: 435-5381, Telex: 26613, Fax: (813) 436-4870, Contact: Hiroyuki Matsumoto, Managing Director, Far East Trade Development

NEW YORK/NEW JERSEY

Continental Europe
>   Leutschenbachstrasse 45, CH-8050 Zurich, Switzerland, Phone: 41-1-302 13 10, Telex: 823678, Fax: 41-1-302 13 68, Contact: John P. Cannizzo

Far East-Pacific Area
>   Kokusai Building, Marunouchi, Chyoda-ku, Tokyo 100, Japan, Phone: 011-81-3 213-2856, Telex: 02222846 PANYNJ, Contact: Keiji Imai

London
>   International House, World Trade Centre, 1 St. Katharine's Way, London E1 9UN, England, Phone: 44-1-481 89 09, Telex: 8814494 PONY G, Fax: 44-1-265 06 74, Contact: Brendan Dugan

NORTH CAROLINA STATE PORTS AUTHORITY

Germany
>   State of North Carolina European Office, Wasserstrasse 2, 4000 Dusseldorf 1, Germany, Phone: (0211) 320533, Telex: 858-1846, Contact: T. Davis Bunn, Director

Hong Kong
  Kenwa Shipping Co., Ltd., 17th Floor, Hing Yip Commercial, Centre, 272-284 Des Voeux Road, Central Hong Kong, Phone: 5-414877, Telex: 62666 KENSCH HX, Contact: Donald S. C. Lam
Japan
  State of North Carolina, Japan Office, Izumi Shiba-Koen Building, 6-8, Shiba-Koen l-chome, Minato-ku, Tokyo 105, Japan, Phone: 03-435-9301, Fax: 03-435-9301, Contact: Atsujiro Fukunaga
Korea
  Korea Maritime International, Inc., 4th Floor, Mediterranean Building, 43-3, l-KA, Pil-Dong, Choong-ku, Seoul, South Korea, Phone: 011-82-2-274-7821/2, Fax: 82-2-755-1790, Contact: K.S. Rim, President
London
  Matheson Shipping Services Limited, 130 Minories, London EC3N lNS, England, Phone: 01-528-4000, Contact: R. C. L. Cooke, Director

OAKLAND CA
Europe
  Van Ommeren Rotterdam, Westerlaan 10, POB 845, 3016 Ck Rotterdam, The Netherlands, Phone: 010-642877, Telex: (844) 21435, Contact: Wilem D. Passenier Representative, Europe
Hong Kong
  No. 7-C Bowen Road, Room 203, Hong Kong, Phone: H-232342, Contact: Peter K.P. Hall, Representative, Hong Kong
Japan
  Yusen Building, 3rd Floor, 3-2, Marunouchi, 2-Chome, Chiyoda-ku, Tokyo, Japan, Phone: (03) 284-6500, Telex: (781) 33613, Fax: 011-81-3-213-5986, Contact: K. Nagao, Director, Far East
Korea
  KAL Building, 20th Floor, 118 Namadaemoon-ro 2ka, Choong-ku, Seoul, South Korea, Phone: 771-03, Telex: (787) 24761, Contact: Pyung Sup Chung, Representative, Korea
Taiwan
  P.O. Box No. 8 Hsi-Chih, Taipei Hsien, Taiwan, Phone: 641-2191, Telex: (785) 31352, Contact: Benson Van, Representative, Taiwan

OLYMPIA WA
Europe
  Sealiner Agencies Holland B.Z., Westblaak 218, 3012 KP Rotterdam, The Netherlands, Fax: 011-31-10-4047182, Contact: Gerard Veilvoye

PORTLAND OR

Hong Kong

Sun Hing Shipping Co., Ltd., 16th, 17th, 18th Floors, Tung Hip Commercial Building, 244-252, Des Voeux Road C., Hong Kong, Phone: 5-8539888, Telex: 73332 SUNAG HX, Fax: 011-852-544-3177, Contact: K. Mok

Korea

Port of Portland, Sam Koo Building, Room 1301, 70 Sogong-Dong Chung-Ku, Seoul, South Korea, Phone: 82-2-753-1349, Telecopier: 82-2-753-S154, Contact: Kim Jin Won

Taiwan

Ocean Pioneer Shipping Co., Ltd., 37, Chi-Nan Road, Section 2, P. O. Box 22650, Taipei, Taiwan, Phone: 02-321-8811/10, Telex: 785-21586/785-11098, Telecopier: 886-2-341-4977, Contact: M. Z. Chen

Tokyo

Port of Portland, Yurakucho Denki Building, North Tower 12F, 1-7-1 Yurakucho, Chiyoda-ku, Tokyo 100, Japan, Phone: 03-201-7533/03-201-7534, Fax: 03-201-7688

SAN FRANCISCO CA

Japan

Nippon Maritime Co., Ltd., Maritime Building, 14-1 Botan l-Chome, Kohtoh-Ku, Tokyo 135, Japan, Phone: 03(641) 7831, Telex: 78122263 NMC

Latin America

Carlos A. Massera, Republica do Peru 124, 401, Copacabana, Rio de Janeiro, Brazil, Phone: (55)(021) 257-0232

Taiwan

Grand World Shipping Agencies, Ltd., 60 Minchuan East Road, Taipei, Taiwan, Phone: (02) 7169555, Telex: 13072 GRANAGEN

SEATTLE WA

Asia

Room 505, Fuji Building, 2-3, Marunouchi 3-chome, Chiyoda-Ku, Tokyo 100, Japan, Phone: (3) 214-5578, Telex: 33288 POST KO, Fax: (3) 285-0770, Contact: Hisashi Imai, Managing Director, Asia

Hong Kong

Swire Shipping (Agencies), Ltd., Swire House, Third Floor, 9, Connaught Road Central, Hong Kong, Phone: (5) 225875, Telex: 86000 SWIRE HX, Fax: (5) 29-9091, Contact: Benjamin P. Wong, Representative

Korea

Room 92, Kwang IL Building, 11, Mookyo-Dong, Chung-Ku, Seoul, South Korea, Phone: (02) 756-0968, Telex: 33218 GAICO, Fax: (2) 756-0970, Contact: Kang-Hyuck Song, Representative

Taiwan
> Dah Tong Transportation & Co., Ltd., 8th Floor, No. 71, Section 2, Nanking East Road, Taipei, Taiwan, Phone: (2) 561-8383, Telex: 22638 TI MARINE, Fax: (2) 561-0625, Contact: Hrong-Nain Lin, Representative

SOUTH CAROLINA STATE PORTS AUTHORITY
Australia-New Zealand
53 Countess St., Mosman 2088, N.S.W., Australia, Phone: (02) 960-1137, Telex:
> 79010101 INSTSY AA21822, Contact: Dudleigh C. Johnson, General Manager

Europe
> Frankfurt Airport Center, P.O. Box 970128 D-600 Frankfurt/Main, Federal Republic of Germany, Contact: Steven A. Nadeau, Director

Far East
> Room 501, Parker House, 72 Queen's Road, Central Hong Kong, Phone: 5-868-0606, Telex: 85176 SCSPA HX, Fax: 5-845-2926, Contact: Thomas E. Lloyd, General Manager

Japan
> Tornomon TBL Building, Suite 902, 19-9, 1 Chome, Toranomon Minatu-ku, Tokyo 105, Japan, Phone: 03-591-1604/5, Telex: 78133478 SCFEO J33478, Contact: Ryuzo Nakada

STOCKTON CA
Japan
> Suzuyo & Co., Ltd., Yusen Building, Suite 403, 3-2, 2-Chome Marunouchi, Chiyoda-ku, Tokyo 100, Japan, Phone: (03) 284-0227, Telex: 246-6705 SUZUYO J

TACOMA WA
Hong Kong
> 2305-6 Sincere Building, 173 Des Voeux Road Central, Hong Kong, Phone: 5-434777, Telex: 75139 KJLSD HX, Fax: 011-852-541-8567, Contact: Bill H.Y. Wong, Hong Kong Consultant

Japan
> Kikyo Bizen Building, Room 405, 1-19-6, Nishi Shinbashi, Minato-ku, Tokyo 105, Japan, Phone: 03-591-5014, Telex: 02222166, Fax: 011-813-504-3317, Contact: Akira Tatara, Far East Regional Sales Manager

South Korea
> 305-1, Banpo-2-Dong, Seocho-ku, Seoul, South Korea, Phone: 82-2-532-9224/5, Telex: DICOSEL K25592, Fax: 82-2-532-6742, Contact: Man Lip Choy, Korea Consultant

Southeast Asia
> 10 Anson Road, 10-18 International Plaza, Singapore 0207, Phone: 2203343/2216444, Telex: RS 23365, Contact: Glenn Wood, S.E. Asia Consultant

VANCOUVER WA
Japan

> Brady (Japan) Ltd., 2-15-23 Todoroki, Setagay-Ku, Tokyo 158, Japan, Contact: John Brady

VIRGINIA PORT AUTHORITY
Brazil

> Rua Marechal Deodoro, 439-1 andar S/3, Caixa Postal, 693, 09700 Sao Bernardo do Campo, Sao Paulo, Brazil, Phone: 011-448-2191, Telex: 1145281 WIDE, Contact: Jose B. Romao, Director

Brussels

> 479 Avenue Louise, Brussels, B-1050, Belgium, Phone: 648-80-82, Telex: 26695, Fax: 648-0698, Contact: Betty Princen-Dignef, Director

Hong Kong

> 2 Exchange Square Central, 11th Floor, Suite 1104A, Hong Kong, Phone: 5-255313, Telex: 81801-VPA HK HX, Fax: 852-5-10-5495, Contact: Wing Hong Li, Director

Japan

> 17th Floor, Fukoku Seimei Building, 2-2, Uchisaiwai-Cho, Chiyoda-Ku, Tokyo 100, Japan, Phone: 508-2750, Telex: 2222531 VASTAT J, Fax: 508-2759, Contact: A. Sakamoto, Director

Korea

> Room No. 1512, Kyobo Building 1, 1-Ka Chongro-Ku, Seoul, South Korea, Phone: 02-739-6248, Telex: 787K25729, Fax: 02-739-6538, Contact: Moon Chi Lee, Director

U.S. Chambers of Commerce Abroad

ARGENTINA

Pablo Baques, American Chamber of Commerce in Argentina, Av. Pte. Roque Saenz Pena 567, P6, 1352 Buenos Aires, Argentina, Phone: (541) 331-3436, Fax: (541) 30-7303, Telex: (390) 21139 BOSBK AR

AUSTRALIA

Robert N. Maher, Executive Director, American Chamber of Commerce in Australia, Level 2, 39-41 Lower Fort Street, Sydney, N.S.W. 2000, Australia, Phone: (612) 241-1907, Fax: 011 61 2 251-5220, Telex: 72729 ATTIAU

Mareylene Williams, Adelaide Manager, AmCham in Australia, 1st Floor, 300 Flinders Street, Adelaide, S.A. 5000, Australia, Phone: (618) 244-0761, Fax: (618) 244-0628

Jeff Lurie, Melbourne Manager, AmCham in Australia, Level 1, 123 Lonsdale Street, Melbourne, Victoria 3000, Australia, Phone: (613) 663-2644, Fax: (613) 663-2473

Jeannette Wallance, Brisbane Manager, AmCham in Australia, 23rd Floor, 68 Queen Street, Brisbane, Queensland 4000, Australia, Phone: (617) 221-8542, Fax: (617) 221-6313

Maureen McCormick, Perth Manager, AmCham in Australia, 6th Floor, 231 Adelaide Terrace, Perth, W.A. 6000, Australia, Phone: (619) 325-9540, Fax: (619) 221-3725

AUSTRIA

Dr. Patricia A. Helletzgruber, Secretary General, American Chamber of Commerce in Austria, Porzellangasse 35, A-1090 Vienna Austria, Phone: (43) 222 31 57 51, Fax: (43) 222 31 57 52/15

BELGIUM

Jo Ann Broger, General Manager, American Chamber of Commerce in Belgium, Avenue des Arts 50, Boite 5, B-1040, Brussels, Belgium, Phone: (32) 2 513 67 70/9, Fax: (32) 2 513 79 28, Telex: 64913 AMCHAM B

BOLIVIA

Carlos Barrero, General Manager, American Chamber of Commerce of Bolivia, Casilla 8268, La Paz, Bolivia, Phone: (5912) 34-2523, Fax: (5912) 34-2523, Telex: (336) 3424 AMCHAM BV

BRAZIL

Augusto de Moura Dinitz, Jr., Executive Vice President, American Chamber of Commerce for Brazil-Rio de Janeiro, C.P. 916, Praca Pio X-15, 5th Floor, 20,040 Rio de Janeiro, RJ Brazil, Phone: (5521) 203 2477, Fax: (5521) 263 4477, Telex: (391) 2134084 AMCH BR

Salvador Ricardo Rubeiz, Executive Director, American Chamber of Commerce for Brazil-Salvador, Rua da Espanha 2, Salas 604-606, 40,000 Salvador, Bahia, Brazil, Phone: (5571) 242-0077; 242-5606, Fax: (5571) 243-9986

John Edwin Mein, Executive VP, American Chamber of Commerce for Brazil-Sao Paulo, Rua Alexandre Dumas 2372, 04717 Sao Paulo, SP. Brazil, Phone: (5511) 246-9199, Fax: (5511) 246-9080, Telex: (391) 1136190 AMCH BR

CHILE

Maria Isabel Jaramillo, Manager, Chilean-American Chamber of Commerce, Av. Americo Vespucio Sur 80, 9 Pisco, 4131 Correo Central, Santiago, Chile, Phone: (562) 48 41 40, Telex: (392) 340260 PBVTR CK (ITT booth; include address)

CHINA (PRC)

R. V. Linton, c/o General Electric (USA) China Co., International Club, Jian Guo Men Wai, Beijing, People's Republic of China, Phone: (861) 5322491/5322559, (861) 5233570, Fax: (861) 512-7345

COLOMBIA

Oscar A. Bradford, President, Colombian-American Chamber of Commerce, Apto. Aereo 8008, Calle 35, No. 6-16, Bogota, Colombia, Phone: (571) 285-7800, Fax: (571) 288-6434, Telex: (396) 43326/45411 CAMC CO

Leyda Lucia Perez B., Executive Director, Colombian-American Chamber of Commerce-Cali, Apdo. Aereo 5943, Cali, Valle, Colombia, Phone: (573) 610-162; 672-993, Fax: (573) 672-992, Telex: (396) 55442 CCCAC CO

Jose Vicente Lodono, Executive Director, Colombian-American Chamber of Commerce-Cartagena, Edificio Banco de Colombia, Of. 500, Apdo. Aereo 20483, Cartagena, Colombia, Phone: (573) 42842, Telex: (396) 37705 ISACO CO

Nicolas de Zubiria, Executive Director, Colombian-American Chamber of Commerce-Medellin, Phone: (573) 268-7491, Telex: (396) 66768

COSTA RICA

Inges Gallegos de Baker, Executive Director, Costa Rican-American Chamber of Commerce , Avda. 2, Calles 30-32 3034, Apdo. 4946, San Jose 1000, Costa Rica, Phone: (506) 33 21 33, Fax: (506) 23 23 49, Telex: (323) 21286 POZUELO CR

DOMINICAN REPUBLIC

Arthur E. Valdez, Executive Director, American Chamber of Commerce of the Dominican Republic, Torre B.H.D., Av. Winston Churchill, PO Box 95-2, Santo Domingo, Dominican Republic, Phone: (809) 544-2222, Fax: (809) 544-0502, Telex: (346) 0958 AMCHAM

ECUADOR

Karl Newlands, Executive Director, Ecuadorian-American Chamber of Commerce, Edificio Multicentra, 4P, La Nina y 6 de Diciembre, Quito, Ecuador, Phone: (5932) 543-512, Fax: (5932) 504-571, Telex: (393) 22298 ECUAME ED

Francisco Rendon, Executive Director, Ecuadorian-American Chamber of Commerce, F. Cordova 812, Piso 3, Oficina 1, Edificio Torres de la Merced, Guayaquil, Ecuador, Phone: (5934) 312-760; 312-865, Fax: (5934) 326-259

EGYPT

Hisham Fahmy, American Chamber of Commerce in Egypt, Cairo Marriott Hotel, Suite 1537, PO Box 33, Zamalek, Cairo, Egypt, Phone: (20) 2 340-8888, Fax: (20) 2 340-8888, Ext. 1543, Telex: 20870 AMCHE UN

EL SALVADOR

Steve Culbertson, Executive Director, American Chamber of Commerce of El Salvador, 65 Avenida Sur, No. 159, PO Box (05) 9, San Salvador, El Salvador, Phone: (503) 23-2419/9604, Fax: (503) 23-6081, Telex: (301) 20768 VERITATEM

GERMANY

Thomas T. Krauss, American Chamber of Commerce in Germany, Rossmarkt 12, Postfach 100 162, D-6000 Frankfurt/Main 1, West Germany, Phone: (49) 69 28 34 01, Fax: (49) 69 28 56 32, Telex: 418679 ACC D

Brita U. Lambert, Assistant Manager, American Chamber of Commerce in Germany, Budapesterstrasse 31, D-1000 Berlin 30, Germany, Phone: (49) 30 261 55 86, Fax: (49) 30 262 26 00

FRANCE

W. Barrett Dower, Executive Director, American Chamber of Commerce in France, 21 Avenue George V, F-75008 Paris, France, Phone: (33) 1 47 23 70 28, (33) 1 47 23 80 26, Fax: (33) 1 47 20 18 62

GREECE

Symeon G. Tsomokos, Genera Manager, American-Hellenic Chamber of Commerce, 16 Kanari Street, 3rd Floor, Athens 106 74, Greece, Phone: (30) 1 36 18 385 /36 36 407, Fax: (30) 1 36 10 170, Telex: 223063 AMCH GR

GUAM

Chairman, Wayne Brown, Guam Chamber of Commerce, 102 Ada Plaza Center, PO Box 283, Agana, Guam 96910, Phone: (671) 472-6311/8001, Telex: 7216160 BOOTH GM

GUATEMALA

Sussanne Egli, Executive Manager, American Chamber of Commerce in Guatemala, Apdo, Postal 832, 7 Avda, 14-44, Zona 9, Nivel 2, Oficina 19, Guatemala City, Guatemala, Phone: (5022) 312-235, Fax: (5022) 312-763, Telex: (305) 5415 DORADO GU

HAITI

Executive Director, Haitian-American Chamber of Commerce & Industry, Complexe 384, Delmas (59), Port-au-Prince, Haiti, Phone: (5091) 60-3164, Telex: (329) 2030001 (public booth; include address)

HONDURAS

Sonia Reyes de Madro, General Manager, Honduran-American Chamber of Commerce, Hotel Honduras Maya, Ap. Pos. 1838, Tegucigalpa, Honduras, Phone: (504) 32-31-91, Ext. 1056, Fax: (504) 3294-43, Telex: (311) 1145 MAYA HO

Liliana de Bendana, Sula Representative, Honduran-American Chamber of Commerce, Edificio Samara, 2 Piso, Of. 5, Blvd. Morazan 16 Ae. SO, Box 1209, San Pedro Sula, Honduras, Phone: (504) 52-2401/2790, Telex: (311) 1145 MAY HO

HONG HONG

Ralph Spencer, Executive Director, American Chamber of Commerce in Hong Kong, 1030 Swire Road, Hong Kong, Phone: (852) 5-260165, Fax: 011-852-810-1289, Telex: 83664 AMCC HX

INDONESIA

Laure Sinclair, Executive Assistant, American Chamber of Commerce in Indonesia, The Landmark Centre, 22nd Floor, Suite 2204, Jl. Jendral Sudirman, Jakarta, Indonesia, Phone: (622) 1-578-0656, Fax: (622) 1-578-2437 Att: L. Sinclair, Telex: 62822 LMARK LA

IRELAND

Robert P. Chalker, Executive Director, American Chamber of Commerce in Ireland, 20 College Green, Dublin 2, Ireland, Phone: (353) 1-79-37-33/1-79-34-02, Fax: (353) 1 60-17-82, Telex: 31187 UCIL EL

ISRAEL

Nina Admoni, Executive Director, Israel-American Chamber of Commerce and Industry, 35 Shaul Hamelech Blvd., PO Box 33174, 64927 Tel Aviv, Israel, Phone: (972) 3 25 23 41/2, Fax: (972) 3 25 12 72, Telex: 32139 BETAM IL

ITALY

Managing Director, American Chamber of Commerce in Italy, Via Cantu 1, 20123 Milano, Italy, Phone: (39) 2 86 90 661, Fax: (39) 2 80 57 737, Telex: 352128 AMCHAM I

IVORY COAST

Mrs. Suzan Cioffi, Secretary, American Chamber of Commerce, Ivory Coast, BP 1083, Abidjan 06, Ivory Coast, Phone: (255) 326 766/785, Telex: 22435 DAM CI

JAMAICA

Dr. Ofe Dudley, Executive Director, American Chamber of Commerce of Jamaica, The Wyndham Hotel, 77 Knutsford Blvd., Kingston 5, Jamaica, Phone: (809) 926-5430, Fax: (809) 929-8597, Telex: (381) 2409 WYNDOTEL JA

JAPAN

Richard E. Cropp, Executive Director, American Chamber of Commerce of Japan, Fukide Bldg., No. 2, 4-1-21 Toranomon, Minato-ku, Tokyo 105, Japan, Phone: (03) 433-5381, Fax: (03) 436-1446, Telex: 2425104 KYLE J

Justin Wentworth III, American Chamber of Commerce in Okinawa, PO Box 235, Okinawa City 904, Japan, Phone: (819) 889-8935-2684, Telex: J79828 SHEROKA, Att: AmCham Okinawa

KOREA

James W. Booth, Executive Vice President, American Chamber of Commerce in Korea, Room 307, Chosun Hotel, Seoul, Korea, Phone: (822) 753-6471/6516, Fax: (822) 755-6577, Telex: 23745; 28432 CHOSUN

MALAYSIA

Erin Ariff, Executive Secretary, American Business Council of Malaysia, 15.01 15th Fl., Amoda, Jalan Imbi, 55100 Kuala Lumpur, Malaysia, Phone: (603) 248-4207/2540, Fax: (603) 243-7682, Telex: MA 32956 KCSKL

MEXICO

John M. Burton, Executive Vice President, American Chamber of Commerce of Mexico, A.C., Lucerna 78-4, Mexico 6, D.F., Mexico, Phone: (905) 705-0995, Fax: (905) 535-3166

Loura Sauceo, Manager, American Chamber of Commerce of Mexico-Guadalajara, Avda. 16 de Septiembre 730-1209, Guadalajara, Jalisco, Mexico, Phone: (5236) 146-300/148-068, Fax: (5236) 425-396, Telex: (383) 0684241 ACHAME

Kathleen Marks Gibler, Manager, American Chamber of Commerce of Mexico A.C.-Monterrey, Picachos 760, Despachos 4 y 6, Colonia Obispado, Monterrey, Nuevo Leon, Mexico, Phone: (52828) 48-7141/4749, Fax: (5283) 4855-74, Telex: (383) 383087 AMCHAME

NETHERLANDS

J.J. van Steenbergen, General Manager, American Chamber of Commerce in the Netherlands, Carnegieplein 5, 2517 KJ The Hague, The Netherlands, Phone: (31) 70 65 98 08/9, Fax: (31) 70 646992, Telex: 18138

NEW ZEALAND

John L. Gordon, Executive Director, American Chamber of Commerce in New Zealand, PO Box 3408, Wellington, New Zealand, Phone: (04) 767081 (Gordon), (04) 727549 (AmCham), Telex: 3514 IMBUSMAC NZ

NICARAGUA

Margarita S. Diaz G., Executive Director, American Chamber of Commerce of Nicaragua, Apdo. 202, Managua, Nicaragua, Phone: (5052) 62-486, Telex: (302) 1255 VIGIL

PAKISTAN

S.R.A. Hashmi, Secretary, American Buiness Council of Pakistan, NIC Building, 6th Floor, Abbasi Shaheed Road off Sharea Faisal, Karachi, Pakistan, Phone: (92) 21-52 1635/5476, Fax: (92) 21-52 6649/3070, Telex: 25620 CHASE PK

PANAMA

Fred Denton, Executive Director, American Chamber of Commerce and Industry of Panama, Apdo. 168, Estafeta Balboa, Panama, Republic de Panama, Phone: (507) 69-3881, Fax: (507) 23-3508

PARAGUAY

George Murphy-Lee, Manager, Paraguayan-American Chamber of Commerce, Edif. Finansud, Av. Mariseal Lopez y Saravi, Asuncion, Paraguay, Phone: (5921) 609-730, Telex: (399) 638 PY LAWYERS

PERU

John B. Ottiker, General Manager, American Chamber of Commerce of Peru, Av. Ricardo Palma 836 Miraflores, Lima 18, Peru, Phone: (5114) 47-9349, Fax: (5114) 47-9352, Telex: (394) 21165 BANKAMER

PHILIPPINES

J. Marsh Thompson, Executive Vice President, American Chamber of Commerce of the Philippines, PO Box 1578, MCC, Manila, The Philippines, Phone: (632) 818-7911, Fax: (632) 816-6359, Telex: (ITT) 45181 AMCHAM PH

PORTUGAL

Dr. Henrique M. Brito do Rio, Secretary General, American Chamber of Commerce in Portugal, Rua de D. Estefania, 155, 5 Esq., Lisbon 1000, Portugal, Phone: (351) 1 57 25 61/82 08, Telex: 42356 AMCHAM P

SAUDI ARABIA

David D. Bosch, Dhahran American Businessmen's Assocation, Eastern Province, c/o ARAMCO, PO Box 1329, Dhahran, Saudi Arabia 31311, Phone: (966) 3 875 2933, Fax: (966) 3-876-1018, Telex: 801220

Andy Constantzos, Chairman, Issues Committee, American Businessmen of Jeddah, Hayatt Regency, PO Box 8483, Jeddah 21482, Saudi Arabia, Phone: (966) 2-651-9800, Ext. 1759, Fax: (966) 2-651-6260, Telex: 602688 HYATT SJ

Richard A. Meade, Chairman, American Businessmen's Group of Riyadh, PO Box 3050, Riyadh 11471, Saudi Arabia 07045, Phone: (966) 1-465-3390, Fax: (966) 1-465-6738, Telex: 401950

SINGAPORE
Donne Petito, Executive Director, American Business Council of Singapore, Scotts Road, 16-07 Shaw Center, Singapore 0922, Phone: (65) 235-0077, Fax: (65) 732-5917, Telex: 50296 ABC SIN

SOUTH AFRICA
Wayne Mitchell, Executive Director, American Chamber of Commerce in South Africa, PO Box 62280, Johannesburg, South Africa, Phone: (27) 11-788-0265, Telex: 429883 SA

SPAIN
Jose A. Manrique, Executive Director, American Chamber of Commerce in Spain, Avda. Diagonal 477, 08036 Barcelona, Spain, Phone: (34) 3 321 81 95/6, Fax: (34) 3 321 81 97

Maria Nieves Hermida, Assistant Executive Director, American Chamber of Commerce in Spain, Hotel EuroBuilding, Padre Damian 23, Madrid 16, Spain, Phone: (34) 1 458-6520

SWITZERLAND
Walter H. Diggelman, Executive Director, Swiss-American Chamber of Commerce, Talacker 41, 8001 Zurich, Switzerland, Phone: (41) 1 211 24 54, Fax: (41) 1 211 95 72, Telex: 813448 IPCO CH

TAIWAN
Loren R. Wolter, Executive Director, American Chamber of Commerce of Taiwan, Room 1012-Chia Hsin Bldg. Annex, 96 Chung Shan N. Rd., Section 2, PO Box 17-277, Taipei, Taiwan, Phone: (886) 2 551-2515, Fax: (886) 2 542-3376, Telex: 27841 AMCHAM

THAILAND
Thomas A. Seale, Executive Director, American Chamber of Commerce in Thiland, PO Box 11-1095, 140 Wireless Road, 7th Floor, Kian Gwan Bridge, Bangkok, Thailand, Phone: (662) 251-9266, Fax: (662) 255-2454, Telex: 82828 KGCOM TH

TURKEY
Ms. Safak Sadullah, Rumeli Cad. No. 63, D7, 4th Floor, Nisantasi 80200, Istanbul, Turkey, Phone: (1) 130 30 81/36 47, Fax: (1) 130 47 34

UNITED ARAB EMIRATES
Vicky Bailey, Executive Director, American Business Council of Dubai, International Trade Center, Ste. 1609, PO Box 9281, Dubai, United Arab Emirates, Phone: (971) 4 377 735, Fax: (971) 4 375 317, Telex: 48244 SERVE EM

UNITED KINGDOM
Robert E. Brunck, Director General, American Chamber of Commerce (United Kingdom), 75 Brook Street, London W1Y 2EB, England, Phone: (44) 493 03 81, Fax: (44) 1 493 23 94, Telex: 23675 AMCHAM

URUGUAY
Carlos Boubet, Manager, Chamber of Commerce Uruguay-U.S.A., Calle Bartolome Mitre 1337, Cassilla de Correo 809, Montevideo, Uruguay, Phone: (5982) 959 059/048, Fax: (5982) 921 735

VENEZUELA
Michael E. Heggie, Executive Director, Venezuelan-American Chamber of Commerce & Industry, Torre Credival, Piso 10, 2da. Avenida de Campo Alegre, Apdo. 5181, Caracas 1010-A, Venezuela, Phone: (582) 32-49-76, Fax: (582) 32-07-64, Telex: (395) 23627 VACCI VC

Foreign Chambers of Commerce and Associations in the United States

ARGENTINA
Argentina-American
Chamber of Commerce
50 West 34th Street
6th Floor, Room C2
New York, NY 10001
(212) 564-3855

ASIA
Asian-US Trade Council
40 East 49th Street
New York, NY 10017
(212) 688-2755

Asia Society
725 Park Avenue
New York, NY 10017
(212) 288-6400

Asia Society
1785 Massachusetts Ave., NW
Washington, DC 20036
(202) 387-6500

AUSTRIA
U.S.-Austrian Chamber
of Commerce, Inc.
165 West 46th Street
New York, NY 10036
(212) 819-0117

BELGIUM
Belgian-American Chamber
of Commerce in the US, Inc.
350 5th Avenue, Suite 703
New York, NY 10118
(212) 967-9898

BRAZIL
Brazilian-American Chamber
of Commerce in the US, Inc.
22 West 48th Street, Room 404
New York, NY 10036
(212) 575-9030

Brazilian-American Chamber
of Commerce, Inc.
801 Brickell
Miami, FL 33131
(305) 377-6700

Brazil-California Trade Association
900 Wilshire, Suite 1434
Los Angeles, CA 90017
(213) 627-0634

CHILE
North-American Chamber
of Commerce, Inc.
220 East 81st Street
New York, NY 10028
(212) 288-5691

CHINA (PRC)
Chinese Chamber of
Commerce New York
Confucius Plaza
33 Bower, Room C203
New York, NY 10002
(212) 226-2795

COLOMBIA
Colombian-American
Association, Inc.
150 Nassau, Suite 2015
New York, NY 10038
(212) 233-7776

DENMARK
Danish-American
Chamber of Commerce
825 3rd Avenue
New York, NY 10019
(212) 980-6240

DOMINICAN REPUBLIC
Dominican Republic Export
Promotion Center
One World Trade Center, Suite 2441
New York, NY 10048
(212) 432-9498

ECUADOR
Ecuadorean-American
Association, Inc.
150 Nassau, Suite 2015
New York, NY 10038
(212) 233-7776

FINLAND
Finnish-American
Chamber of Commerce
540 Madison Avenue, 18th Floor
New York, NY 10022
(212) 832-2588

Finnish-American Chamber
of Commerce of the Midwest
321 N. Clark Street, Suite 2880
Chicago, IL 60610
(312) 670-4700

FRANCE
French-American Chamber
of Commerce in the U.S.
509 Madison Avenue, Suite 1900
New York, NY 10022
(212) 371-4466

GERMANY
German-American
Chamber of Commerce
666 Fifth Avenue
New York, NY 10103
(212) 974-8830

German-American Chamber
of Commerce of Chicago
104 South Michigan Avenue
Chicago, IL 60603-5978
(312) 782-8557
Fax (312) 782-3892

German-American Chamber
of Commerce of Los Angeles, Inc.
One Park Plaza Building, Suite 1612
3250 Wilshire Blvd.
Los Angeles, CA 90010
(213) 381-2236

German-American Chamber of
Commerce of the Pacific Coast, Inc.
465 California Street, Suite 910
San Francisco, CA 94104
(415) 392-2262

Representative for German
Industry and Trade
One Farragut Square South
Washington, DC 20006
(202) 347-0247
Fax (202) 628-3685

GREECE
Hellenic-American
Chamber of Commerce
29 Broadway, Room 1508
New York, NY 10006
(212) 629-6380

INDIA
India Chamber
of Commerce of America
445 Park Avenue
New York, NY 10022
(212) 755-7181

INDONESIA
American-Indonesian
Chamber of Commerce, Inc.
12 East 41st Street, Suite 701
New York, NY 10017
(212) 637-4505

IRELAND
Ireland-United States Council
for Commerce and Industry, Inc.
460 Park Avenue, 22nd Floor
New York, NY 10022
(212)751-2660

ISRAEL
American-Israel Chamber
of Commerce and Industry, Inc.
350 Fifty Avenue, Suite 1919
New York, NY 10118
(212) 971-0310

American-Israel Chamber
of Commerce and Industry, Inc.
Metropolitan Chicago
180 N. Michigan Avenue, Suite 911
Chicago, IL 60601
(312) 641-2937

ITALY
Italian Chamber of
Commerce of Chicago
126 West Grand Avenue
Chicago, IL 60610
(312) 661-1336

Italy-American
Chamber of Commerce, Inc.
350 Fifth Avenue, Suite 3015
New York, NY 10118
(212) 279-5520

JAPAN
Honolulu-Japanese
Chamber of Commerce
2454 South Beretania Street
Honolulu, HI 96826
(808) 949-5531

Japan Business Association
of Southern California
345 South Figueroa Street
Los Angeles, CA 90071
(213) 485-0160
Fax (213) 626-5526

Japanese Chamber of
Commerce and Industry of Chicago
401 North Michigan Avenue
Room 602
Chicago, IL 60611
(312) 332-6199

Japanese Chamber
of Commerce of New York, Inc.
115 E. 57th
New York, NY 10022
(212) 935-0303

Japanese Chamber of
Commerce of Southern California
244 South San Pedro Street, Room 504
Los Angeles, CA 90012
(213) 626-3067

KOREA
Korean Chamber of Commerce
30000 W. Olympic Blvd., Suite 200
Los Angeles, CA 90006
(213) 480-1115

US-Korea Society
725 Park Avenue
New York, NY 10021
(212) 517-7730

LATIN AMERICA
Council of the Americas
680 Park Avenue
New York, NY 10021
(212) 628-3200

Houston-Inter-American
Chamber of Commerce
1520 Texas Avenue, Suite ID
Houston, TX 77002

Latin American
Chamber of Commerce
P.O. Box 30240
New Orleans, LA 70190
(504) 488-7425

Latin Chamber of Commerce
1417 West Flagler Street
Miami, FL 33135
(305) 642-3870

Latin American
Manufacturing Association
4919 New Jersey Avenue, SE
Washington, DC 20003
(202) 546-3808

Pan American Society of
San Francisco World Affairs Center
312 Sutter Street
San Francisco, CA 94108

Pan American Society of the US, Inc.
680 Park Avenue
New York, NY 10021
(212) 249-8950

MEXICO
Mexican Chamber of
Commerce of Arizona
P.O. Box 626
Phoenix, AZ 85001
(602) 252-6448

Mexican Chamber of Commerce
of the County of Los Angeles
125 Paseo de La Plaza, Room 404
Los Angeles, CA 90012
(213) 688-7330

United States-Mexico
Chamber of Commerce
1900 L Street, NW, Suite 612
Washington, DC 20036
(202) 296-5198

Americas Society
680 Park Avenue
New York, NY 10021
(212) 249-8950

MIDDLE EAST
American Mid-East
Business Association
80 Park Avenue, Suite 17N
New York, NY 10017
(212) 986-7229

Mid-American-Arab
Chamber of Commerce, Inc.
135 South LaSalle Street, Suite 2050
Chicago, IL 60603
(312) 782-4654

National Council
on U.S.-Arab Relations
1735 I Street, NW, Suite 515
Washington, DC 20006
(202) 293-0801

US-Arab Chamber of Commerce
One World Trade Center, Suite 4657
New York, NY 10048
(212) 432-0655

US-Arab Chamber of Commerce
1825 K Street, NW, Suite 1107
Washington, DC 20006
(202) 331-8010

US-Arab Chamber
of Commerce, Pacific
P.O. Box 11239
1 Hellidie Plaza, Suite 504
San Francisco, CA 94101-7239
(415) 398-9200

US-Arab Chamber of Commerce
505 North Belt Drive, Suite 405
Houston, TX 77060
(713) 447-2673

NETHERLANDS
Netherlands Chamber of
Commerce in the U.S., Inc.
One Rockefella Plaza, 11th Floor
New York, NY 10020
(212) 265-6460

NIGERIA
Nigerian-American
Chamber of Commerce, Inc.
575 Lexington Avenue
New York, NY 10020
(212) 715-7200

NORWAY
Norwegian-American
Chamber of Commerce, Inc.
World Trade Center
350 South Figueroa Street, Suite 360
Los Angeles, CA 90017

Norwegian-American
Chamber of Commerce, Inc.
Upper Midwest Chapter
229 Foshay Tower
Minneapolis, MN 55402
(612) 332-3338

Norweigan-American
Chamber of Commerce
Two Embarcadero Center, Suite 2930
San Francisco, CA 94111
(415) 986-0766

Norwegian-American
Chamber of Commerce, Inc.
800 Third Avenue
New York, NY 10022
(212) 421-9210

PAKISTAN
U.S.-Pakistan Economic Council
c/o Zuckerman and Dunn, PC
1140 Avenue of the Americas
New York, NY 10036
(212) 921-2929

PERU
Peruvian-American Association
500 West 34th Street
6th Floor, Suite C2
New York, NY 10001
(212) 564-3855

PHILIPPINES
Philippine-American
Chamber of Commerce, Inc.
711 3rd Avenue, 17th Floor
New York, NY 10017
(212) 972-9326

Philippine-American
Chamber of Commerce
c/o Phillipine Consulate
447 Sutter Street
San Francisco, CA 94108
(415) 433-6666

PORTUGAL
Portugal-U.S. Chamber of Commerce
5 West 45th Street, 4th Floor
New York, NY 10036
(212) 354-4627

PUERTO RICO
Puerto Rico Chamber of Commerce
5 West 45th Street, 4th Floor
New York, NY 10023
(212) 724-4731

SAUDI ARABIA
Saudia Arabia Council of
Chambers of Commerce and Industry
c/o Hamed Jared, Washington
Representative
Embassy of Saudi Arabia
601 New Hampshire Ave., NW
Washingotn, DC 20037

SPAIN
Spain-U.S. Chamber of Commerce
350 5th Avenue, Room 3514
New York, NY 10118
(212) 967-2170

SWEDEN
Swedish-American
Chamber of Commerce, Inc.
825 3rd Avenue, 22nd Floor
New York, NY 10022
(212) 838-5530

Swedish-American Chamber of
Commerce of Western U.S., Inc.
Ferry Building
World Trade Center, Suite 268
San Francisco, CA 94111
(415) 781-4188

SWITZERLAND
Swiss-Ameican Chamber of
Commerce, New York Chapter
347 5th Avenue, Room 1008
New York, NY 10016
(212) 213-0482

TRINIDAD & TOBAGO
Trinidad and Tobago Chamber
 of Commerce of the USA, Inc.
c/o Trintoc Services Ltd.
400 Madison Avenue, Room 803
New York, NY 10017
(2312) 759-3388

UNITED KINGDOM
British-American
Chamber of Commerce
275 Madison Avenue, Room 1714
New York, NY 10016
(212) 889-0680

British-American
Chamber of Commerce
41 Sutter Street, Suite 303
San Francisco, CA 94104
(415) 296-8645

British-American
Chamber of Commerce & Trade
Center of the Pacific Southwest
1640 5th Street, Suite 224
Santa Monica, CA 90401
(213) 394-4977

VENEZUELA
Venezuelan-American
Association of the US, INc.
150 Nassau, Suite 2015
New York, NY 10038
(212) 233-7776

YUGOSLAVIA
U.S.-Yugoslav Economic Council
818 18th Street, NW, Suite 818
Washington, DC 20006
(202) 857-0170

U.S. Government Printing Office Bookstores

The U.S. Government Printing Office operates bookstores all around the country, where you can browse through the shelves and buy and take books home with you. Naturally, these stores can't stock all of the more than 21,000 titles in the USGPO inventory, but they do carry the ones you're most likely to be looking for. And they'll be happy to order any government book currently offered for sale and have it sent directly to you. All government bookstores accept VISA, MasterCard, and Superintendent of Documents deposit account orders. For more information, please write to your nearest USGPO bookstore.

ALABAMA

O'Neill Building, 2021 Third Avenue, North Birmingham AL 35203, 205-731-1056

CALIFORNIA

ARCO Plaza C-Level, 505 South Flower Street, Los Angeles CA 90071, 213-894-5841

Room 1023 Federal Building, 450 Golden Gate Avenue, San Francisco CA 94102, 415-556-0643

COLORADO

Room 117, Federal Building, 1961 Stout Street, Denver CO 80294, 303-844-3964

World Savings Building, 720 North Main Street, Pueblo CO 81003, 719-544-3142

DISTRICT OF COLUMBIA

U.S. Government Printing Office, 710 North Capitol Street NW, Washington DC 20401, 202-275-2091

1510 H Street NW, Washington DC 20005, 202-653-5075

FLORIDA

Room 158, Federal Building, 400 West Bay Street, Jacksonville, FL 32202, 904-791-3801

GEORGIA

Room 100, Federal Building, 275 Peachtree Street NE, P.O. Box 56445, Atlanta GA 30343, 404-331-6947

ILLINOIS

Room 1365, Federal Building, 219 S. Dearborn Street, Chicago IL 60604, 312-353-5133

MARYLAND

Warehouse Sales Outlet, 8660 Cherry Lane, Laurel MD 20707, 301-953-7974/792-0262

MASSACHUSETTS
Thomas P. O'Neill Building, 10 Causeway Street, Room 179, Boston MA 02222, 617-565-6680

MICHIGAN
Suite 160, Federal Building, 477 Michigan Avenue, Detroit MI 48226, 313-226-7816

MISSOURI
120 Bannister Mall, 5600 East Bannister Road, Kansas City MO 64137, 816-765-2256

NEW YORK
Room 110, 26 Federal Plaza, New York NY 10278, 212-264-3825

OHIO
Room 1653, Federal Building, 1240 East 9th Street, Cleveland OH 44199, 216-522-4922

Room 207, Federal Building, 200 N. High Street, Columbus OH 43215, 614-469-6956

OREGON
1305 SW First Avenue, Portland, OR 97201-5801, 503-221-6217

PENNSYLVANIA
Robert Morris Building, 100 North 17th Street, Philadelphia PA 19103, 215-597-0677

Room 118, Federal Building, 1000 Liberty Avenue, Pittsburgh PA 15222, 412-644-2721

TEXAS
Room 1C46, Federal Building, 1100 Commerce Street, Dallas TX 75242, 214-767-0076

Texas Crude Building, 801 Travis Street, Suite 120, Houston TX 77002, 713-653-3100

WASHINGTON
Room 194, Federal Building, 915 Second Avenue, Seattle WA 98174, 206-442-4270

WISCONSIN
Room 190, Federal Building, 517 East Wisconsin Avenue, Milwaukee WI 53202, 414-291-1304

Abrasive Products, Graylin Presbury, tel 202-482-5157, Rm H4055, Cluster BI, Cable Code 6330.

Accounting, J. Marc Chittum, tel 202-482-0345, Rm H1110, Cluster SERV, Cable Code 6243

Adhesives/Sealants, Raimundo Prat, tel 202-482-0128, Rm H4033, Cluster BI, Cable Code 6310.

ADP Support for Aerospace, Harlan Westover, tel 202-482-3068, Rm H6733, Cluster AERO, Cable Code 6600

Advertising, Dwight Umstead, tel 202-482-3050, Rm H1120, Cluster SERV, Cable Code 6242.

Aerospace Financing Issues, Marci Kenney, tel 202-482-8228, Rm H6887, Cluster AERO, Cable Code 6600.

Aerospace Industry Information, Analysis and Data, Gene Kingsbury, tel 202-482-0678, Rm H6733, Cluster AERO, Cable Code 6600.

Aerospace Market Development and Support, David C. Bowie, tel 202-482-8228, Rms H6877 and H6883, Cluster AERO, Cable Code 6600.

Aerospace Market Promo, Claudette Sarsfield, John White, tel 202-482-2835, Rm H6898C, Cluster AERO, Cable Code 6600.

Aerospace Marketing Support, George Driscoll, tel 202-482-8228, Rm H6883, Cluster AERO, Cable Code 6600.

Aerospace Policy & Analysis, Sally H. Bath, tel 202-482-8228, Rm H6887, Cluster AERO, Cable Code 6600.

Aerospace Trade Policy Issues, Sally H. Bath, tel 202-482-8228, Rm H6881, Cluster AERO, Cable Code 6600.

Aerospace Trade Promo, John C. White, tel 202-482-3353, Rm H6898C, Cluster AERO, Cable Code 6600.

Aerospace-Space Programs, Marci Kenney, tel 202-482-8228, Rm H6877, Cluster AERO, Cable Code 6600.

Agribusiness (Major Proj), Richard Bell, tel 202-482-2460, Rm H2013, Cluster CGIC, Cable Code 6930.

Agricultural Chemicals, Francis P. Maxey, tel 202-482-0128, Rm H4029A, Cluster BI, Cable Code 6310.

Agricultural Machinery (incl Trade Promo), Mary Weining, tel 202-482-4708, Rm H2107, Cluster CGIC, Cable Code 6910.

Air Conditioning Eqpmt, Tyrena Holley, tel 202-482-3509, Rm H2104, Cluster CGIC, Cable Code 6910.

Air Pollution Control Eqpmt, Loretta Jonkers, tel 202-482-0564, Rm H2811, Cluster CGIC, Cable Code 6920.

Air Traffic Control (Market Support), George Driscoll, tel 202-482-8228, Rm H6877, Cluster AERO, Cable Code 6600.

Air, Gas Compressors, Edward McDonald, tel 202-482-0680, Rm H2122, Cluster CGIC, Cable Code 6910.

Air, Gas Compressors (Trade Promo), George Zanetakos, tel 202-482-0552, Rm H2126, Cluster CGIC, Cable Code 6910.

Aircraft & Aircraft Engines (Market Support), George Driscoll, tel 202-482-8228, Rm H6883, Cluster AERO, Cable Code 6600.

Aircraft & Aircraft Engines (Trade Promo), John C. White, tel 202-482-3353, Rm H6898C, Cluster AERO, Cable Code 6600.

Aircraft Auxiliary Equipment (Market Support), George Driscoll, tel 202-482-8228, Rm H6883, Cluster AERO, Cable Code 6600.

Aircraft Parts (Market Support), George Driscoll, tel 202-482-8228, Rm H6883, Cluster AERO, Cable Code 6600.

Aircraft Parts/Aux Eqpmt (Trade Promo), John C. White, tel 202-482-3353, Rm H6898C, Cluster AERO, Cable Code 6600.

Airlines, Randall E. Miller, tel 202-482-5071, Rm H1120, Cluster SERV, Cable Code 6242.

Airport Equipment (Market Support), George Driscoll, tel 202-482-8228, Rm H6883, Cluster AERO, Cable Code 6600.

Airport Equipment (Trade Promo), John C. White, tel 202-482-3353, Rm H6898C, Cluster AERO, Cable Code 6600.

Airports, Ports, Harbors (Major Proj), Deboorne Piggot, tel 202-482-3352, Rm H2011, Cluster CGIC, Cable Code 6930.

Alcoholic Beverages, Cornelius Kenney, tel 202-482-2428, Rm H4320, Cluster AACG, Cable Code 6810.

Alum Extrud/Alum Rolling, David Cammarota, tel 202-482-0575, Rm H4053, Cluster BI, Cable Code 6330.

Alum Forgings, Electro, David Cammarota, tel 202-482-0575, Rm H4053, Cluster BI, Cable Code 6830.

Alum Sheet, Plate/Foil, David Cammarota, tel 202-482-0575, Rm H4053, Cluster BI, Cable Code 6330.

Ammunition, Small Arms (Trade Promo), Charles Cummings, tel 202-482-5361, Rm H2126, Cluster CGIC, Cable Code 6910.

Analytical Instruments, Margaret Donnelly, tel 202-482-5466.

Analytical Instruments (Trade Promo), G.P. Gwaltney, tel 202-482-3090, Rm H1010, Cluster S&E, Cable Code 6730.

Animal Feeds, William V. Janis, tel 202-482-2250, Rm H4318, Cluster AACG, Cable Code 6810.

Apparel, William Dulka, tel 202-482-4058, Rm H3117, Cluster T&A, Cable Code 6510.

Asbestos/Cement Prod, Charles Pitcher, tel 202-482-0132, Rm H4514, Cluster BI, Cable Code 6320.

Asl & Disk Drives, Victoria Kader, tel 202-482-0571, Rm 1002, Cluster S&E, Cable Code 6710.

Assembly Equipment, Edward Abrahams, tel 202-482-0312, Rm H2128, Cluster CGIC, Cable Code 6920.

Audio Visual Equipment (Export Promo), Reginald Backham, tel 202-482-5478, Rm H4327, Cluster AACG, Cable Code 6810.

Audio Visual Services, John
Siegmund, tel 202-482-4781, Rm
H11146, Cluster SERV, Cable Code
6241.

Auto Ind Affairs Parts Suppliers,
Robert O. Reck, tel 202-482-1419,
Rm H4044, Cluster AACG, Cable
Code 6820,
Loretta M. Allison, tel 202-482-4019,
Rm H4008, Cluster AACG, Cable
Code 6820,
Deborah Semb, tel 202-482-1418,
Rm H4044, Cluster AACG, Cable
Code 6820,
Heather Jones, tel 202-482-1418, Rm
H4044, Cluster AACG, Cable Code
6820.

Auto Industry Affairs, Stuart Keitz, tel
202-482-0554, Rm H4036, Cluster
AACG, Cable Code 6820.

Aviation and Helicopter Services,
Randall Miller, tel 202-482-5071, Rm
H1120, Cluster SERV, Cable Code
6242.

Avionics Marketing, George Driscoll,
tel 202-482-8228, Rm H6877, Cluster
AERO, Cable Code 6600.

Bakery Products, William V. Janis, tel
202-482-2250, Rm H4318, Cluster
AACG, Cable Code 6810.

Ball Bearings, William E. Fletcher, tel
202-482-0309, Rm H2107, Cluster
CGIC, Cable Code 6910.

Basic Paper & Board Mfg, Donald W.
Butts, tel 202-482-0382, Rm H4512,
Cluster BI, Cable Code 6320.

Batteries, Primary, Jonathan Streeter,
tel 202-482-2132, Rm H4325, Cluster
AACG, Cable Code 6810.

Bauxite, Alumina, Prim Alum, David
Cammarota, tel 202-482-0575, Rm
H4053, Cluster BI, Cable Code 6320.

Belting & Hose, Raimundo Prat, tel
202-482-0128, Rm H4033, Cluster BI,
Cable Code 6310.

Beryllium, Brian Duggan, tel 202-482-
0575, Rm H4053, Cluster BI, Cable
Code 6330.

Beverages, Cornelius Kenney, tel 202-
482-2428, Rm H4320, Cluster
AACG, Cable Code 6810.

Bicycles, John Vanderwolf, tel 202-482-
0348, Rm H4319, Cluster AACG,
Cable Code 6810.

Biotechnology, Emily Arakaki, tel 202-
482-3888, Rm H4043, Cluster BI,
Cable Code 6310.

Biotechnology (Trade Promo), G.P.
Gwaltney, tel 202-482-3090, Rm
H1010, Cluster S&E, Cable Code
6730.

Blowers and Fans, Loretta Jonkers, tel
202-482-0564, Rm H2811, Cluster
CGIC, Cable Code 6920.

Boat Building (Major Proj), Deboorne
Piggot, tel 202-482-3352, Rm H2011,
Cluster CGIC, Cable Code 6930.

Boat Building/Repairing, Leonard
Heimowitz, tel 202-482-0558, Rm
H2122, Cluster CGIC, Cable Code
6910.

Boats, Pleasure, John Vanderwolf, tel
202-482-0348, Rm H4319, Cluster
AACG, Cable Code 6810.

Books, William S. Lofquist, tel 202-
482-0379, Rm 4316, Cluster AACG,
Cable Code 6810.

Builders Hardware, Franklin
Williams, tel 202-482-0132, Rm
H4514, Cluster BI, Cable Code 6320.

Building Materials & Construction,
Charles B. Pitcher, tel 202-482-0132,
Rm H4514, Cluster BI, Cable Code
6320.

Building Materials (Trade Policy), Mary Ann Smith, tel 202-482-0132, Rm H4520, Cluster BI, Cable Code 6320.

Business Forms, Rose Marie Bratland, tel 202-482-0380, Rm 4316, Cluster AACG, Cable Code 6810.

Cable Broadcasting, John Siegmund, tel 202-482-4781, Rm H1114, Cluster SERV, Cable Code 6241.

CAD/CAM (Trade Promo), Franc Manzolillo, tel 202-482-2991, Rm H2128, Cluster CGIC, Cable Code 6920.

CAD/CAM, Patrick McGibbon, tel 202-482-0314, Rm H2128, Cluster CGIC, Cable Code 6920.

Canned Fruits, Specialties, Vegetables, Donald A. Hodgen, tel 202-482-3346, Rm H4320, Cluster AACG, Cable Code 6810.

Capital Goods (Trade Promo), Jerry Morse, tel 202-482-5097, Rm H2001B, Cluster CGIC, Cable Code 6930.

Capital Goods DAS, Jon M. Huntsman, tel 202-482-5023, Rm H2001B, Cluster CGIC, Cable Code 6930.

Carbon Black, Raimundo Prat, tel 202-482-0128, Rm H4033, Cluster BI, Cable Code 6310.

Cement, Charles Pitcher, tel 202-482-0132, Rm H4514, Cluster BI, Cable Code 6320.

Cement Plants (Major Proj), Barbara White, tel 202-482-4160, Rm H2007, Cluster CGIC, Cable Code 6930.

Ceramics (Advanced), Moira Shea, tel 202-482-0128, Rm H4033, Cluster BI, Cable Code 6310.

Ceramics Machinery, Eugene Shaw, tel 202-482-3494, Rm H2104, Cluster CGIC, Cable Code 6910.

Cereals, William V. Janis, tel 202-482-2250, Rm H4318, Cluster AACG, Cable Code 6810.

Chemicals (Liaison & Policy), Michael J. Kelly, tel 202-482-0128, Rm H4033, Cluster BI, Cable Code 6310.

Chemicals & Allied Products, Vincent Kamenicky, tel 202-482-0128, Rm H4033, Cluster BI, Cable Code 6310.

Chemical Plants (Major Proj), Wally Haraguchi, tel 202-482-4877, Rm H2007, Cluster CGIC, Cable Code 6930.

Chinaware, Judy Corea, tel 202-482-0311, Rm H4321, Cluster AACG, Cable Code 6810.

Civil Aircraft Agreement, Marci Kenney, tel 202-482-8228, Rm H6883, Cluster AERO, Cable Code 6600.

Civil Aviation, Randall Miller, tel 202-482-5071, Rm H1120, Cluster SERV, Cable Code 6242.

Coal Exports, Charles L. Oddenino, Joseph J. Yancik, tel 202-482-1466, Rm H4411, Cluster BI, Cable Code 6340.

Cobalt, David Cammarota, tel 202-482-0575, Rm H4053, Cluster BI, Cable Code 6330.

Cocoa and Coffee Products, C. Littleton, tel 202-482-5124, Rm H4412, Cluster BI, Cable Code 6330.

Commercial Aircraft (Trade Policy), Marci Kenney, tel 202-482-8228, Rm H6883, Cluster AERO, Cable Code 6600.

Commercial Lighting Fixtures, Richard A. Whitley, tel 202-482-0682, Rm H2807, Cluster CGIC, Cable Code 6920.

Commercial Printing, William Lofquist, tel 202-482-0379, Rm H4316, Cluster AACG, Cable Code 6810.

Commercial/Indus Refrig Eqpmt, Tyrena Holley, tel 202-482-3509, Rm H2104, Cluster CGIC, Cable Code 6910.

Commercialization of Space (Market), David C. Bowie, tel 202-482-8228, Rm H6877, Cluster AERO, Cable Code 6600.

Commercialization of Space (Services), Friedrich R. Crupe, tel 202-482-4781, Rm H1114, Cluster SERV, Cable Code 6241.

Commonline/Standstill, George Grafeld, tel 202-482-8228, Rm H6887, Cluster AERO, Cable Code 6600.

Composite MTL in Metal Working, tel 202-482-0316, Rm H2128, Cluster CGIC, Cable Code 6920.

Composites, Advanced, James Manion, tel 202-482-5157, Rm H4059, Cluster BI, Cable Code 6330.

Computer and DP Services, Mary Inoussa, tel 202-482-5820, Robert G. Atkins, tel 202-482-4781, Rm H1116, Cluster SERV, Cable Code 6241.

Computer Eqpmt & Software, Clay Woods, tel 202-482-0571/3013, Rm H1104, Cluster S&E, Cable Code 6710,
Timothy O. Miles, tel 202-482-0574, V. Spathopoulos, tel 202-482-0572, Heidi M. Hoffman, tel 202-482-2053, Rm H1004, Cluster S&E, Cable Code 6710.

Computers & Business Eqpmt, Joyce V. Watson, tel 202-482-3360, Rm H1002, Cluster S&E, Cable Code 6710.

Computers & Business Eqpmt, Office of, John E. McPhee, tel 202-482-0572, Rm H1104, Cluster S&E, Cable Code 6710.

Computers (Trade Promo), Judy A. Fogg, tel 202-482-4936, Vera A. Swann, tel 202-482-0396, Rm H1004, Cluster S&E, Cable Code 6710.

Confectionery Products, Cornelius Kenney, tel 202-482-2428, Rm H4320, Cluster AACG, Cable Code 6810.

Construction Machinery (Trade Promo), Leonard Heimowitz, tel 202-482-0558, Rm H2122, Cluster CGIC, Cable Code 6910.

Construction, Domestic, Patrick MacAuley, tel 202-482-0132, Rm H4514, Cluster BI, Cable Code 6310.

Consumer Electronics, Jonathan Streeter, tel 202-482-2132, Rm H4325, Cluster AACG, Cable Code 6810.

Consumer Electronics (Export Promo), Edward K. Kimmel, tel 202-482-3640, Rm H4327, Cluster AACG, Cable Code 6810.

Consumer Goods, John H. Boyd, tel 202-482-0337, Rm H4312, Cluster AACG, Cable Code 6810.

Containers & Packaging, Kim Copperthite, tel 202-482-0595, Rm H4053, Cluster BI, Cable Code 6330.

Contract Machining, Patrick McGibbon, tel 202-482-0314, Rm H2128, Cluster CGIC, Cable Code 6920.

Conventional Fossil Fuel Power (Major Proj), Robert Dollison, tel 202-482-2783, Rm H2015B, Cluster CGIC, Cable Code 6930.

Converted Paper Prod, Gary Stanley, tel 202-482-0375, Rm H4512, Cluster BI, Cable Code 6310.

Conveyors/Conveying Eqmt, Mary Weining, tel 202-482-4708, Rm H2107, Cluster CGIC, Cable Code 6910.

Conveyors/Conveying Eqmt (Trade Promo), Mary Weining, tel 202-482-4708, Rm H2107, Cluster CGIC, Cable Code 6910.

Copper, Copper/Brass Mills, Copper Wire Mills, Brian Duggan, tel 202-482-0575, Rm H4053, Cluster BI, Cable Code 6330.

Corn Products, William V. Janis, tel 202-482-2250, Rm H4318, Cluster AACG, Cable Code 6810.

Cosmetics, Leo R. McIntyre, tel 202-482-0128, Rm H4033, Cluster BI, Cable Code 6310.

Costume Jewelry, John M. Harris, tel 202-482-1178, Rm H4325, Cluster AACG, Cable Code 6810.

Cottonseed Oil, William V. Janis, tel 202-482-2250, Rm H4318, Cluster AACG, Cable Code 6810.

Current-Carrying Wiring Devices, Richard A. Whitley, tel 202-482-0682, Rm H2807, Cluster CGIC, Cable Code 6920.

Cutlery, Judith Corea, tel 202-482-0311, Rm H4323, Cluster AACG, Cable Code 6810.

Dairy Products, William V. Janis, tel 202-482-2250, Rm H4318, Cluster AACG, Cable Code 6810.

Data Processing Services, Robert G. Atkins, tel 202-482-1114, Rm H1116, Cluster SERV, Cable Code 6241.

Database Services, Mary C. Inoussa, tel 202-482-1114, Rm H1116, Cluster SERV, Cable Code 6241.

Dolls, Judy Corea, tel 202-482-0311, Rm H4321, Cluster AACG, Cable Code 6810.

Drilling Mus/Soft Compounds, Damon Greer, tel 202-482-0564, Rm H2811F, Cluster CGIC, Cable Code 6920.

Drugs, Leo R. McIntyre, tel 202-482-0128, Rm H4033, Cluster BI, Cable Code 6310.

Durable Goods, Gerald F. Gordon, tel 202-482-1176, Rm H4312, Cluster AACG, Cable Code 6810.

Earthenware, Judy Corea, tel 202-482-0311, Rm H2007, Cluster AACG, Cable Code 6810.

Education Facilities (Major Proj), Barbara White, tel 202-482-4160, Rm H2007, Cluster CGIC, Cable Code 6930.

Educational/Training, Simon Francis, tel 202-482-0350, Rm H1112, Cluster SERV, Cable Code 6241.

Electric Industrial Apparatus Nec, Richard A. Whitley, tel 202-482-0682, Rm H2807, Cluster CGIC, Cable Code 6920.

Elec/Power Gen/Transmission & Dist Eqt (Trade Promo), Jay Brandes, tel 202-482-0560, Rm H2807R, Cluster CGIC, Cable Code 6920.

Electrical Power Plants (Major Proj), Robert Dollison, tel 202-482-2733, Rm H2015B, Cluster CGIC, Cable Code 6930.

Electrical Test & Measuring, Margaret T. Donnelly, tel 202-482-5466, Rm H1202, Cluster S&E, Cable Code 6720.

Electricity, William Sugg, tel 202-482-1466, Rm H4411, Cluster BI, Cable Code 6340.

Electro-optical Instruments, Margaret T. Donnelly, tel 202-482-5466, Rm H1202, Cluster S&E, Cable Code 6720.

Electro-optical Instruments (Trade Promo), G. P. Gwaltney, tel 202-482-3090, Rm H1010, Cluster S&E, Cable Code 6720.

Electronic (Legislation), E. MacDonald Nyhen, tel 202-482-0570, Rm H1012, Cluster S&E, Cable Code 6720.

Electronic Components, Marguerite Markey, tel 202-482-8411, Rm H1015, Cluster S&E, Cable Code 6720.

Electronic Components/Production & Test Equip, Joseph J. Burke, tel 202-482-5014, Rm H1015, Cluster S&E, Cable Code 6720.

Elevators, Moving Stairways (incl Trade Promo), Mary Weining, tel 202-482-4708, Rm H2107, Cluster CGIC, Cable Code 6910.

Employment, Simon Francis, tel 202-482-0350, Rm H1112, Cluster SERV, Cable Code 6243.

Energy (Commodities), Joseph J. Yancik, tel 202-482-1466, Rm H4415, Cluster BI, Cable Code 6340.

Energy, Renewable, John Rasmussen, tel 202-482-1466, Rm H4411, Cluster BI, Cable Code 6340.

Engineering/Construction Services (Trade Promo), Robert Ruan, tel 202-482-0359, Rm H2005, Cluster CGIC, Cable Code 6930.

Entertainment Industries, John Siegmund, tel 202-482-4781, Rm H1116, Cluster SERV, Cable Code 6241.

Explosives, Francis P. Maxey, tel 202-482-0128, Rm H4033, Cluster BI, Cable Code 6310.

Export Trading Companies, George Mueller, tel 202-482-5131/5618, Cluster SERV, Cable Code 6200.

Fabricated Metal Construction Materials, Franklin Williams, tel 202-482-0132, Rm H4514, Cluster BI, Cable Code 6320.

Farm Machinery (incl Trade Promo), Mary Weining, tel 202-482-4708, Rm H2107, Cluster CGIC, Cable Code 6910.

Fasteners (Industrial), Richard Reise, tel 202-482-3489, Rm 2107, Cluster CGIC, Cable Code 6910.

Fats and Oils, William V. Janis, tel 202-482-2250, Rm H4318, Cluster AACG, Cable Code 6810.

Fencing (Metal), Robert Shaw, tel 202-482-0132, Rm H4514, Cluster BI, Cable Code 6320.

Ferroalloys Products, Graylin Presbury, tel 202-482-0609, Rm 4414, Cluster BI, Cable Code 6330.

Ferrous Scrap, Robert Sharkey, tel 202-482-0606, Rm H4414, Cluster BI, Cable Code 6330.

Fertilizers, Francis P. Maxey, tel 202-482-0128, Rm H4033, Cluster BI, Cable Code 6310.

Filters/Purifying Eqmt, Loretta Jonkers, tel 202-482-0564, Rm H2811, Cluster CGIC, Cable Code 6920.

Finance & Management Industries, Wray O. Candilis, tel 202-482-0339, Rm H1110, Cluster SERV, Cable Code 6243.

Fisheries (Major Proj), Richard Bell, tel 202-482-2460, Rm H1110, Cluster CGIC, Cable Code 6930.

Flexible Mfg Systems (Trade Promo), Franc Manzolillo, tel 202-482-2991, Rm H2128, Cluster CGIC, Cable Code 6920.

Flexible Mfg Systems, Patrick McGibbon, tel 202-482-0314, Rm H2128, Cluster CGIC, Cable Code 6920.

Flour, William V. Janis, tel 202-482-2250, Rm H4318, Cluster AACG, Cable Code 6810.

Fluid Power, Edward McDonald, 202-482-0680, Rm H2122, Cluster CGIC, Cable Code 6910.

Food Products Machinery, Irvin Axelrod, 202-482-0310, Rm H2107, Cluster CGIC, Cable Code 6910.

Food Retailing, Cornelius Kenney, 202-482-2428, Rm H4320, Cluster AACG, Cable Code 6810.

Footwear, James Byron, 202-482-4034, Rm H4318, Cluster AACG, Cable Code 6810.

Forest Products, Donald W. Butts, 202-482-0375, Rm H4512, Cluster BI, Cable Code 6320.

Forest Products, Domestic Construction, Chris Kristensen, 202-482-0384, Rm H4520, Cluster BI, Cable Code 6320.

Forest Products (Trade Policy), Michael Hicks, 202-482-0375, Rm H4520, Cluster BI, Cable Code 6320.

Forgings, Semifinished Steel, Charles Bell, 202-482-0609, Rm H4414, Cluster BI, Cable Code 6330.

Fossil Fuel Power Generation (Major Proj), Robert Dollison, 202-482-2733, Rm H2015B, Cluster CGIC, Cable Code 6930.

Foundry Eqmt, Barbara Comer, tel 202-482-0316, Rm H2128, Cluster CGIC, Cable Code 6930.

Foundry Industry, Charles Bell, tel 202-482-0609, Rm H4414, Cluster BI, Cable Code 6330.

Franchising, J. Marc Chittum, tel 202-482-0345, Rm H1100, Cluster SERV, Cable Code 6243.

Fur Goods, Joe Enright, tel 202-482-3459, Rm H4323, Cluster AACG, Cable Code 6810.

Furniture, Kevin Ellis, tel 202-482-1140, Rm H4319, Cluster AACG, Cable Code 6810.

Gallium, David Cammarota, tel 202-482-0575, Rm H4053, Cluster BI, Cable Code 6330.

Games & Children's Vehicles, tel 202-482-5479, Rm H4321, Cluster AACG, Cable Code 6810.

Gaskets/Gasketing Materials, William E. Fletcher, tel 202-482-0309, Rm H2107, Cluster CGIC, Cable Code 6910.

General Aviation Aircraft (Industry Analysis), Gene Kingsbury, tel 202-482-0677, Rm H6883, Cluster AERO, Cable Code 6600.

General Industrial Machinery, William Donahoe, tel 202-482-5455, Rm H2805, Cluster CGIC, Cable Code 6920.

General Industrial Machinery Nec, Exc 35691, Eugene Shaw, tel 202-482-3494, Rm H2104, Cluster CGIC, Cable Code 6910.

Generator Sets/Turbines (Major Proj), Robert Dollison, tel 202-482-2733, Rm H2015B, Cluster CGIC, Cable Code 6930.

Germanium, David Cammarota, tel 202-482-0575, Rm H4053, Cluster BI, Cable Code 6330.

Giftware (Export Promo), Reginald Beckham, tel 202-482-5478, Rm H4327, Cluster AACG, Cable Code 6810.

Glass, Flat, Franklin Williams, tel 202-482-0132, Rm H4518, Cluster BI, Cable Code 6320.

Glassware, Judy Corea, tel 202-482-0311, Rm H4321, Cluster AACG, Cable Code 6810.

Gloves (work), Joe Enright, tel 202-482-3459, Rm H4323, Cluster AACG, Cable Code 6810.

Grain Mill Products, William V. Janis, tel 202-482-2250, Rm H4318, Cluster AACG, Cable Code 6810.

Greeting Cards, Rose Marie Bratland, tel 202-482-0380, Rm H4316, Cluster AACG, Cable Code 6810.

Guns & Ammunition, John Vanderwolf, tel 202-482-0348, Rm H4319, Cluster AACG, Cable Code 6810.

Hand Saws, Saw Blades, Eugene Shaw, tel 202-482-3494, Rm H2104, Cluster CGIC, Cable Code 6910.

Hand/Edge Tools Ex Mach TI/Saws, Eugene Shaw, tel 202-482-3494, Rm H2104, Cluster CGIC, Cable Code 6910.

Handbags, Joseph Enright, tel 202-482-3459, Rm H4323, Cluster AACG, Cable Code 6810.

Hard Surfaced Floor Coverings, Robert Shaw, tel 202-482-0132, Rm H4514, Cluster BI, Cable Code 6320.

Hardware (Export Promo), Charles E. Johnson, tel 202-482-3422, Rm H4327, Cluster AACG, Cable Code 6810.

Health, Simon Francis, tel 202-482-0350, Rm H1112, Cluster SERV, Cable Code 6243.

Heat Treating Equipment, Barbara Comer, tel 202-482-0316, Rm H2128, Cluster CGIC, Cable Code 6920.

Heating Eqmt Ex Furnaces, Tyrena Holley, tel 202-482-3509, Rm H2104, Cluster CGIC, Cable Code 6910.

Heavy Eqmt, Max Miles, tel 202-482-0679, Rm H2124, Cluster CGIC, Cable Code 6910.

Helicopters, Gene Kingsbury, tel 202-482-0677, Rm H6883, Cluster AERO, Cable Code 6600.

Helicopters (Market Support), George Driscoll, tel 202-482-8228, Rm H6883, Cluster AERO, Cable Code 6600.

Helicopter Services, Randall E. Miller, tel 202-482-5071, Rm H1120, Cluster SERV, Cable Code 6242.

High Tech Trade, U.S. Competitiveness, Victoria L. Hatter, tel 202-482-3913, Rm H2225, Cluster TIA, Cable Code 6410.

Hoists, Overhead Cranes (incl Trade Promo), Mary Wiening, tel 202-482-4708, Rm H2107, Cluster CGIC, Cable Code 6910.

Hose & Belting, Raimundo Prat, tel 202-482-0128, Rm H4033, Cluster BI, Cable Code 6310.

Hotel & Restaurants (Export Promo), Edward K. Kimmel, tel 202-482-3640, Rm 4327, Cluster AACG, Cable Code 6810.

Hotels and Motels, J. Richard Sousane, tel 202-482-4582, Rm H1120, Cluster SERV, Cable Code 6240.

Household Appliances, Housewares (Export Promo), Charles E. Johnson, tel 202-482-3422, Rm H4327, Cluster AACG, Cable Code 6810.

Household Appliances, John M. Harris, tel 202-482-1178, Rm H4325, Cluster AACG, Cable Code 6810.

Household Furniture, Kevin Ellis, tel 202-482-1140, Rm H4319, Cluster AACG, Cable Code 6810.

Housing & Urban Development (Major Proj), Barbara White, tel 202-482-4160, Rm H2013, Cluster CGIC, Cable Code 6930.

Housing Construction, Patrick Cosslett, tel 202-482-0132, Rm H2007, Cluster BI, Cable Code 6320.

Industrial Controls, Richard A. Whitley, tel 202-482-0682, Rm H2807, Cluster CGIC, Cable Code 6920.

Industrial Drives/Gears, William E. Fletcher, tel 202-482-0309, Rm H2107, Cluster CGIC, Cable Code 6910.

Industrial Gases, Antonios Kostalas, tel 202-482-0128, Rm H4033, Cluster BI, Cable Code 6310.

Industrial Organic Chemicals, Leo McIntyre, tel 202-482-0128, Rm H4033, Cluster BI, Cable Code 6310.

Industrial Process Controls, Margaret T. Donnelly, tel 202-482-5466, Rm H1010, Cluster S&E, Cable Code 6730.

Industrial Robots, Patrick McGibbon, tel 202-482-0314, Rm H2128, Cluster CGIC, Cable Code 6920.

Industrial Robots (Trade Promo), Franc Manzolillo, tel 202-482-2991, Rm H2128, Cluster CGIC, Cable Code 6920.

Industrial Sewing Machines, Tyrena Holley, tel 202-482-3509, Rm H2104, Cluster CGIC, Cable Code 6910.

Industrial Structure, Lester A. Davis, tel 202-482-4924, Rm H2224, Cluster TIA, Cable Code 6410.

Industrial Trucks (Incl Trade Promo), Mary Wiening, tel 202-482-4608, Rm H2107, Cluster CGIC, Cable Code 6910.

Information Industries, Friedrich R. Crupe, tel 202-482-4781, Rm H1114, Cluster SERV, Cable Code 6241.

Information Services, Mary C. Inoussa, tel 202-482-5820, Rm H1114, Cluster SERV, Cable Code 6241.

Inorganic Chemicals, Kevin Donahue, tel 202-482-0128, Rm H4033, Cluster BI, Cable Code 6310.

Inorganic Pigments, Kevin Donahue, tel 202-482-0128, Rm H4033, Cluster BI, Cable Code 6310.

Insulation, Robert Shaw, tel 202-482-0132, Rm H4514, Cluster BI, Cable Code 6320.

Insurance, Bruce McAdam, tel 202-482-0346, Rm H1108, Cluster SERV, Cable Code 6243.

Intellectual Property Rights (Services), John E. Siegmund, tel 202-482-4781, Rm H1114, Cluster SERV, Cable Code 6241.

Internal Combustion Engines, Nec (Trade Promo), Charles Cummings, tel 202-482-5361, Rm H2126, Cluster CGIC, Cable Code 6910.

International Commodities, Fred
Siesseger, tel 202-482-5124, Rm
H4515, Cluster BI, Cable Code 6330.

International Major Projects, Robert
Thibeault, tel 202-482-5225, Rm
H2015B, Cluster CGIC, Cable Code
6930.

Investment Management, Bruce
McAdam, tel 202-482-0346, Rm
H1108, Cluster SERV, Cable Code
6243.

Irrigation (Major Proj), Richard Bell,
tel 202-482-2460, Rm H2013, Cluster
CGIC, Cable Code 6930.

Irrigation Equipment, Damon Greer,
tel 202-482-0564, Rm H2811F,
Cluster CGIC, Cable Code 6920.

Jams & Jellies, Donald A. Hodgen, tel
202-482-3346, Rm H4320, Cluster
AACG, Cable Code 6810.

Jewelry, John Harris, tel 202-482-1178,
Rm H4325, Cluster AACG, Cable
Code 6810.

Jewelry (Export Promo), Reginald
Beckham, tel 202-482-5478, Rm
H4327, Cluster AACG, Cable Code
6810.

Jute Products, Diani Tasnadi, tel 202-
482-5124, Rm H4515, Cluster BI,
Cable Code 6330.

Kitchen Cabinets, Mitchel Auerbach,
tel 202-482-0375, Rm H4508, Cluster
BI, Cable Code 6320.

Laboratory Instruments, Margaret T.
Donnelly, tel 202-482-5466, Rm
H1202, Cluster S&E, Cable Code
6720.

Laboratory Instruments (Trade
Promo), G. P. Gwaltney, tel 202-482-
3090, Rm H1010, Cluster S&E,
Cable Code 6720.

Lamp Bulbs, Jonathan Streeter, tel 202-
482-2132, Rm H4325, Cluster
AACG, Cable Code 6810.

Lasers (Trade Promo), G. P. Gwaltney,
tel 202-482-3090, Rm H1010, Cluster
S&E, Cable Code 6720.

Lawn & Garden Equipment, Jonathan
Streeter, tel 202-482-2132, Rm 4325,
Cluster AACG, Cable Code 6810.

Lead Products, David Larrabee, tel
202-482-0575, Rm H4053, Cluster BI,
Cable Code 6330.

Leasing Equipment & Vehicles, Bruce
McAdam, tel 202-482-0346, Rm
H1108, Cluster SERV, Cable Code
6243.

Leather Products, Joe Enright, tel 201-
277-3459, Rm H4323, Cluster
AACG, Cable Code 6810.

Leather Tanning, James E. Byron, tel
202-482-4034, Rm H4318, Cluster
AACG, Cable Code 6810.

Legal Services, J. Marc Chittum, tel
202-482-0345, Rm H1110, Cluster
SERV, Cable Code 6243.

LNG Plants (Major Proj), Janet
Thomas, tel 202-482-4146, Rm
H2007, Cluster CGIC, Cable Code
6930.

Logs, Wood, Michael Hicks, tel 202-
482-0375, Rm H4512, Cluster BI,
Cable Code 6320.

Luggage, Joe Enright, tel 202-482-3459,
Rm H4323, Cluster AACG, Cable
Code 6810.

Lumber, Barbara Wise, tel 202-482-
0375, Rm H4512, Cluster BI, Cable
Code 6320.

Machine Tool Accessories, Patrick McGibbon, tel 202-482-0314, Rm H2128, Cluster CGIC, Cable Code 6920.

Magnesium, David Cammarota, tel 202-482-0575, Rm H4053, Cluster BI, Cable Code 6330.

Man-made Fiber, William Dulka, tel 202-482-4058, Rm H3117, Cluster TEXA, Cable Code 6510.

Management Consulting, J. Marc Chittum, tel 202-482-0345, Rm H1110, Cluster SERV, Cable Code 6243.

Manifold Business Forms, Rose Marie Bratland, tel 202-482-0380, Rm H4316, Cluster AACG, Cable Code 6810.

Margarine, William V. Janis, tel 202-482-2250, Rm 4318, Cluster AACG, Cable Code 6810.

Marine Insurance, C. William Johnson, tel 202-482-5012, Rm H1120, Cluster SERV, Cable Code 6242.

Marine Recreational Equipment (Export Promo), Reginald Beckham, tel 202-482-5478, Rm H4327, Cluster AACG, Cable Code 6810.

Maritime Shipping, C. William Johnson, tel 202-482-5012, Rm H1120, Cluster SERV, Cable Code 6242.

Marketing Promo (Basic Ind), Donald R. Trafton, tel 202-482-2493, Rm H4043, Cluster BI, Cable Code 6300.

Materials, Advanced, David Cammarota, tel 202-482-0575, Rm H4053, Cluster BI, Cable Code 6330.

Mattresses & Bedding, Kevin Ellis, tel 202-482-1140, Rm H4319, Cluster AACG, Cable Code 6810.

Meat Products, Donald A. Hodgen, tel 202-482-3346, Rm H4320, Cluster AACG, Cable Code 6810.

Mech Power Transmission Eqmt, Nec, William E. Fletcher, tel 202-482-0309, Rm H2107, Cluster CGIC, Cable Code 6910.

Medical Facilities (Major Proj), Barbara White, tel 202-482-4160, Rm H2007, Cluster CGIC, Cable Code 6930.

Medical Instruments, Michael Fuchs, tel 202-482-0550, Rm H1010, Cluster S&E, Cable Code 6720.

Medical Instruments (Trade Promo), George B. Keen, tel 202-482-2010, Rm H1014, Cluster S&E, Cable Code 6720.

Mercury, Fluorspar, James J. Manion, tel 202-482-5157, Rm H4055, Cluster BI, Cable Code 6330.

Metal Building Products, Franklin Williams, tel 202-482-0132, Rm H4514, Cluster BI, Cable Code 6320.

Metal Cookware, Judy Corea, tel 202-482-0311, Rm H4321, Cluster AACG, Cable Code 6810.

Metal Cutting Machine Tools, Patrick McGibbon, tel 202-482-0314, Rm H2128, Cluster CGIC, Cable Code 6920.

Metal Cutting Machine Tools (Trade Promo), Franc Manzolillo, tel 202-482-2991, Rm H2128, Cluster CGIC, Cable Code 6920.

Metal Cutting Tools for Machine Tools, Barbara Comer, tel 202-482-0316, Rm H2128, Cluster CGIC, Cable Code 6920.

Metal Forming Machine Tools, Patrick McGibbon, tel 202-482-0314, Rm H2128, Cluster CGIC, Cable Code 6920.

Metal Forming Machine Tools (Trade Promo), Franc Manzolillo, tel 202-482-2991, Rm H2128, Cluster CGIC, Cable Code 6920.

Metal Powders, Brian Duggan, tel 202-482-0575, Rm H4053, Cluster BI, Cable Code 6330.

Metals, Secondary, Ralph Thompson, tel 202-482-0606, Rm H4513, Cluster BI, Cable Code 6330.

Metalworking Eqmt Nec, Patrick McGibbon, tel 202-482-0314, Rm H2128, Cluster CGIC, Cable Code 6920.

Metalworking, John Mearman, tel 202-482-0315, Rm H2128, Cluster CGIC, Cable Code 6920.

Millwork, Mitchel Auerbach, tel 202-482-0375, Rm H4508, Cluster BI, Cable Code 6320.

Mineral-based Construction Materials (Clay, Concrete, Gypsum, Asphalt, Stone), Charles B. Pitcher, tel 202-482-0132, Rm H4514, Cluster BI, Cable Code 6320.

Mining Machinery (Trade Promo), George Zanetakos, tel 202-482-0552, Rm H2126, Cluster CGIC, Cable Code 6910.

Mining Machinery, Edward McDonald, tel 202-482-0680, Rm H2122, Cluster CGIC, Cable Code 6910.

Mobile Homes, Patrick Cosslett, tel 202-482-0132, Rm H4514, Cluster BI, Cable Code 6320.

Molybdenum, David Cammarota, tel 202-482-0575, Rm H4053, Cluster BI, Cable Code 6330.

Monorails (Trade Promo), Mary Wiening, tel 202-482-4708, Rm H2107, Cluster CGIC, Cable Code 6910.

Motion Pictures, John Siegmund, tel 202-482-4781, Rm H1114, Cluster SERV, Cable Code 6241.

Motor Vehicles Auto Ind Affairs, John W. Hartman, tel 202-482-0669, Rm H4044, Cluster AACG, Cable Code 6820,
Edward Leviton, tel 202-482-0669, Rm H4040, Cluster AACG, Cable Code 6820,
Robin Gaines, tel 202-482-0669, Rm H4040, Cluster AACG, Cable Code 6820,
Ann Bybee, tel 202-482-0669, Rm H4036, Cluster AACG, Cable Code 6820.

Motor Vehicles, Albert T. Warner, tel 202-482-0669, Rm H4036, Cluster AACG, Cable Code 6820.

Motorcycles, John Vanderwolf, tel 202-482-0348, Rm H4319, Cluster AACG, Cable Code 6810.

Motors, Elect, Richard A. Whitley, tel 202-482-0682, Rm H2807, Cluster CGIC, Cable Code 6920.

Music, John Siegmund, tel 202-482-4781, Rm H1114, Cluster SERV, Cable Code 6241.

Musical Instruments, Judy Corea, tel 202-482-0311, Rm H4321, Cluster AACG, Cable Code 6810.

Mutual Funds, Bruce McAdam, tel 202-482-0346, Rm H1108, Cluster SERV, Cable Code 6243.

Natural Gas, Douglas Perry, tel 202-482-1466, Rm H4413, Cluster BI, Cable Code 6340.

Natural, Synthetic Rubber, Leo McIntyre, tel 202-482-0128, Rm H4033, Cluster BI, Cable Code 6310.

Newspapers, Rose Marie Bratland, tel 202-482-0380, Rm H4316, Cluster AACG, Cable Code 6810.

Nickel Products, Graylin Presbury, tel 202-482-0575, Rm H4053, Cluster BI, Cable Code 6330.

Non-alcoholic Beverages, Cornelius Kenney, tel 202-482-2428, Rm H4320, Cluster AACG, Cable Code 6810.

Noncurrent Carrying Wiring Devices, Richard A. Whitley, tel 202-482-0682, Rm H2807, Cluster CGIC, Cable Code 6920.

Nondurable Goods, Nazir Bhagat, tel 202-482-0341, Rm H4314, Cluster AACG, Cable Code 6810.

Nonelectric Engines, Charles Cummings, tel 202-482-5361, Rm H2126, Cluster CGIC, Cable Code 6910.

Nonferrous Foundries, Brian Duggan, tel 202-482-0610, Rm H4414, Cluster BI, Cable Code 6330.

Nonferrous Metals, James Manion, tel 202-482-0575, Rm H4053, Cluster BI, Cable Code 6330.

Nonmetallic Minerals Nec, James J. Manion, tel 202-482-5157, Rm H4053, Cluster BI, Cable Code 6330.

Nonresidential Construction, Domestic, Patrick MacAuley, tel 202-482-0132, Rm H4053, Cluster BI, Cable Code 6320.

Nuclear Power Plants (Major Proj), Robert Dollison, tel 202-482-2733, Rm H2015B, Cluster CGIC, Cable Code 6930.

Numerical Controls for Machine Tools, Patrick McGibbon, tel 202-482-0314, Rm H2128, Cluster CGIC, Cable Code 6920.

Nuts, Bolts, Washers, Richard Reise, tel 202-482-3489, Rm H2107, Cluster CGIC, Cable Code 6910.

Nuts, edible, William V. Janis, tel 202-482-2250, Rm H4318, Cluster AACG, Cable Code 6810.

Ocean Shipping, C. William Johnson, tel 202-482-5012, Rm H1120, Cluster SERV, Cable Code 6242.

Oil & Gas (Fuels Only), Douglas Perry, tel 202-482-1466, Rm H4413, Cluster BI, Cable Code 6340.

Oil & Gas Development & Refining (Major Proj), Janet Thomas, tel 202-482-4146, Rm H2007, Cluster CGIC, Cable Code 6930.

Oil Field Machinery (Trade Promo), Charles Cummings, tel 202-482-5361, Rm H2126, Cluster CGIC, Cable Code 6910.

Oil Field Machinery, Edward McDonald, tel 202-482-0680, Rm H2122, Cluster CGIC, Cable Code 6910.

Oil Shale (Major Proj), Janet Thomas, tel 202-482-4146, Rm H2007, Cluster CGIC, Cable Code 6930.

Operations & Maintenance, J. Marc Chitum, tel 202-482-0345, Rm H1110, Cluster SERV, Cable Code 6243.

Organic Chemicals, Leo McIntyre, tel 202-482-0128, Rm H4033, Cluster BI, Cable Code 6310.

Outdoor Lighting Fixtures, Richard A. Whitley, tel 202-482-0682, Rm H2807, Cluster CGIC, Cable Code 6920.

Outdoor Power (Export Promo), Charles E. Johnson, tel 202-482-3422, Rm H4327, Cluster AACG, Cable Code 6810.

Packaging & Containers, Kim Copperthite, tel 202-482-0575, Rm H4053, Cluster BI, Cable Code 6330.

Packaging Machinery, Irvin Axelrod, tel 202-482-0310, Rm H2107, Cluster CGIC, Cable Code 6310.

Paints/Coatings, Raimundo Prat, tel 202-482-0128, Rm H4033, Cluster BI, Cable Code 6310.

Paper And Board Packaging, Leonard S. Smith, tel 202-482-0375, Rm H4512, Cluster BI, Cable Code 6320.

Paper Industries Machinery, Edward Abrahams, tel 202-482-0312, Rm H2128, Cluster CGIC, Cable Code 6920.

Paper, Donald Butts, tel 202-482-0375, Rm H4512, Cluster BI, Cable Code 6320.

Pasta, William V. Janis, tel 202-482-2250, Rm H4318, Cluster AACG, Cable Code 6810.

Paving Materials (Asphalt & Concrete), Charles Pitcher, tel 202-482-0132, Rm H4514, Cluster BI, Cable Code 6320.

Pectin, William V. Janis, tel 202-482-2250, Rm H4318, Cluster AACG, Cable Code 6810.

Pens/Pencils, etc., John Harris, tel 202-482-1178, Rm H4325, Cluster AAG, Cable Code 6810.

Periodicals, Rose Marie Bratland, tel 202-482-0380, Rm H4316, Cluster AACG, Cable Code 6810.

Pet Food, William V. Janis, tel 202-482-2250, Rm H4318, Cluster AACG, Cable Code 6810.

Petrochemicals, Cyclic Crudes, Leo McIntyre, tel 202-482-0128, Rm H4033, Cluster BI, Cable Code 6310.

Petrochemicals Plants (Major Proj), Wally Haraguchi, tel 202-482-4877, Rm H2007, Cluster CGIC, Cable Code 6930.

Petrochemicals, Leo McIntrye, tel 202-482-0128, Rm H4033, Cluster BI, Cable Code 6310.

Petroleum, Crude & Refined Products, Douglas Perry, tel 202-482-1466, Rm H4413, Cluster BI, Cable Code 6340.

Pharmaceuticals, Leo McIntyre, tel 202-482-0128, Rm H4033, Cluster BI, Cable Code 6310.

Photographic Eqmt & Supplies, Joyce Watson, tel 202-482-0574, Rm H1002, Cluster S&E, Cable Code 6720.

Pipelines (Major Proj), Janet Thomas, tel 202-482-4146, Rm H2007, Cluster CGIC, Cable Code 6930.

Plastic Construction Products (Most), Franklin Williams, tel 202-482-0132, Rm H4514, Cluster BI, Cable Code 6320.

Plastic Materials, Moira Shea, tel 202-482-0128, Rm H4033, Cluster BI, Cable Code 6310.

Plastic Products Machinery, Eugene Shaw, tel 202-482-3494, Rm H2104, Cluster CGIC, Cable Code 6910.

Plastic Products, Raimundo Prat, tel 202-482-0128, Rm H4033, Cluster BI, Cable Code 6310.

Plumbing Fixtures & Fittings, Robert Shaw, tel 202-482-0132, Rm H4514, Cluster BI, Cable Code 6320.

Plywood/Panel Products, Mitchel Auerbach, tel 202-482-0375, Rm H4512, Cluster BI, Cable Code 6320.

Point-of-Use Water Treatment, Damon Greer, tel 202-482-0564, Rm H2811, Cluster CGIC, Cable Code 6920.

Pollution Control Equipment, Loretta Jonkers, tel 202-482-0564, Rm H2811, Cluster CGIC, Cable Code 6920.

Porcelain Electrical Supplies (Part), Richard A. Whitley, tel 202-482-0682, Rm H2807, Cluster CGIC, Cable Code 6920.

Pottery, nec, Judy Corea, tel 202-482-0311, Rm H4321, Cluster AACG, Cable Code 6810.

Poultry Products, Donald A. Hodgen, tel 202-482-3346, Rm H4320, Cluster AACG, Cable Code 6810.

Power Hand Tools, Edward Abrahams, tel 202-482-0312, Rm H2128, Cluster CGIC, Cable Code 6920.

Precious Metal Jewelry, John M. Harris, tel 202-482-1178, Rm H4325, Cluster AACG, Cable Code 6810.

Prefabricated Buildings (Metal), Franklin Williams, tel 202-482-0132, Rm H4514, Cluster BI, Cable Code 6320.

Prefabricated Buildings (Wood), Patrick Cosslett, tel 202-482-0132, Rm H4514, Cluster BI, Cable Code 6320.

Prepared Meats, Donald A. Hodgen, tel 202-482-3346, Rm H4320, Cluster AACG, Cable Code 6810.

Primary Commodities, Fred Siesseger, tel 202-482-5124, Rm H4515, Cluster BI, Cable Code 6330.

Printing & Publishing, William S. Lofquist, tel 202-482-0379, Rm H4316, Cluster AAG, Cable Code 6810.

Printing Trade Services, Rose Marie Bratland, tel 202-482-0380, Rm H4316, Cluster AACG, Cable Code 6810.

Printing Trades Mach/Eqmt, Alexis Kemper, tel 202-482-5956, Rm H2104, Cluster CGIC, Cable Code 6910.

Process Control Instruments, Margaret T. Donnelly, tel 202-482-5466, Rm H1202, Cluster S&E, Cable Code 6720.

Process Control Instruments (Trade Promo), G. P. Gwaltney, tel 202-482-3090, Rm H1010, Cluster S&E, Cable Code 6720.

Processing & Special Eqmt, William Fletcher, tel 202-482-0309, Rm 2107, Cluster CGIC, Cable Code 6910.

Pulp And Paper Mills (Major Proj), Barbara White, tel 202-482-4160, Rm H1007, Cluster CGIC, Cable Code 6930.

Pulpmills, Gary Stanley, tel 202-482-0375, Rm H4512, Cluster BI, Cable Code 6320.

Pumps, Pumping Eqmt, Edward McDonald, tel 202-482-0680, Rm H2122, Cluster CGIC, Cable Code 6910.

Pumps, Valves, Compressors (Trade Promo), George Zanetakos, tel 202-482-0552, Rm H2126, Cluster CGIC, Cable Code 6910.

Radio & TV Broadcasting, John Siegmund, tel 202-482-4781, Rm H1114, Cluster SERV, Cable Code 6241.

Radio & TV Communications Eqmt, Linda Gossack, tel 202-482-2872, Rm H1003A, Cluster S&E, Cable Code 6730.

Railroad Eqpmt (Trade Promo), Leonard Heimowitz, tel 202-482-0558, Rm H2122, Cluster CGIC, Cable Code 6910.

Railroad Services, J. Richard Sousane, tel 202-482-4582, Rm H1120, Cluster SERV, Cable Code 6242.

Recreational Eqmt (Export Promo), Thomas Cox, tel 202-482-5852, Rm H4327, Cluster AACG, Cable Code 6810.

Refractory Products, Brian Duggan, tel 202-482-0610, Rm H4414, Cluster BI, Cable Code 6330.

Renewable Energy Eqpmt, Les Garden, tel 202-482-0556, Rm H2811R, Cluster CGIC, Cable Code 6920.

Research & Development, James B. Price, tel 202-482-4781, Rm H1114, Cluster SERV, Cable Code 6241.

Residential Lighting Fixtures, Richard A. Whitley, tel 202-482-0682, Rm H2807, Cluster CGIC, Cable Code 6920.

Retail Trade, Marvin J. Margulies, tel 202-482-5086, Rm H1120, Cluster SERV, Cable Code 6242.

Rice Milling, William V. Janis, tel 202-482-2250, Rm H4318, Cluster AACG, Cable Code 6810.

Roads, Railroads, Mass Trans (Major Proj), Jay L. Smith, tel 202-482-4642, Rm H2011, Cluster CGIC, Cable Code 6930.

Robots, Patrick McGibbon, tel 202-482-0314, Rm H2128, Cluster CGIC, Cable Code 6930.

Roller Bearings, William E. Fletcher, tel 202-482-0309, Rm H2107, Cluster CGIC, Cable Code 6910.

Rolling Mill Machinery, Barbara Comer, tel 202-482-0316, Rm H2128, Cluster CGIC, Cable Code 6920.

Roofing, Asphalt, Charles Pitcher, tel 202-482-0132, Rm H4514, Cluster BI, Cable Code 6320.

Rubber, Rubber Products, Raimundo Prat, tel 202-482-0128, Rm H4033, Cluster BI, Cable Code 6310.

Saddlery & Harness Products, Joe Enright, tel 202-482-3459, Rm H4323, Cluster AACG, Cable Code 6810.

Safety & Security Equip (Trade Promo), Howard Fleming, tel 202-482-5163, Rm H1014, Cluster S&E, Cable Code 6720.

Satellites & Space Vehicles (Marketing), David C. Crowe, tel 202-482-8228, Rm H6877, Cluster AERO, Cable Code 6600.

Satellites, Communication, Timothy Shea, tel 202-482-4466, Rm H1001A, Cluster S&E, Cable Code 6720.

Scientific Instruments (Trade Promo), G.P. Gwaltney, tel 202-482-3090, Rm H1010, Cluster S&E, Cable Code 6720.

Scientific Measurement/Control Eqpmt, Margaret Donnelly, tel 202-482-5466, Rm H1202, Cluster S&E, Cable Code 6720.

Screw Machine Products, Richard Reise, tel 202-482-3489, Rm H2107, Cluster CGIC, Cable Code 6910.

Screws, Washers, Richard Reise, tel 202-482-3489, Rm H2107, Cluster CGIC, Cable Code 6910.

Security & Commodity Brokers, Thomas R. Fenwick, tel 202-482-0347, Rm H1108, Cluster SERV, Cable Code 6243.

Security Management Svcs., J. Marc Chittum, tel 202-482-0345, Rm H1112, Cluster SERV, Cable Code 6243.

Semiconductor Prod Eqmt & Materials, Peggy Haggerty, tel 202-482-3360, Rm H1202, Cluster S&E, Cable Code 6720.

Semiconductors, Marguerite Markey, tel 202-482-8411, Rm H1015, Cluster S&E.

Service Industries (Urugay Round), Jay Dowling, tel 202-482-1134, Rm 1124, Cluster SERV, Cable Code 6240.

Service Industries, Brant W. Free, tel 202-482-3575, Rm H1124, Cluster SERV, Cable Code 6240.

Services Data Base Development, David McMeans, tel 202-482-0351, Rm H1108, Cluster SERV, Cable Code 6243, Robert G. Atkins, tel 202-482-4781, Rm H1114, Cluster SERV, Cable Code 6241.

Services, DAS, R. David Luft, tel 202-482-5261, Rm H1128, Cluster SERV, Cable Code 6200.

Shingles (Wood), Barbara Wise, tel 202-482-0375, Rm H4512, Cluster BI, Cable Code 6320.

Silverware, John Harris, tel 202-482-1178, Rm H4325, Cluster AACG, Cable Code 6810.

Sisal Products, Clinton R. Shaw, tel 202-482-5124, Rm H4511, Cluster BI, Cable Code 6330.

Snackfood, William V. Janis, tel 202-482-2250, Cluster AACG, Cable Code 6810.

Soaps, Detergents, Cleaners, Leo R. McIntyrė, tel 202-482-0128, Rm H4033, Cluster BI, Cable Code 6310.

Software (Export Promo), Judy Fogg, tel 202-482-4936, Rm H1008, Cluster S&E, Cable Code 6730.

Software, Clay Woods, tel 202-482-0571, Rm H1104, Cluster S&E, Cable Code 6730, Heidi C. Hijikata, tel 202-482-0571, Rm H1104, Cluster S&E, Cable Code 6730.

Solar Cells, Photovoltaic Devices, Ocean Solar Equipment, Biomass, Geothermal, Les Garden, tel 202-482-0556, Rm H2811R, Cluster CGIC, Cable Code 6920.

Soy Products, William V. Janis, tel 202-482-2250, Rm H4318, Cluster AACG, Cable Code 6810.

Space Commercialization (Equipment), David C. Bowie, tel 202-482-8228, Rm H6877, Cluster AERO, Cable Code 6600.

Space Commercialization (Services), Friedrich R. Crupe, tel 202-482-4781, Rm H1114, Cluster SERV, Cable Code 6241.

Space Policy Development, Marci Kenney, tel 202-482-8228, Rm H6877, Cluster AERO, Cable Code 6600.

Space Policy Development (Services), Friedrich R. Crupe, tel 202-482-4781, Rm H1114, Cluster SERV, Cable Code 6241.

Space Services, Friedrich R. Crupe, tel 202-482-4781, Rm H11146, Cluster SERV, Cable Code 6241.

Special Industry Machinery, Nec, Eugene Shaw, tel 202-482-3494, Rm H2104, Cluster CGIC, Cable Code 6910.

Special Industry Machinery, tel 202-482-0302, Rm H2102, Cluster CGIC, Cable Code 6910.

Speed Changers, William E. Fletcher, tel 202-482-0309, Rm H2107, Cluster CGIC, Cable Code 6910.

Sporting & Athletic Goods, John Vanderwolf, tel 202-482-0348, Rm H4319, Cluster AACG, Cable Code 6810.

Sporting Goods (Export Promo), Thomas Cox, tel 202-482-5852, Rm H4327, Cluster AACG, Cable Code 6810.

Steel Industry Products, Charles Bell, tel 202-482-0608, Rm H4414, Cluster BI, Cable Code 6330.

Steel Industry, Ralph F. Thompson, tel 202-482-0606, Rm H4414, Cluster BI, Cable Code 6330.

Steel Markets, Charles Bell, tel 202-482-0608, Rm H4414, Cluster BI, Cable Code 6330.

Storage Batteries, David Larabee, tel 202-482-0575, Rm H4053, Cluster BI, Cable Code 6330.

Sugar Products, Diana Tasnadi, tel 202-482-5124, Rm H4515, Cluster BI, Cable Code 6330.

Supercomputers, Lauren J. Kelley, tel 202-482-0571, Rm H1104, Cluster S&E, Cable Code 6710.

Superconductor electronics, Phil Marcus, tel 202-482-1330, Rm H1016, Cluster S&E, Cable Code 6720.

Superconductors, Roger Chiarado, tel 202-482-0402, Rm H1209, Cluster SE, Cable Code 6720.

Switchgear & Switchboard Apparatus, Richard A. Whitley, tel 202-482-0682, Rm H2807, Cluster CGIC, Cable Code 6920.

Tea, William V. Janis, tel 202-482-2250, Rm H4318, Cluster AACG, Cable Code 6810.

Technology Affairs, Edwin B. Shyking, tel 202-482-4694, Rm H4043, Cluster BI, Cable Code 6300.

Telecommunications, Roger Stechschulte, tel 202-482-4466, Rm H1001A, Cluster S&E, Cable Code 6730.

Telecommunications (Cellular), Linda Gossack, tel 202-482-4466, Rm H1001A, Cluster S&E, Cable Code 6730.

Telecommunications (CPE), John Henry, tel 202-482-4466, Rm H1001A, Cluster S&E, Cable Code 6730.

Telecommunications (Fiber Optics), James McCarthy, tel 202-482-4466, Rm H1001A, Cluster S&E, Cable Code 6730.

Telecommunications (Major Projects), Rick Paddock, tel 202-482-4466, Rm H1001A, Cluster S&E, Cable Code 6730.

Telecommunications (Network Equip), John Henry, tel 202-482-4466, Rm H1001A, Cluster S&E, Cable Code 6730.

Telecommunications (Radio, Satellite), Linda Gossack, tel 202-482-4466, Rm H1001A, Cluster S&E, Cable Code 6730.

Telecommunications (Services), Ivan Shefrin, tel 202-482-4466, Rm H1001A, Cluster S&E, Cable Code 6730, Robert G. Atkins, tel 202-482-4781, Rm H1114, Cluster SERV, Cable Code 6241.

Telecommunications (Trade Promo), Theresa E. Rettig, tel 202-482-4466, Rm H1001A, Cluster S&E, Cable Code 6730.

Telecommunications (TV Broadcast), Richard Paddock, tel 202-482-4466, Rm H4318, Cluster AACG, Cable Code 6810.

Teletext Services, Mary Inoussa, tel 202-482-5820, Rm H1114, Cluster SERV, Cable Code 6241.

Textile Machinery, Tyrena Holley, tel 202-482-3509, Rm H2104, Cluster CGIC, Cable Code 6910.

Textiles, William A. Dulka, tel 202-482-4058, Rm H3117, Cluster TEXA, Cable Code 6510.

Timber Products (Tropical), Clinton R. Shaw, tel 202-482-5124, Rm H4511, Cluster BI, Cable Code 6330.

Tin Products, Jon Manager, tel 202-482-5124, Rm H4513, Cluster BI, Cable Code 6330.

Tires, Raimundo Prat, tel 202-482-0128, Rm H4033, Cluster BI, Cable Code 6310.

Tobacco Products, Cornelius Kenney, tel 202-482-2428, Rm H4320, Cluster AACG, Cable Code 6810.

Tools/Dies/Jigs/Fixtures, Patrick McGibbon, tel 202-482-0314, Rm H2128, Cluster CGIC, Cable Code 6920.

Tourism (Major Proj), Barbara White, tel 202-482-4160, Rm H2007, Cluster CGIC, Cable Code 6930.

Tourism Services, J. Richard Sousane, tel 202-482-4582, Rm H1120, Cluster SERV, Cable Code 6242.

Toys & Games (Export Promo), Reginald Beckham, tel 202-482-5478, Rm H4327, Cluster AACG, Cable Code 6810.

Toys, Judy Corea, tel 202-482-0311, Rm H4321, Cluster AACG, Cable Code 6810.

Trade Related Employment, Lester A. Davis, tel 202-482-4924, Rm H2224, Cluster TIA, Cable Code 6410.

Transborder Data Flows, Mary C. Inoussa, tel 202-482-5820, Rm H1114, Cluster SERV, Cable Code 6241.

Transformers, Richard A. Whitley, tel 202-482-0682, Rm H2807, Cluster CGIC, Cable Code 6920.

Transportation Industries, Albert Alexander, tel 202-482-4581, Rm H1120, Cluster SERV, Cable Code 6242.

Travel & Tourism, J. Richard Sousane, tel 202-482-4582, Rm H1120, Cluster SERV, Cable Code 6242.

Tropical Commodities, Diana Tasnadi, tel 202-482-5124, Rm H4515, Cluster BI, Cable Code 6330.

Trucking Services, J. Richard Sousane, tel 202-482-4581, Rm H1122, Cluster SERV, Cable Code 6242.

Tungsten Products, Jon Manager, tel 202-482-5124, Rm H4513, Cluster BI, Cable Code 6330.

Uranium, William Sugg, tel 202-482-1466, Rm H4411, Cluster BI, Cable Code 6340.

Value-added Telecommunications Serv, Robert G. Atkins, tel 202-482-4781, Rm H1114, Cluster SERV, Cable Code 6241.

Valves, Pipe Fittings Ex Brass, Richard Reise, tel 202-482-3489, Rm H2107, Cluster CGIC, Cable Code 6910.

Vegetables, Donald A. Hodgen, tel 202-482-3346, Rm H4320, Cluster AACG, Cable Code 6810.

Videotax Services, John Siegmund, tel 202-482-4781, Mary C. Inoussa, tel 202-482-5820, Rm H1114, Cluster SERV, Cable Code 6241.

Wallets, Billfolds, Flatgoods, Joe Enright, tel 202-482-3459, Rm H4323, Cluster AACG, Cable Code 6810.

Warm Air Heating Eqmt, Tyrena Holley, tel 202-482-3509, Rm H2104, Cluster CGIC, Cable Code 6910.

Wastepaper, Gary Stanley, tel 202-482-0375, Rm H4512, Cluster BI, Cable Code 6320.

Watches, John Harris, tel 202-482-1178, Rm H4325, Cluster AACG, Cable Code 6810.

Water and Sewerage Treatment Plants (Major Proj), Mary Alice Healey, tel 202-482-4643, Rm H2013, Cluster CGIC, Cable Code 6930.

Water Resource Eqmt, Damon Greer, tel 202-482-0564, Rm H2811F, Cluster CGIC, Cable Code 6920.

Welding/Cutting Apparatus, Barbara Comer, tel 202-482-0316, Rm H2128, Cluster CGIC, Cable Code 6910.

Wholesale Trade, Dwight Umstead, tel 202-482-3050, Rm H1110, Cluster SERV, Cable Code 6242.

Windmill Components, Les Garden, tel 202-482-0556, Rm H2811R, Cluster CGIC, Cable Code 6920.

Wire & Wire Products, Ralph Thompson, tel 202-482-0606, Rm H4414, Cluster BI, Cable Code 6330.

Wire Cloth, Franklin Williams, tel 202-482-0132, Rm H4516, Cluster BI, Cable Code 6330.

Wire Cloth, Industrial, William E. Fletcher, tel 202-482-0309, Rm H2107, Cluster CGIC, Cable Code 6910.

Wood Containers, Wood Preserving, Michael Hicks, tel 202-482-0375, Rm H4512, Cluster BI, Cable Code 6320.

Wood Products, Donald Butts, tel 202-482-0375, Rm H4412, Cluster BI, Cable Code 6320.

Woodworking Machinery, Edward McDonald, tel 202-482-0680, Rm H2122, Cluster CGIC, Cable Code 6910.

Yeast, William V. Janis, tel 202-482-2250, Rm H4318, Cluster AACG, Cable Code 6810.

Important Contacts for Major Foreign Markets

New exporters often have a need to obtain information about a particular country market. Libraries have country indexes and these are very useful. In addition, however, a firm interested in securing answers to specific market questions should consult with our embassy and consulate personnel.

Additionally, foreign country embassies in the U.S. are often pleased to answer inquiries. American Chambers of Commerce are also fruitful sources of country market information. Important contacts for selective foreign markets are listed below to assist managers in their pursuit of country information.

ARGENTINA
American Embassy Commercial Section, 4300 Columbia, 1425, Buenos Aires, Argentina, Tel 54-1-774-7611/8811/9911, Telex 18156 USICA AR.

American Chamber of Commerce in Argentina, Virrey Loreto 2477/81, 1426 Buenos Aires, Argentina, Tel 782-6016, Telex 21517 CIARG AR.

Embassy of Argentina Commercial Section, 1667 K Street, N.W., Suite 610, Washington, DC, 20006, Tel (202) 939-6400, Telex 89-2537 EMBARG WSH.

AUSTRALIA
American Embassy Commercial Section, Moonah Pl., Canberra, A.C.T. 2600, Australia, Tel 61-62-705000, Telex 62104 USAEMB.

American Consulate General, Melbourne Commercial Section, 24 Albert Road, South Melbourne, Victoria 3205, Australia, Tel 61-3-697-7900, Telex 30982 AMERCON.

American Consulate General, Sydney Commercial Section, 36th Floor, T&G Tower, Hyde Park Square, Park and Elizabeth Sts., Sydney 2000, N.S.W., Australia, Tel 61-2-264-7044, Telex 74223 FCSSYD.

American Consulate General, Perth Commercial Section, 246 St. George's Ter., Perth, WA 6000, Australia, Tel 61-9-322-4466.

American Chamber of Commerce in Australia, 60 Margaret Street, Sydney, N.S.W.,2000, Australia, Tel 221-3055, Telex 72729.

Embassy of Australia Commercial Section, 1601 Massachusetts Avenue N.W., Washington, DC 20036, Tel (202) 797-3201.

AUSTRIA
American Embassy Commercial Section, Boltzmanngasse 16, A-1091, Vienna, Austria, Tel 43-222-31-55-11, Telex 114634.

U.S. Export Development Office, Schmidgasse 14, A-1080, Vienna, Austria, Telex I 1 6103.

BAHAMAS

American Embassy Commercial Section, Mosmar Building, Queen Street, P.O. Box N-8197, Nassau, Bahamas, Tel 809-322-4753 thru 56, Telex 20-138 AMEMB NS138.

Embassy of the Bahamas Commercial Section, 600 New Hampshire Avenue N.W., Suite 865, Washington, DC 20037, Tel (202)338-3940, Telex 440 244 BHMS.

BELGIUM

American Embassy Commercial Section, 27 Boulevard du Regent, B-1000 Brussels, Belgium, Tel 32-2-513-3830, Telex 846-21336.

U.S. Mission to the European Communities, 40 Boulevard du Regent, B-1000 Brussels, Belgium, Tel 32-2-513-4450, Telex 21336.

American Chamber of Commerce in Belgium, c/o Essochem, B-1040 Brussels, Belgium, Tel 02-720-9130, Telex 62788.

Embassy of Belgium Commercial Section, 3330 Garfield Street, N.W., Washington, DC 20008, Tel (202) 333-6900, Telex 89 566 AMBEL WSH.

BRAZIL

American Embassy Commercial Section, Avenida das Nocoes, Lote 3, Brasilia, Brazil, Tel 55-61-223-0120, Telex 061-1091.

American Consulate General Rio de Janeiro, Commercial Section, Avenida Presidente Wilson, 147, Rio de Janeiro, Brazil, Tel 55-21-292-7117, Telex AMCONSUL 21-22831.

American Consultate General Sao Paulo, Commercial Section, Rua Padre Joao Manoel, 933, P.O. Box 8063, Sao Paulo, Brazil, Tel 55-11-881-6511, Telex 11-31574.

American Chamber of Commerce in Brazil--Rio de Janeiro, 20.040 Rio de Janiero, RJ, Brazil, Tel 203-2477, Telex 2123539 RJRT BR.

American Chamber of Commerce in Brazil--Sao Paulo, Caixa Postal 1980, 01051, Sao Paulo, SP, Brazil, Tel 011-212-3132, Telex 1132311 CASE BR.

Embassy of Brazil Commercial Section, 3006 Massachusetts Avenue, N.W., Washington, DC 20008, Tel (202) 745-2700, Telex 440371 BRASMB 89430 BRASMB.

CANADA

American Embassy Commercial Section, 100 Wellington Street, Ottawa, Ontario, Canada, K1p5T1, Tel (613) 238-5335, Telex 0533582.

American Consulate General Calgary, Commercial Section, 615 Macleod Trail S.E., Room 1050, Calgary, Alberta, Canada T2G 4T8, Tel (403) 266-8962, Telex 038-21332.

American Consulate General Montreal, Commercial Section, Suite 1122, South Tower, Place Desjardins, Montreal, Canada, H5B1G1, Tel (514)281-1866, Telex 05-268751.

American Consulate General Toronto, Commercial Section, 360 University Avenue, Toronto, Ontario, Canada 15G1S4, Tel (416) 595-1700, Telex 065-24132.

American Consulate General Vancouver, Commercial Section, 1075 West George Street, 21st Floor, Vancouver, British Columbia, Canada V6E4E9, Tel (604)685-4311, Telex 04-55673.

Embassy of Canada Commercial Section, 1746 Massachusetts Avenue N.W., Washington, DC 20036, Tel (202) 785-1400, Telex 8 9664 DOMCAN A WSH.

CHILE

American Embassy Commercial Section, Edificio Codina, Agustinas 1343, Santiago, Chile, Tel 56-2-710133/90 and 710326/75, Telex 240062-USIS-CL.

American Chamber of Commerce in Chile, Pedro de Valdivia 291, Santiago, Chile, Tel 223-3037, Telex 645129 CMDLC CZ.

Embassy of Chile Commercial Section, 1732 Massachusetts Avenue, N.W., Washington, DC 20036, Tel (202) 785-1746, Telex 89-2663 EMBACHILE WSH.

CHINA, PEOPLE'S REPUBLIC OF

American Embassy Commercial Section, Guang Hua Lu 17, Beijing, People's Republic of China, Tel 86-1-523831, Telex AMEMB CN 22701.

American Consultate General Guangzou, Commercial Section, Dong Fang Hotel, Box 100, Guangzou, People's Republic of China, Tel 86-20-669900, ext. 1000, Telex GZDSHCN 44439.

American Consulate General Shanghai, Commercial Section, 1469 Huai Hai Middle Road, Box 200, Shanghai, People's Republic of China, Tel 86-21-379880, Telex USCGCN 33383.

American Consulate General Shenyang, Commercial Section, 40 Lane 4, Section 5, Sanjing Street, Heping District, Box 45, Shenyang, People's Republic of China, Tel 86-24-290000, Telex 80011 AMCS CN.

American Chamber of Commerce in China, Jtan Guo Hotel, Jtan Guo Men Wai, Beijing, People's Republic of China, Tel 59-5261, Telex 210179 GJPEK CN.

Embassy of the People's Republic of China, Commercial Section, 2300 Connecticut Avenue S.W., Washington, DC 20008, Tel (202) 328-2520.

COLUMBIA

American Embassy Commercial Section, Calla 38, No. 8-61, Bogota, Columbia, Tel 57-1-285-1300/1688, Telex 44843.

American Chamber of Commerce in Columbia-Bogata, Trv. 18, No. 78-80, Apartado Aereo 75240, Bogata, Columbia, Tel 256-8800, Telex 44635.

American Chamber of Commerce in Columbia-Cali, Apartado Aereo 101, Cali, Valle, Columbia, Tel 689-506, 689-409, Telex 55442.

Embassy of Columbia Commercial Section, 2118 Leroy Place N.W., Washington, DC 20008, Tel (202) 387-8338, Telex 197 624 COLE UT.

COMMONWEALTH OF INDEPENDENT STATES (former U.S.S.R.)

American Embassy Commercial Section, Ulitsa Chaykovskogo 19/21/23, Moscow, Russia, Tel 7 096-252-24-51 thru 59, Telex 41316OUSGSO SU.

CIS Trade Representative in the U.S., 2001 Connecticut Avenue, N.W., Washington, DC 20008, Tel (202) 232-2917.

DENMARK

American Embassy Commercial Section, Dag Hammarskjolds Ahe 24, 2100 Copenhagen, Denmark, Tel 45-1-423144, Telex 22216.

Embassy of Demark Commercial Section, 3200 Whitehaven Street, N.W., Washington, DC 20008, Tel (202) 234-4300, Telex 089525 DEN EMB WSH, 64444 DEN EMB WSH.

EGYPT

American Embassy Commercial Section, 5 Sharia Latin America, Cairo, Arab Republic of Egypt, Tel 20-2-355-7371, Telex 93773 AMEMB.

American Consulate General Alexandria, Commercial Section, 110 Avenue Horreya, Alexandria, Arab Republic of Egypt, Tel 20-3-4821911.

American Chamber of Commerce in Egypt, Cairo Marriott Hotel, Suite 1537, Cairo, Arab Republic of Egypt, Tel 340-8888, Telex 20870.

Embassy of Egypt Commercial Section, 2715 Connecticut Avenue, N.W., Washington, DC 20008, Tel (202) 265-9111, Telex 89-2481 COMRAU WSH, 64-251 COMRAU WSH.

FRANCE

American Embassy Commercial Section, 2 Avenue Gabriel, 75382 Paris Cedex 08, Paris, France, Tel 33-1-42-96-12-02, 42-61-80-75, Telex 650-221.

American Consulate General Marseille, Commercial Section, No. 9 Rue Armeny 13006, 13006 Marseille, France, Tel 52-92-00, Telex 430597.

American Consulate General Strasbourg, Commercial Section, 15 Avenue D'Alsace, 67082 Strasbourg, Cedex, Strasbourg, France, Tel 88-35-31-04, Telex 870907.

American Chamber of Commerce in France, 53, Avenue Montaigne, 75008 Paris, France, Tel 1-359-2349.

Embassy of France Commercial Section, 4101 Reservoir Road, N.W., Washington, DC 20007, Tel (202) 944-6000, Telex 248320 FRCC UR.

GERMANY

American Embassy Commercial Section, Deichmanns Avenue, 5300 Bonn 2, Federal Republic of Germany, Tel 49-228-3391, Telex 885-452.

American Mission--Berlin Commercial Section, Clayalle 170, D-1000 Berlin 33 (Dahlem), Federal Republic of Germany, Tel 030-819-7561, Telex 183-701 USBER D.

American Consulate General Dusseldorf, Commercial Section, Cecilienalle 5, 4000 Dusseldorf 30, Federal Republic of Germany, Tel 49-211-490081, Telex 8584246.

American Consulate General Frankfurt, am Main Commercial Section, Seismayerstrasse 21, 6000 Frankfurt, Federal Republic of Germany, Tel 49-69-75305-0 or 75304-0, Telex 412589 USCON-D.

American Consulate General Hamburg, Commercial Section, Alsterufer 27/28, 2000 Hamburg 36, Federal Republic of Germany, Tel 49-40-441061, Telex 213777.

American Consulate General Munich, Commercial Section, Koeniginstrasse 5, 8000 Muenchen 22, Federal Republic of Germany, Tel 49-89-23011, Telex 5-22697 ACGM-D.

American Consulate General Stuttgart, Commercial Section, Urbanstrasse 7, 7000 Stuttgart, Federal Republic of Germany, Tel 49-711-210221, Telex 07-22945.

American Chamber of Commerce in Germany, Flying Tigers, Flughafen, Luftfrachtzentrum, 6000 Frankfurt 75, Federal Republic of Germany, Tel, Telex.

Embassy of the Federal Republic of Germany, 4645 Reservoir Road, Washington, DC 20007, Tel (202) 298-4000, Telex 8 9481 DIPLOGERMA WSH.

HONG KONG

American Consulate General Hong Kong, Commercial Section, 26 Garden Road, Hong Kong, Tel 852 5 239011, Telex 63141 USDOC HX.

American Chamber of Commerce in Hong Kong, Lark International, Ltd., 15/F World Commerce Center, Harbour City, 11 Canton Road, TST Kowloon, Hong Kong, Tel 5-26595.

Hong Kong Office/British Embassy, 3100 Massachusetts Avenue, N.W., Washington, DC 20008, Tel (202) 898-4591, Telex 440484 HK WSH UY.

INDIA

American Embassy Commercial Section, Shanti Path, Chanakyapuri, 110021 New Delhi, India, Tel 91 11 600651, Telex 031-65269 USEM IN.

American Consulate General Bombay, Commercial Section, Lincoln House, 78 Bhulabhai Desai Road, Bombay 400026, India, Tel 91 022 822-3611, Telex 011-75425 ACON IN.

American Consulate General Madras, Commercial Section, Mount Road, Madras 600006, India, Tel 91-44-473-040/477-542.

Embassy of India Commercial Section, 2536 Massachusetts Avenue, N.W., Washington, DC 2O0O08, Tel (202) 939-7000.

IRELAND

American Embassy Commercial Section, 42 Elgin Road, Ballsbridge, Dublin, Ireland, Tel 353-1-688777, Telex 93684.

American Chamber of Commerce in Ireland, 20 College Green, Dublin 2, Ireland, Tel 712733, Telex 31187 UCIL/EL.

Embassy of Ireland Commercial Section, 2234 Massachusetts Avenue, N.W., Washington, DC 20008, Tel (202) 462-3939, Telex 64160 HIBERNIA 64160.

ISRAEL

American Embassy Commercial Section, 71 Hayarkon Street, Tel Aviv, Israel, Tel 972-3-03-654338, Telex 33376 OR 371386 US FCS IL.

American Chamber of Commerce in Israel, 35 Shaul Hamelech Blvd., P.O. Box 33174, Tel Aviv, Israel, Tel 03-252341/2, Telex 32139 BETAM IL.

Embassy of Israel Commercial Section, 1621 22nd Street, NW., Washington, DC 20008, Tel (202) 364-5400.

ITALY

American Embassy Commercial Section, Via Veneto 119/A, 00187 Rome, Italy, Tel 39-6-46741, Telex 622322 AMBRMA.

American Consulate General Milan, Commercial Section, Via Principe Amedeo, 20121 Milano, Italy, Tel 39-2-652-841 thru 5.

American Chamber of Commerce in Italy, c/o Peat, Marwick, Mitchell & Company, Via San Paolo 15, 20121 Milano, Italy, Tel, Telex.

Embassy of Italy Commercial Section, 1601 Fuller Street, N.W., Washington, DC 20009, Tel (202) 328-5500, Telex 90-4076 ITALY EMB WSH.

JAPAN

American Embassy Commercial Section, 10-1 Akasaka, 1-chome, Minato-ku (107), Tokyo, Japan, Tel 81-3-583-7141, Telex 2422118.

U.S. Export Development Office, 7th Floor World Import Mart, 1-3, Higashi Ilkebukuro 3-chome, Toshimna-ku, Tokyo 170, Japan, Tel 81-3-987-2441, Telex 2722446.

American Consulate General Osaka, Commercial Section, SAnkei Building, 9th Floor, 4-9, Umeda 2 chome, Kita-ku, Osaka (530), Japan, Tel (06) 341-2754/7.

American Chamber of Commerce in Japan--Okinawa, P. 0. Box 235, Koza, Okinawa City (904), Japan, Tel 098935-2684, Telex J79873 NANSEI OK.

MEXICO

American Embassy Commercial Section, Paseo de la Reforma 305, Mexico 5 D. F., Mexico, Tel 52-5-211-0042, Telex 017-73-091 and 017-75-685.

U.S. Export Development Office, 31 Liverpool, Mexico 6 D.F., Mexico, Tel 52-5-591-01-55, Telex 01773471.

American Chamber of Commerce in Mexico, Embotelladora Tarahumara, S.A. de C.V., Rio Amazonas No. 43, 06500 Mexico, D.F., Mexico, Tel 591-0066, Telex 1775481 CCDFME.

Embassy of Mexico Commercial Section, 2829 16th Street, N.W., Washington, DC 20009, Tel (202) 234-6000, Telex 90 4307 OCCMEX.

NETHERLANDS

American Embassy Commercial Section, Lange Voorhout 102, The Hague, the Netherlands, Tel 31-70-62-49-11, Telex (044) 31016.

American Consulate General Amsterdam, Commercial Section, Museumplein 19, Amsterdam, the Netherlands, Tel 31-20-64-56-61 or 79-03-21, Telex (044) 16176 CGUSA NL.

American Chamber of Commrce in the Netherlands, 2517 Kj The Hague, the Netherlands, Tel 023-339020, Telex 41219.

Embassy of the Netherlands, Commercial Section, 4200 Linnean Avenue, N.W., Washington, DC 20008, Tel (202) 244-5300.

NEW ZEALAND

American Embassy Commercial Section, 29 Fitzherbert Terrace, Thorndon, Wellington, New Zealand, Tel 64-4-722-068, Telex NZ 3305.

The American Chamber of Commerce in New Zealand, P.O. Box 33-246 Takapuna, Auckland 9, New Zealand, Tel 444-4760, Telex nz 2601.

Embassy of New Zealand, Commercial Section, 37 Observatory Circle, Washington, DC 20008, Tel (202) 328-4800, Telex 8 9526 TOTARA WSH.

NORWAY

American Embassy Commercial Section, Drammensveien 18, Oslo 2, Norway, Tel 47-2-44-85-50, Telex 78470.

Embassy of Norway Commercial Section, 2720 34th Street, N.W., Washington, DC 20008, Tel (202) 333-6000, Telex 89-2374 NORAMB WSH.

PORTUGAL

American Embassy Commercial Section, Avenida das Forcas Armadas, 1600 Lisbon, Portugal, Tel 351-1-726-6600, 726-6659, Telex 12528 AMEMB.

American Chamber of Commerce in Portugal, Avenida Marcechal Gomes de Costa 33, 1800 Lisbon, Portugal, Tel 853996, Telex 12599 AUTOREX P.

Embassy of Portugal Commercial Section, 2125 Kalorama Road, N.W., Washington, DC 20008, Tel (202) 328-8610, Telex 64399 PORT EMB P.

SAUDI ARABIA

American Embassy Commercial Section, Sulaimaniah District, P.O. Box 9041, Riyadh, Saudi Arabia, Tel 966-1-488-3800, Telex 406866AMEMB SJ.

American Chamber of Commerce in Saudi Arabia, c/o Saudi Business Systems, P.O. Box 4992, Dhahran, Saudi Arabia, Tel 864-5838, Telex 670418 SABSYS SJ.

Embassy of Saudi Arabia, Commercial Section, 601 New Hampshire Avenue, N.W., Washington, DC 20037, Tel (202) 483-2100.

SINGAPORE

American Embassy Commercial Section, 30 Hill Street, Singapore 0617, Tel 338-0251.

American Chamber of Commerce in Singapore, 11 Dhoby Ghaut, 08-04 Cathay Building, Singapore 0922.

Embassy of Singapore Commercial Section, 1824 R Street, N.W., Washington, DC 20009, Tel (202) 667-7555, Telex 440024 SING EMB.

SOUTH KOREA

American Embassy Commercial Section, 82 Sejong-Ro; Chongro-ku, Korea, Tel 82-2-732-2601 thru 18, Telex AMEMB 23108.

Embassy of Korea, 2320 Massachusetts Avenue, N.W., Washington, DC 20008, Tel, Telex.

SPAIN

American Embassy Commercial Section, Serrano 75, Madrid, Spain, Tel 34-1-276-3400/3600, Telex 27763.

American Chamber of Commerce in Spain, Paseo de Gracia 95, Barcelona 8. Spain, Tel 319-9550, Telex 52672.

Embassy of Spain Commercial Section, 2558 Massachusetts Avenue, N.W., Washington, DC 20008, Tel (202) 265-8600, Telex 89 2747 SPAIN WSH.

SWEDEN

American Embassy Commercial Section, Strandvagen 101, Stockholm, Sweden, Tel 46-8-7835300, Telex 12060 AMEMB S. Embassy of Sweden Commercial Section, 600 New Hampshire Avenue, N.W., Washington, DC 20037, Tel (202) 298-3500, Telex 89 2724 SVENSK WSH.

TAIWAN

American Institute in Taiwan, 7 Lane 134 Hsin Yi Road, Section 3, Taipei, Taiwan, Republic of China, Telex 23890 USTRADE.

American Chamber of Commerce in Taiwan, P.O. Box 17-277, Taipei, Taiwan, Republic of China.

UNITED KINGDOM

American Embassy Commercial Section, 24/31 Grosvenor Square, London W. 1A 1AE, England, Tel 44-01-499-9000, Telex 266777.

Codes:
(Af) Affiliate Membership of WTCA
(C) World Trade Center Club
(D) Display and Exhibit Facilities
(E) Trade Education Services
(G) Group Trade Missions
(H) Hotel
(K-O) World Trade Center Operating

(M) Meeting Facilities
(N) WTC NETWORK Access
(NSR) No Services Reported
(O) Temporary Offices
(R-IP) World Trade Center In Progress
(R-P) World Trade Center Planned
(S) Temporary Secretaries
(T) Translating Services

AARHUS
World Trade Center Aarhus (R-IP), c/o Kurt Thorsen Totalentreprise A/S, Daigas Avenue 42, DK 8000 Aarhus, Denmark, Fax: 45 8612 72 89, WTC NETWORK: VVTCAA, Telephone: 45 8612 72 00.

ABIDJAN
World Trade Center of Abidjan (R-O), (Centre de Commerce International Abidjan), P.O. Box V. 68, Abidjan, Ivory Coast, Telex: 23 460 CCICI, Fax: (225) 22 71 12, WTC NETWORK: WTCAJ, Telephone: (225) 21 30 92, 21 43 7X, 21 61 81.

ADELAIDE
World Trade Center Adelaide (R-P), Fricker Development Pty. Ltd., 64 Hindmarsh Square, Adelaide, So. Australia 5000, Fax: (08) 232-1441, Telephone: (08) 236-4131, Joe Walker, Executive Director, (NSR).

AIX-LES-BAINS
Academie Europeenne Des Affaires (Af), Mairie d'Aix-les-Bains, Place Maurice Mollard, 73100 Aix-Les-Bains, France, Telex: 980015, Fax: (3378) 79882748, Telephone: (3378) 79350795, Gratien Ferrari, Mayor, (NSR).

AMMAN
Amman World Trade Center (R-P), Federation of Jordanian Chambers of Commerce, Amman, Jordan, Telex: 24103 FJCC JO, Cable: CHAMBERSW Amman, Fax: (96-26) 686-947, 685-997, Telephone: (96-26) 665-492, 674-495, Mohammed Asfour, Chairman of Preparatory, Committee, (NSR).

AMSTERDAM
World Trade Center Amsterdam (R-O), Strawinskylaan 1, 1077 XW Amsterdam, The Netherlands, Telex: 12808 WTCAM NL, Cable: WORLDTRADER

AMSTERDAM, Fax: 31 (20) 6627255, WTC NETWORK: WTCAM, Telephone: 31 (20) 575 9111, Rolf Draak, Managing Director, Services: INCEMDGHOST.

ANCHORAGE
World Trade Center Anchorage (R-P), Alaska Center for International Business, University of Alaska - Ankorage, 4201 Tudor Centre Dr., Suite 320, Anchorage, Alaska 99508 U.S.A., Telex: 981 074 WTCA AHG UD, Fax: (907) 561-1541, WTC NETWORK: WTCAK, Telephone: (907) 561-1615 Dr. John Choon Kim, Director, Services: INEMOST.

ANTWERP
N.V. The World Trade Center Association, of Antwerp (R-O), Branderijstraat 12-14-16, 2000 Antwerp, Belgium, Telex: 72308 VITCAB, Cable: WORLDTREDCENT, Fax: 03/234-3166, WTC NETWORK: WTCAN, Telephone: 03/231-8071, 03/231-8072, Paula Marckx, General Manager, Services: INCMGHOST.

ARCHAMPS
World Trade Center Archamps (R-P), 108 Avenue Louis Casai, 1215 Geneva, Switzerland, Telex: 289959 WTCG CH, Telephone: 41 (22) 989 989, Morris Saady, (NSR).

ATHENS
World Trade Center Athens (R-P), c/o Kurt Thorsen Totalentreprise A/S, World Trade Aarhus, Dalgas Avenue 42, Aarhus, Denmark 8000, Fax: 45 86 116990, WTC NETWORK: WTCAA, Telephone: 45 86 116900, Ebbe Johansen, Managing Director, (NSR).

ATLANTA
World Trade Center Atlanta (R-O), 240 Peachtree Street, N.E., Suite 2200, Atlanta, Georgia 30303 U.S.A, Telex: 4611133)WCATL, Fax: (404) 220-3030, WTC NEWTOWRK: WTCAT, Telephone: (404) 525-4144, Janis M. Basists, Executive Director, Services; INCEMDH.

AUCKLAND
World Trade Center Auckland (R-P), Level 4, 46 Edward Street, Brisbane, Queensland, Australia, Fax: (617) 221-7651, Telephone: (617) 221-8666, Adrian Black, Managing Director, (NSR).

BAHRAIN
World Trade Center Bahrain (R-P), P.O. Box 669, Bahrain. Arabian Gulf, Telex: 8243 NASCON BN, Cable: ANASCON, Fax: 973-728184, Telephone: 725522, Nadhirn Hanna Sheikh, Managing Director, Services: IG.

BALTIMORE
The World Trade Center Baltimore (R-O), Suite 2100, 401 East Pratt Street, Baltimore, Maryland 21202 U.S.A., Telex: 87581 VvrTCBALT, WTC

NETWORK: WTCBL, Telephone: (301) 333-4544, Pearl Chou, Director, Services: INCEMDGHOST.

BANGKOK

World Trade Center Bangkok (R-IP), 8th Floor Sinthon Building, 132 Wireles Road, Bangkok, 10330, Thailand, Telex: 21369 Vy7CB TH, Cable: METROBANK-CODES:, PETERSON 4TH EDITION: PRIVATE, Fax: 66(2) 2534488, WTC NETWORK: WTCBK, Telephone: 66(2) 254-1801, 255-7722, Dr. Arun Panupong, Chair-man of Executive, Board, Services: INEMGHOST.

BARCELONA

World Trade Center Barcelona (R-P), Mallorca, 214, 4, 1st, 08008 Barcelona, Spain, Fax: 30254-5766, WTC NETWORK: WTCBC, Telephone: 3-253-5408/5409, Javier Gil-Robles, President, Services: N.

BARI

World Trade Center Bari (R-P), Societa Italcontruzioni S.r.l., Via Sparano 115, Bari 70100, Italy, Fax: (80) 670130, Telephone: (80) 670140, Viterbi Ciacoma, Managing Director, (NSR).

BASEL

World Trade Center Basel (R-O), Isteinerstrasse 53, CH-402 1 Basel, Switzerland, Telex: 964074 V;TCC CH, Cable: FAIRS CH, Fax: (61) 692-0617, WTC NETWORK: WTCBA, Telephone: (61) 691-2029, Philippe Levy, Director General, Services: INCEMDGHOST.

World Trade Center Club of Switzerland, Basel (Af), Isteinerstrasse 53, CH-4021 Basel, Switzerland, Telex: 964074 WTCC CH, Cable: FAIRS CH, Fax: (61) 692-0617, WTC NETWORK: WTCBA, Telephone: (61) 691-2029, Dr. Gustav E. Grisard, President, Services: CI.

BEAUPORT

World Trade Center Quebec-Beauport (R-P), c/o Mr. Francois-Xavier Simard, Jr., 2635, Boulevard Hochelaga, Suite 960, Ste.-Foy, Quebec, Canada GlV 4W2, Fax: (418-654-0566, WTC NETWORK: WTCQB, Telephone: (418) 654-0550, Francois-Xavier Simard, Jr., (NSR).

BEIJING

China World Trade Center (Beijing) Ltd., (R-IP), No. 1 Jian Guo Men Wai Avenue, Level 4, China World Tower Beijing, 100004, P.R.C., Telex: 210087, Fax: 86 (1) 505-1002, Telephone: 86 (1) 505-2288/8408, Feng Zhi Cheng, Managing Director, Services: MDGHST.

World Trade Centre Beijing (R-P), Rm. 409 4/F. 2nd Central Building, Hualong Street, Nanheyan, East City District, Beijing, P.R.C., Telex: 210333 BCPIT CN, Cable: BJCCPIT, Fax: 86 (1) 512-5176, Liu Hui Lin, Vice Chair, Services: INMGHST.

BERLIN

World Trade Center Berlin (R-P), c/o held and Francke, Kurfurstendamm 179, 1000 Berlin-15, West Germany, Fax: (30) 882-2789, Telephone: (30) 882-6376, Peter Kern, Director, (NSR).

BILBAO

World Trade Center Bilbao (R-P), Alameda de Urquijo 10,1, 48008 Bilbao, Spain, Telex: 83132568 E CHEK, Fax: (344) 416-6012, Telephone: (344) 415-7033, Jose Maria Escondrillas, President, (NSR).

BOGOTA

World Trade Center Bogota (R-O), Calle 98 No. 9-03, Bogota, Columbia, S.A., Telex: 45666 CEMCO, Cable: WORLDTRADE, Fax: (57) (1) 218-3020, WTC NETWORK: WTCBT, Telephone: (57) (1) 218-4411, Camilo Estefan, President, Services: INCEMDGHOST.

BOMBAY

World Trade Center Bombay (R-O), M. Visvesvaraya Industrial, Research & Development Centre, Centre 1, 31st Floor, Cuffe Parade, Bombay 400 005, India, Telex: 6846 WTCB IN, 5023 WTCB IN, Cable: VIRDCOM, Fax: (91) (22) 202 3906, Telephone: (91) (22) 2144 34/21 28 71, P.K. Akerkar, Executive Director, Services: IEMHT.

BORDEAUX

World Trade Center Bordeaux (R-P), SOCAFIM, Societe Auxiliaire D'Entreprises (SAE), 57 Cours Pasteur, 33000 Bordeaux, France, Fax: 56 9176 64, Telex: 540 250, Telephone: 56 3145 00, Marcel Guiraud, Director General, (NSR).

BOSTON

World Trade Center Boston (R-O), Boston, Massachusetts 02210-2004, U.S.A., Fax: (617) 439-5033, WTC NETWORK: WTCBO, Telephone: (617) 439-5000, John Drew, President, Services: INCEMDGOST.

BRIDGEPORT

World Trade Center Bridgeport (R-P), Lafayette Square, 350 Fairfield Avenue, Bridgeport, Connecticut 06604 U.S.A., Fax: (203) 331-9006, WTC NETWORK: WTCBP, Telephone: (203) 366-8500, Frederick K. Biebel, President, CWTA, Services: IEMGH.

BRISBANE

World Trade Center Brisbane (R-P), Port Centre, 369 Ann Street, or, G.P.O. Box 2931, Brisbane, Queensland Australia, 4001, Fax: (617) 835-2033, WTC NETWORK: WTCBB, Telephone: (617) 831-2033, Adrian R. Black, Manager, Services: INMDHOS.

BRUGGE
International Club of West Flanders, De Hanze (Af), Zilverstraat 43, B-8000 Brugge, Belgium, Telex: 81 282 KABRUG B ATT INTERN.CLUB, Telephone: (32) 50 33 47 99, Nicole van Nieuwenhuyse, Services: ICMDS.

BRUSSELS
World Trade Center Association Brussels, A.S.B.L.(R - O), 162 Boulevard Emile Jacqmain-Boite 12, B-1210 Brussels, Belgium, Telex: 65471 WTCB, Cable: WORLDTRADE BRUSSELS, Fax: (32) (2) 217-2820, WTC NETWORK: WTCBR, Telephone: (32) (2) 219-4400, Dominique F.G. Houtart, Vice President, Services: INCEMDGHOST.

BUDAPEST
World Trade Center Budapest (R-O), Hungarian Chamber of Commerce, Kossuth Lajos Ter 6-8, Budapest, Hungary H-1055, P.O. Box 106, Budapest, Hungary 1055, Telex: 22-4745 MKKH, Cable: KAMARA BUDAPEST, Fax: (36) (1) 153-1285, WTC NETWORK: WTCBU, Telephone: (36) (1)153-3333,153-2503, Andras Gabor, President, Services: INCMGHO.

BUENOS AIRES
World Trade Center Buenos Aires, S.A., (R-IP), Moreno 584, 9th Floor, 1091 Buenos Aires, Argentina S.A., Telex: (33) 22036 JECON AR, Fax: (541) 331-0223, WTC NETWORK: WTCBN, Telephone: (541) 34-3216/3283/3408, Jorge E. Castex, President, Services: INDGHST.

BUFFALO
Buffalo World Trade Centre (R-P), Triple Vision Group, Inc., Olympic Towers, 300 Pearl Street, Suite 200, Buffalo, New York 14202 U.S.A., Fax: (716) 842-6049, Telephone: (716) 842-6065, Larry Griffiths, President, (NSR).

CAIRO
World Trade Center Co., Cairo (R-IP), 1113 Comich El-Nil, P.O. Box 2007, Cairo, Egypt, Telex: 2, 2612 WTCAI UN, Fax: 391-6233, WTC NETWORK: WTCCI, Telephone: 748092n480941748096/748054, Amgad Moussa Sabry, VHC Administrator, Services: INMGH.

CALGARY
World Trade Centre Calgary (R-P), Stock Exchange Tower, Suite 3, 300-1111 Melville Street, Vancouver, B.C. Canada V6E 4H7, Telex: 04-54467 RBS VCR, Fax: (604) 688-3830, WTC NETWORK: WTCVN, Telephone: (604) 682-3830, Charles Hopkins, President, (NSR).

CALI
World Trade Center de Cali (R-P), Calle 13, #4 25 Piso 17, P.O. Box 7795, Cali-Valle Columbia, S.A., Fax: 923-805272, WTC NETWORK: WTCCA, Telephone: 923-894882, Cable: AA 7795, Jorge Enrique Botero, President, (NSR).

CAPE VERDE

World Trade Center Cape Verde (R-P), Praia-CP No. 211, Republic of Cape
    Verde, Telex: 6041 COMERC CV, Telephone: 611124/611342, Virgilio B.
    Fernandes, Secretary of State, (NSR).

CARACAS

World Trade Center Caracas (R-P), P.O. Box 64978, CCCT, Caracas 1061,
    Venezuela Telex: 39523553 VIBRAS, Cable: VICOM, Fax: (582) 926676, WTC
    NETWORK: WTCCC, Telephone: (582) 928686/929620, Franklin D. Koppel
    Benchimol, Managing Director, Services: INEMGOT.

CARDIFF

Cardiff World Trade Center, Wales (R-IP), C/o Harlech Court, Bute Terrace,
    Cardiff, Wales, U.K., Telex: 497492 CHACOMG, Fax: (222) 395398, Telephone:
    (222)464141, John Lord, Director, Services: MDHOST.

CEDAR RAPIDS

Cedar Rapids World Trade Center (R-O), 312 - 8th Street, Suite 200, Des Moines,
    Iowa 50309 U.S.A., Telex: 627-80053 PRO SECS, Fax: (515) 246-6014, WTC
    NETWORK: VITCCR, Telephone: (515) 246-6000, Bruce W. Gerleman,
    President, Services: INEMDGOST.

CHARLESTON

World Trade Center Charleston (R-P), Charleston Trident Chamber of
    Commerce, P.O. Box 975, Charleston, South Carolina 29402 U.S.A., Fax: (803)
    723-4853, WTC NETWORK: WTCCL, Telephone: (803) 577-2510 Ext. 3056,
    Virginia M. Norvell, Vice President, Services: INEGT.

CHARLOTTE

World Trade Center Charlotte (R-P), Box 220814, Charlotte, North Carolina 28222
    U.S.A., Telex: 802187 HQ CHA, Fax: (704) 332-3464, Telephone: (704) 335-0000,
    William K. Machielsen, Chairman, (NSR).

CHATTANOOGA

World Trade Center Chattanooga (R-P), 1001 Market Street, Chattanooga,
    Tennessee 37402 U.S.A., Fax: (615) 752-4322, WTC NETWORK: WTCCG,
    Telephone: (615) 752-4316, J. Michael Thatcher, WTC Director, (NSR).

CHENGDU

World Trade Center Club Chengdu (Af), Sichuan Jin Jiang Hotel, No. 36 Section
    2, Ren Min Nan Road, Chengdu, Sichuan, P.R.C., Telex: 60216 WTCCD CN,
    Cable: 4481 CHENGDU, Fax: (86) (28) 66-4325, Telephone: (86) (28) 58-
    2222/2232/2233/2234, Cai Li, Deputy Manager, Services: ICEMGHOST.

CHICAGO

Illinois World Trade Center Chicago (R-O), 321 North Clark Street, Suite 550,
    Chicago, Illinois 60610-4714 U.S.A., Fax: (312) 793-4979, WTC NETWORK:

WTCCH, Telephone: (312) 793-4982, Lt. Governor George H. Ryan, Chairman, Services: INCEMGHOST.

Club International (Af), The Drake Hotel, 140 East Walton Place, Chicago, Illinois 60611 U.S.A., Telex: 270278, Cable: DRAKEHO CFHCAGO, Telephone: (312) 787-2200, Victor T. Burt, General Manager, Services: CNMHST.

CHONGQING

World Trade Center Club Chongqing (Af), Room 3213-3214, Renmin Hotel, No. 175 Renmin Road, Chongqing, Sichuan Province, PRC, Telex: 62224 WT CCQCN, Cable: 4406, Fax:351456, Telephone: 351456, Xin Xian-Ping, Deputy General Manager, (NSR).

COLOGNE

World Trade Center Koln GmbH. (R-P), Bruckenstr. 17, D-5000 Koln I, F.R.G., Fax: 221/20594-19, Telephone: 221/20594-02, Dr. Ing Helmuth Leitzgen, General Manager, (NSR).

Asia Pacific Center (Af), Stadtsparkasse Koln, Kaiser-Wilhelm-Ring 20, 5000 Cologne, F.R.G., Telex: 1722 14204 ASIA, Fax: 221/13 76 51, WTC NETWORK: APC, Telephone: 221/16 02 10, Hans F. Berner, Director, Services: EEMGOS.

COLORADO SPRINGS

Rocky Mountain World Trade Center (R-P), P.O. Box 65.i9, Colorado Springs, Colorado 80934 U.S.A., Telex: 4992665, Telephone: (719) 633-9041, John S. Bock, President, Services: OS.

COLUMBUS

International Trade Development Office, (R-P), Columbus Area Chamber of Commerce, 37 North High Street, Columbus, Ohio 43215 U.S.A., Telex: 687-4646 INTRADE COL, Fax: (614) 469-8250, WTC NETWORK: WTCCO, Telephone: (614) 221-1321, R. Michael McCarthy, Vice President, Economic Development, Services: IEMG.

COPENHAGEN

World Trade Center Copenhagen (R-P), C/0 Kurt Thorsen Totalentreprise A/S, Dalgas Avenue 42, DK 8000 Aarhus, Denmark, Fax: 45 (86)12 72 89, WTC NETWORK: WTCCP, Telephone: 45 (86)12 72 00, Ebbe Johansen, Managing Director, (NSR).

CURACAO

International Trade Center, Curacao, (ITCC) (R-O), Piscadera Bay, P.O. Box 6005, Curacao, Netherlands Antilles, Dutch Caribbean, Telex: 1454 ITCC NA, Fax: 599-9-624408, WTC NETWORK: WTCCU, Telephone: 599-9-624433, John W. Sellers, Managing Director, Services: ICMDGHOST.

CYPRUS

Cyprus World Trade Centre, Nicosia (R-O), Chamber Building, 38, Grivas Dhigenis Avenue & 3, Deligiorgis Street, P.O. Box 1455, Nicosia, Cyprus,

Telex: 2077 CHAMBER CY, Cable: CHAM13ER, Fax: 357-2-449048, WTC NETWORK: WTCCY, Telephone: 02-449500 and 02-462312, Panayiotis Loizides, Secretary General, Services: IEMDGOST.

DENVER
World Trade Center Denver (R-O), 1625 Broadway, Suite 680, Denver, Colorado 80202 U.S.A., Fax: (303) 892-3820, WTC NETWORK: WTCDN, Telephone: (303) 592-5760, John J. Reardon, President/CEO, Services: INCEMHOST.

DES MOINES
Iowa World Trade Center - Des Moines, (R-P), 3200 Ruan Center 666 Grand Avenue, Des Moines, Iowa 50309 U.S.A., Telex: 283078 BTC IEITC DMS UR, Cable: BANKTRUST, Fax: (515) 245-3878, Telephone: (515) 245-2555, John Ruan, President, Services: IMDHOS.

Iowa Department of Economic Development (Af), Division of Community Progress, 200 East Grand Avenue, Des Moines, Iowa 50309 U.S.A., Telex: 478466 DEV COM DMS, WTC NETWORK: IDED, Telephone: (515) 281-3251, Cynthia B. Lidgett, Division Administrator, Services: IE.

DETROIT
World Trade Center of Detroit/Windsor, (R-P), 150 W. Jefferson, Suite 1510, Detroit, Michigan 48226 U.S.A., Fax: (313) 965-1525, WTC NETWORK: WTCDT, Telephone: (313) 965-6500, William I. Spencer, President, Services: N.

DUBAI
Dubai World Trade Centre (R-O), P.O. Box 9292, Dubai. United Arab Emirates, Telex: (0893) 47474 DITC EM, Fax: 97 14 372200, WTC NETWORK: WTCDU, Telephone: 97 14 372200, Ian J. Luxton, General Manager, Services: INCEMDHOST.

DUSSELDORF
World Trade Center Dusseldorf (R-P), c/o WTCGG SA, 14, Chemin Rieu, 1208 Geneva, Switzerland, Telex: 429389, Telephone: 4122/476552, Morris Saady, (NSR).

EDMONTON
World Trade Center Edmonton (R-O), P.O. Box 1480, Edmonton, Alberta, Canada T5J 2N5, Telex: 03742611 VZTC EDM, Fax: (403) 477-0128, WTC NETWORK: WTCED, Telephone: (403) 471-7283, Howard S. Crosley, General Manager, Services: PXNMHOST.

EINDHOVEN
World Trade Center Eindhoven N.V. (R-O), Bogert 1, P.O. Box 2085, 5600 CB Eindhoven, The Netherlands, Telex: 59046, Fax: 31-40-449041, Telephone: 31-40-653653, Dr. C.J.M. Rooijmans, Managing Director, Services: ICEMDGHOST.

FORT-DE-FRANCE

World Trade Centre Martinique (R-P), c/o Chambre de Commerce et d'Industrie, de la Martinique, 50 Rue Ernest Deproge, B.P. 478, 97241 Fort de France Cedex, Martinique, French West Indies, Telex: 912 633 MR, Fax: (596) 60 66 68, WTC NETWORK: WTCMQ, Telephone: (596) 55 28 00, Jocelyne Gospodnetic, Head of Economic Action, Department, C.C.I.M., Services: INEMGHT.

FORT LAUDERDALE

World Trade Center Fort Lauderdale, Florida (R-O), P.O. Box 13065, 1100 Lee Wagener Blvd., Fort Lauderdale International Airport, Fort Lauderdale, Florida 33315 U.S.A., Fax: (305) 359-0277, WTC NETWORK: WTCFL, Telephone: (305) 359-3615, Henrietta Frankel, Director, Services: INEMDGOS.

FRANKFURT

World Trade Center Frankfurt (R-P), c/o WTCGG SA, 14, Chemin Rieu, 1208 Geneva, Switzerland, Telex: 429389, Telephone: 4122/476552, Morris Saady, (NSR).

GENEVA

World Trade Center Geneva (R-O), 10, Route de l'Aeroport, P.O. Box 306, 1215 Geneva 15, Switzerland, Telex: 41 54 40 V;TCG CH, Fax: 4122/79410885, WTC NETWORK: WTCGV, Telephone: 4122n98 99 89, Philippe Doubre, Secretary General, Services: INCNMHOST.

GENOA

World Trade Center Genoa S.p.A. (R-O), Torre WTC -19th Floor, 16149 Genoa, Italy, Telex: 275851 CETEX I, Fax: (39) (10) 456802, WTC NETWORK: WTCGN, Telephone: (39) (10) 2423001, Giovanni Sancristoforo, Managing Director, Services: INCMGHOST.

GHENT

International Club of Flanders (Af), Sint-Pietersplein, 11, 9000 Ghent, Belgium, Fax: (091) 21 79 43, Telephone: 091/22 96 68 or 091/21 79 43, Hilaire Dewulf, Secretary General, Services: CMDH.

GLASGOW

World Trade Center Glasgow (R-P), c/o World Trade Centre (Holdings) Ltd., 17 Walter Road, Swansea, SA1 5NG United Kingdom, Fax: 0792-648821, WTC NETWORK: WTCGL, Telephone: 0792-473646, Stuart Williams, Director, (NSR).

GOTHENBURG

Scandinavian World Trade Center (R-O), Massans Gata 18, P.O. Box 5253, 402 25 Gothenburg, Sweden, Telex: 5427430 GOTCHAM, Fax: 46 31835936, WTC NETWORK: WTCGO, Telephone: 46 31835900, Aake Ahlstroem, Managing Director, Services: INCEMDGHOST.

GREAT FALLS

The Great Falls World Trade Center (R-P), P.O. Box 1668, Great Fails, Montana 59403 U.S.A., WTC NETWORK: WTCGF, Telephone: (406) 452-6982/9767, Arthur W. Renander, Director, (NSR).

GREENSBORO

World Trade Center Greensboro (R-P), Piedmont Triad Airport Authority, P.O. Box 35005, Greensboro, North Carolina 27425 U.S.A., Telephone: (919) 665-5600, Stanley Frank, Chairman of the Board, (NSR).

GREENVILLE-SPARTANBURG

The Greenville-Spartanburg, World Trade Center (R-P), The Jenkins Companies, 315 Old Boiling Springs Road, Greer, South Carolina 29650 U.S.A., Telephone: (803) 297-8600, R. Patrick Jenkins, Proprietor, (NSR).

GRENOBLE

World Trade Center Grenoble (R-P), GREX, 1, Place Andre Malraux BP 297, 38016 Grenoble Cedex, France, Telex: 320 824 F, Fax: (33) 76 87 73 11, WTC NETWORK: WTCGR, Telephone: (33) 76 47 20 36/76 46 06 67, Odile Arnould, Executive Manager, Services: ICEMG.

GUADALAJARA

Guadalajara World Trade Center (R-O), Av. Mariano Otero 1499, 44560 Guadalajara, Jalisco, Mexico, Apdo. Postal (P.O. Box 33-29), Fax: (52) (36) 47 58 87, WTC NETWORK: WTCGU, Telephone: (52) (36) 47 50 50/47 50 90/47 05 97, Miguel Cervantes, Chief Executive Director, Services: ICDG.

GUAM

World Trade Center Guam (R-P), P.O. Box 692, Agana, Guam 96910, Fax: (671) 649-1540, Telephone: (671) 649-0216, Albert M. Chaco, Director, (NSR).

GUANGZHOU

World Trade Centre Club Guangzhou (Af), Garden Tower, Garden Hotel, Room 834-837, Guangzhou, P.R.C., Telex: 44341)WCG CN, Fax: (86) (20) 338999 ext. 7835/7836/7837, Wang Yuan Xue, Secretary General, Services: EEMDGHOST.

HALIFAX

World Trade Center Halifax (R-O), 1800 Argyle Street, 8th Floor, P.O. Box 955, Halifax, Nova Scotia, Canada B3J 2V9, Fax: (902) 422-2922, WTC NETWORK: WTCHA, Telephone: (902) 428-7233, Chirstopher J. Thomley, Manager, Services: INCEMWHOST.

HAMBURG

World Trade Center Hamburg (R-O), Neuer Wall 50, 2000 Hamburg 36, Federal Republic of Germany, Fax: 49 (40) 36 48 82, WTC NETWORK: WTCHH, Telephone: 49 (40) 37 26 30, Herman H. Schurink, Managing Director, Services: INMHST.

HANGZHOU

Zhejiang World Trade Centre, Hangzhou, (R-IP), 15 Shuguang Road, Hangzhou, P.R.C, Telex: 35037 FFTRA CN, Cable: 0083 HANGZHOU, Fax: 86 (571) 553447, Telephone: 86 (571) 753287, Zhuang Yumin, Chairman, (NSR).

HARTFORD

Connecticut World Trade Association, Hartford (R-IP), Capitol Center, 370 Asylum Street, Hartford, Connecticut 06103 U.S.A., Fax: (203) 527-6762, WTC NETWORK: WTCHD, Telephone: (203) 727-8541, Frederick K. Biebel, President, Services: INEMGH.

HAVANA CITY

Chamber of Commerce, of the Republic of Cuba (R-P), Calle 21 No. 701/661, Esq. A, Vedado, P.O. Box 4237, Havana, Cuba, Telex: 511752 CAMAR CU, Telephone: 30-4436 and 30-3356/58, Julio A. Garcia Oliveras, President, Services: IMDG.

HEFEI

Hefei World Trade Centre Club (Af), Imp/Exp Bldg., Room 202, Jinzhai Road, Hefei, Anhui Province, P.R.C., Telex: 90204 ATTEC CN, Cable: 1397 HEFEI, Fax: 86 (0551) 331210/332705, Telephone: 86 (0551) 332712, Zuo Bing, Liaison Officer, Services: IEMDGHOST.

HELSINKI

World Trade Center Helsinki (R-P), c/o The Central Chamber of Commerce of Finland, Ms. Sirpa Rissa-Anttilainen, Deputy Director, P.O. Box 1000 SF-00101 Helsinki, Finland, Telex: 123814 chamb sf, Fax: (3580) 650303, Telephone: (3580) 650133, Sirpa Rissa-Anttilainen, Deputy Director, Central Chamber of Commerce of Finland, (NSR).

HONG KONG

World Trade Centre Club Hong Kong (R-O), 2M/F & 3/F World Trade Centre, Causeway Bay, Hong Kong, Telex: 71729 VVTCHEN HX, Cable: WTCENTRE HONG KONG, Fax: (852) 895-2692, WTC NETWORK: WTCHK, Telephone: (852) 779528, Ronnie Chow, General Manager, Services: INCMDHOST.

HONOLULU

World Trade Center Honolulu (R-P), Suite 110, 521 Ala Moana Boulevard, Honolulu, Hawaii 96813 U.S.A., Fax: (808) 537-4488, WTC NETWORK: WTCHO, Telephone: (808) 599-3969, Randall Ho, Executive Director, (NSR).

Department of Business, and Economic Development (Af), Business Services Division, 250 South King Street, P.O. Box 2359, Honolulu, Hawaii 96804 U.S.A., Telex: 7430250 HIDPED, Cable: FUSAS, Fax: (808) 523-8637, Telephone: (808) 548-4608, Thomas J. Smyth, Division Head, Services: IIEG.

HOUSTON

Houston World Trade Association (R-O), A Division of the Greater Houston Partnership, 1100 Milam, 25th Floor, Houston, Texas 77002 U.S.A., Fax: (713) 658-2429, WCT NETWORK: WTCHS, Telephone: (713) 658-2401, Miguel R. San Juan, Vice President, Services: INCEMGHOST.

INDIANAPOLIS

World Trade Center Indianapolis (R-P), Baize Development Corporation, 3905 Vincennes Road, Suite 500, Indianapolis, Indiana 46268 U.S.A., Fax: (317) 876-3905, Telephone: (317) 871-6807, James E. Baize, President (NSR).

ISTANBUL

World Trade Center Istanbul (R-IP), Atatiirk Hava Limani Yani, Cobancesme Kavsagi, P.O. Box 40, 34830 Havalimani, Istanbul, Turkey, Telex: 28531 IDTM TR, Telephone: (901) 573-0099; 573-3979; 574-5459, Ege Onganer, Project Manager, Services: I.

JACKSONVILLE

Jacksonville World Trade Center, Association (R-IP), Jacksonville Chamber of Commerce, 3 Independent Drive, Jacksonville, Florida 32202 U.S.A., Telex: 7401076JAXC, Fax: (904) 632-0617, WTC NETWORK: WTCJX, Telephone: (904) 353-0300, Arnie Frankel, Director, International Development Department, Services: INEMG.

JAKARTA

World Trade Center Jakarta (R-O), Wisma Metropolitan 11, L. 16, Jalan Jend., Sudirman Kav. 31, P.O. Box 5/KBYMP, Jakarta 12920, Indonesia, Telex: 62838 VffCJKT IA, Cable: WORLDTRADE JAKARTA, Fax: 62 (021) 5781673, WTC NETWORK: WTCJK, Telephone: 62 (021) 5781945/302/312, Harjo Nimpoeno, Executive Director, Services: INCEMDGHOST.

JAMAICA

JAMPRO Ltd. (Af), Jamaica Economic Development Agency, 35 Trafalgar Road, Kingston 10, Jamaica, West Indies, Telex: 2222 JANIPROJA, Cable: EXPROM, Fax: (809) 924-9650, Telephone: (809) 929-7190/8217/8235, Corrine McCarty, President, Services: ICEMDGHOST.

JOHANNESBURG

World Trade Centre Johannesburg (R-O), Jurgens Park, Jones Road, Jet Park, P.O. Box 500, Kempton Park 1620, Republic of South Africa, Telex: 74-0931 SA, Cable: WORLDTCSA, Fax: 27 (11) 975-9415, WTC NETWORK: WTCJO, Telephone: 27 (11) 975-8011, C.P. Swart, Executive Chairman, Services: INEMDGHOST.

South African Foreign Trade Organization, (SAFTO) (Af), P.O. Box 782706, 5th Floor, Export House, Cnr, Maud & West Streets, Sandton, 2146, Republic of

South Africa, Telex: 4-24111 SA, Fax: 27 (11) 883-6569, Telephone: 27 (11) 883-3737, W.B. Holtes, Chief Executive, Services: ICEMGHOST.

JONKOPING

Jonkoping World Trade Center (R-P), Jonkoping Chamber of Commerce, Elmiavagen, S-552 44, Jonkoping, Sweden, Telex: 70164 HKAM, Fax: 46 (36)129579, Telephone: 46 (36) 160310, Coran Kinnander, President, (NSR).

KANSAS CITY

Municipal Government, of Greater Kansas City (Af), 29th Floor, City Hall, 414 E. 12th Street, Kansas City, Missouri 64106 U.S.A., Fax: (816) 221-7440, Telephone: (816) 274-2595, Richard L. Berkley, Mayor, (NSR).

KARACHI

World Trade Center Karachi (R-P), Khayaban-E-Roomi, KDA Scheme No. 5, Clifton, Karachi, Pakistan, Telex: 2712 ARFIN PK, Fax: 92 (21) 514594, Telephone: 92 (21) 539345, Shahid Firoz, Managing Director, (NSR).

KIEL

World Trade Center Kiel GmbH (R-P), Neuer Wan 50, 2000 Hamburg 36, F.R.G., Fax: 49 (40) 36 48 82, WTC NETWORK: WTCHH, Telephone: 49 (40) 37 26 30, Herman H. Schurink, Managing Director, (NSR).

KUALA LUMPUR

Putra World Trade Centre (R-O), Level 3, PWTC-UMNO Complex, 41 Jalan Tun Ismail, 50480 Kuala Lumpur, Malaysia, Telex: PUTRA MA 28 1 00, Fax: (603) 442-2959, WTC NETWORK: WTCKL, Telephone: (603) 442-2999, Kamarulzaman Bahadun, President, Services: INCMDGHOST.

LAGOS

World Trade Center of Nigeria, Ltd. (R-O), Western House, 8th Floor, 8/10 Broad Street, P.O. Box 4466, Lagos, Nigeria, Telex: (905) 23282 WTCN NG, and (905) 21622 CIGRUP NG, Cable: WORLDTRADERS, LAGOS NIGERIA, Telephone: 234 (1) 632221/632293/635128, Shirley Fiberesima, Services: IMDGS.

LAS PALMAS

World Trade Center Canary Islands S.A., Las Palmas (R-P), c/Los Balcones, 8-5', 35001 Las Palmas de Gran Canaria, Canary Islands, Spain, Fax: (928) 321629, WTC NETWORK: WTCIC, Telephone: (92X) 320 747, Borja Benitez de Lugo y Massieu, Executive Director, (NSR).

LAS VEGAS

Nevada World Trade Center, Las Vegas (R-O), 3920 S. Eastern Avenue, Building C, Suite 472, Las Vegas, Nevada 89109 U.S.A., Fax: (213) 622-6485, WTC NETWORK: WTCLV, Telephone: (702) 876-5806, Alexander Vari, Chairman of the Board, Services: INCMDHOST.

LE HAVRE

Le Havre World Trade Center (R-O), Quai George V, 76600 Le Havre, France, Telex: 190637 WTCLH, Fax: 33 (35) 21-06-81, WTC NETWORK: WTCLH, Telephone: 33 (35) 214341, Francis P. Genot, Director, Services: INEMDGHOST.

LEIDEN

World Flower Trade Center (R-O), Verbeekstraat 11, P.O. Box 9324, 2300 PH Leiden, The Netherlands, Telex: 30264 WFFC NL, Fax: 31 (71) 314842, Telephone: 31 (71) 31 20 31, C.J.M. Buis, President, Services: IMDGHOST.

LEIPZIG

World Trade Center Leipzig (GDR) (R-P), c/o Dr. Rainer Buhr, World Trade Center Ruhr Valley, Sparkassenstr.1, 4650 Gelsenkirchen, F.R.G., Telex: 824840 RWE D, Fax: 49 (209) 144285, WTC NETWORK: WTCRV, Telephone: 49 (209) 22097, Dr. Rainer Buhr, Executive Director, (NSR).

LEXINGTON

World Trade Center Lexington (R-P), 410 West Vine Street, Suite 290, Lexington, KY 40507 U.S.A., Fax: (606) 233-0658, WTC NETWORK: WTCLE, Telephone: (606) 258-3139, Kenneth A. Current, Executive Director, Services: IMOST.

LILLE

World Trade Center Lille (R-O), 112 Rue de L'Hopita Militaire BP 209, 59029 Lille Cedex, France, Telex: CCI LRT 136 321F, Fax: 22 (02) 40 0455, WTC NETWORK: WTCLL, Telephone: 22 (20) 57 0507, Patrick Van Den Schriek, President, Services: INCMHOS.

LIMA

World Trade Center Lima (P-R), Av. de la Marina 2355, Lima 32, Peru, Telex 25504 PE FERIA, Fax 51 (14) 523907, WTC NETWORK: WTCLM, Telephone 51 (14) 528140, Carlos Ruibal Franco, Executive Director, Services: ICEMWHOST.

LISBON

World Trade Center Lisbon (R-O), Av. do Brasil, 1, 1700 Lisboa, Portugal, Telex: 12326 WTCLIS P or 15584 WTCLIS P, Fax: 35 (11) 768-436/793-0394, WTC NETWORK: WTCLI, Telephone: 35 (11) 793-3571, Maria Armanda Adao e Silva, President, Services: INCEMWHOST.

LIVERPOOL

World Trade Centre Liverpool (R-P), Trafalgar Wharf Development Initiative Ltd., Suite No. C4 Brunswick Enterprise Ctr., Brunswick Business Park, Liverpool L3 4BD, Merseyside, Great Britain, Fax: (51) 709-2843, Telephone: (51) 709-4759, Timothy Wale, Chairman, (NSR).

LJUBLIJANA
World Trade Center Ljublijana (R-P), SMELT Global Project Management, Titova 184, 61113 Ljublijana, Yugoslavia, Telex: 31376 SMELT YU, Fax: 38 (61) 34 12 16, WTC NETWORK: WTCLJ, Telephone: 38 (61) 371231, Joze Zagar, President, (NSR).

LONDON
London World Trade Center Association (R-O), Intemation House, 1 St. Katharine's Way, London, E1 9UN, United Kingdom, Cable: WORLDTRADE LDN, Fax: 44 (71) 265-0459, WTC NETWORK: WTCLD, Telephone: 44 (71) 488-2400, Christopher J. Lemay, Director, Services: INCEMGHOST.

LONG BEACH
Greater Los Angeles World Trade Center, Association, Long Beach (R-O), One World Trade Center, Suite 295, Long Beach, Califomia 90831-0295 U.S.A., Telex: 333339, Fax: (213) 495-7071, WTC NETWORK: WTCLB, Telephone: (213) 495-7070, Merry Tuten, President, CEO, Services: INCEMDGOST.

LOS ANGELES
Los Angeles World Trade Center (R-O), 350 So. Figueroa Street, Suite 240, Los Angeles, California 90071 U.S.A., Fax: (213) 680-4184, For Services: (213) 495-7070 (Michael Klesh), GLAWTCA, Al Dougal, Building Manager (213) 489-3337, Services: IIEGHOST.

LUGANO
World Trade Center Lugano (R-IP), CRC Society of Estate Promotion, Palazzo Banca dello Stato, CH-6982 Agno, Switzerland, Fax: (4191) 506137, Telephone: (4191) 595962, Renato P. Dellea, Director, (NSR).

LUXEMBOURG
World Trade Center Luxembourg (R-IP), RR-3, rue de la loge, L-1945 Luxembourg, Telex: 60182 RORELU, Fax: 460-752, WTC NETWORK: WTCLU, Telephone: 00352 475-178, Dr. Rolphe L. Reding, Services: INCMDGHOST.

LYON
Lyon Commerce International (R-O), 16 rue de la Republique, 69289 Lyon, Cedex 02, France, Telex: (42) 310828F CECOMEX, Fax: 33 (7) 837-9400, WTC NETWORK: WTCLY, Telephone: 33 (7) 240 5752, Robert Maury, Managing Director, Services: INCEMDHCO.

MACAU
World Trade Center Macau SARL (R-O), Rua de Peking, No. 183, Edificio Marina Plaza, 5th Floor Apt. A & B, Macau, Telex: 88831 WTCOM, Fax: (853) 563398, WTC NETWORK: WTCMC, Telephone: (853) 565225/562151, Antonio Leca Da Veiga Paz, Managing Director, Services: INGHSTC.

MADISON

Madison World Trade Center (R-P), 2130 Pinehurst Drive, Middleton, Wisconsin 53562 U.S.A., Fax: (608) 836-6669, Telephone: (608) 836-3600, Jeffrey Straubel, Director, (NSR).

MADRID

World Trade Center Madrid, S.A. (R-IP), Paseo de la Habana, 26-30-40, 28036 Madrid, Spain, Fax: 341 262 4004, WTC NETWORK: WTCMA, Telephone: 341 411 6145, Antonio Trueba, President, Services: INMGHOST.

MALMO

World Trade Center Malmo (R-P), Chamber of Commerce of Southern, Sweden, Skeppsbron 2, S-211 20, Malmo, Sweden, Telex: 333 88 CHAMBERS, Fax: 040 11 86 09, Telephone: 040 735 50, Per-Inge Olsson, Vice President, Services: IEMDGO.

MANCHESTER

Manchester Chamber of Commerce and Industry (Af), 56 Oxford Street, Manchester, M60 7HJ, United Kingdom, Telex: 667822 CHACOM G, Cable: COMMERCE MANCHESTER, Fax: 061 236-4160, Telephone: 061 236-3210, Simon G. Sperryn, Chief Executive, Services: IMDGO.

MANILA

World Trade Center, Metro Manila (R-P), 5th Floor, Pacific Star Building, Makati Ave., Makati, Metro Manila, Philippines, Telex: 45959 WTCPHIL PM, Fax: 63(2) 819-7205, WTC NETWORK: W-FCMM, Telephone: 63(2) 819-, 7297/7232/7204 Lilia B. DeLima, Chief Operating Officer &, Executive Vice President, Services: INEMGOS.

MARSEILLE

Mediterranean World Trade, Center, Marseille/CMCI (R-O), CMCI-2 Rue Henri Barbusse, 13241 Marseille Cedex 01, France, Telex: 441247, Fax: 33 9139 33 60, WTC NETWORK: WTCMR, Telephone: 33 91 39 33 50, Bernard Cazes, General Manager, Services: INCEMDGHOST.

MELBOURNE

World Trade Centre, Association Melbourne (R-O), Suite 609, Bldg. D, World Trade, Centre, P.O. Box 461, Melbourne, Victoria, Australia, 3005, Telex: AA34211 HARBOR, Cable: HARBOR, Fax: 61 3629-7202, WTC NETWORK: WTCME, Telephone: 61 3614-8626, Nicholas M. Loukides, Executive Manager, (NSR).

METZ

World Trade Center Metz (R-P), 10/12, Avenue Foch, BP 330, 57000 Metz Cedex 1, France, Telex: 860 362, Fax: (33) 87 52 31 99, Telephone: (33) 87 52 31 00, Gerard Schmitt, Vice President, Services: IEM.

MEXICO CITY

World Trade Center Mexico, City (R-IP), Montecito 38-Piso 34, Col. Napoles, C.P. 03810 Mexico, D.F., Fax: (905) 682-7779, WTC NETWORK: WTCMX, Telephone: (905) 687-7592/660-4042, Guillermo Gutierrez-Muro, Managing Director, Services: INEMDGHOST.

MIAMI

World Trade Center Miami (R-O), One World Trade Plaza, Suite 1800, 80 S.W. 8th Street, Miami, Florida 33130 U.S.A., Telex: 153797 WTCMIA, WTC NETWORK: WTCMI, Telephone: (305) 579-0064, Charlotte Gallogly, Executive, Director, Services: INEMDHOST.

Execucentre International (Af), 444 Brickell Avenue, Suite 407, Miami, Florida 33131 U.S.A., Telex: 910 250 3923, Cable: EXECUCENTRE, Telephone: (305) 374-8300, Carol Evanco, Managing Director, Services: OS.

MILAN

World Trade Center Italy SRL, Milan (R-O), Palazzo WTC, Centro Direzionale Milanofiori, 20090 Assago (Milan) Italy, Telex: 340422 WTC INF I, Fax: (02) 824-1605, Telephone: (02) 824-4086, Agostino Giorgi, Services: MDH.

W.T.C. Trading, S.R.L., Milan (Af), Palazzo WTC, Centro Direzionale Milanofiori, 20090 Assago (Milan) Italy, Telex: 340422 WTC INF I, Fax: (02) 824-1605, Telephone: (02) 824-4086/89 200 463, Dr. Arnaldo Berera, Chairman, Services IH.

MILWAUKEE

Wisconsin World Trade Center, at Milwaukee (R-O), Pfister Hotel, 424 E. Wisconsin Avenue, Milwaukee, Wisconsin 53202 U.S.A., WTC NETWORK: WTCMK, Fax: (414) 274-3846, Telephone: (414) 274-3840, Charles C. Mulcahy, President, Services: INEMGHOST.

MONTERREY

World Trade Center Monterrey (R-P), Edificio Omega, Campos Eliseos No. 345 5o. Piso, Col. Chapultepec Polanco, Mexico D.F., CP 11560, Fax: 202-8961/9009, Telephone: 202-1921/6950/8907/8283/7569/7203, Alfredo Suarez Ruiz, Vice President, (NSR).

MONTPELLIER

World Trade Center Montpellier (R-P), Pelege S.A., 15, rue du Rocher F 75008, Paris, France, Telex: 648262 F, Fax: 33 (14) 293-5368, Telephone: 33 (14) 293-4950, Michel Pelege, President, (NSR).

MONTREAL

World Trade Centre Montreal (R-O), 1253 McGill College Avenue, Suite 404, Montreal, Quebec, Canada H3B 2Y5, Telex: 055-62324 WTC/CH-MTL, Fax: (514) 393-3140, WTC NETWORK: WTCMT, Telephone: (514) 393-3355, Jacques Saint-Pierre, Executive Director, Services: INEMGOST.

MOSCOW

World Trade Center Moscow (R-O), v/o SOVINCENTR, 12, Krasnopresnenskaya
    nab., 123610 Moscow U.S.S.R., Telex: 411486 SOVIN SU, Fax: (7095) 2302-761,
    WTC NETWORK: WTCMO, Telephone: 256 63 03, Alexander N. Podvolotsky,
    Director General, Services: INCEMDGHOST.

MUNICH

World Trade Center Munich (R-P), c/o WTCGG SA, 14, Chemin Rieu, 1208
    Geneva, Switzerland, Telex: 429389, Telephone: 4122/47 65 52, Morris Saady,
    (NSR).

NANJING

World Trade Centre Club Nanjing (Af), c/o Jinling Hotel, 2 Hanzhong Road,
    Nanjing, 210005 P. R. C., Telex: 341 lo JEHNJ CN, Cable: 6855 NANJING CN,
    Fax: 86 (25) 643396, Telephone: 86 (25) 741999 742888, Ext. 4615/4611, Pu
    Kunyu, Deputy General Manager, Services: ICEMDGHOST.

NANTES

World Trade Center Nantes (R-O), Centre Atlantique de Commerce
    International, 16 Quai Ernest Renaud. BP 718, 44027 Nantes Cedex 04, France,
    Telex: 710586F, Fax: 40 44 6090, WTC NETWORK: WTCNA, Telephone: (40)
    44 60 80, Francois Marion, Manager, Services: INCEMDGOST.

NEW DELHI

Trade Development Authority (Af), Bank of Baroda Building, 16 Sansad Marg,
    P.O. Box 767, New Delhi, 110001, India, Telex: 3165155 ADEP-IN, Cable:
    ADEPT, Telephone: (91) 11-3322819/3320214, K. Obayya, Executive Director,
    Services: IMD.

NEW ORLEANS

World Trade Center of New Orleans (R-O), 2 Canal Street, Suite 2900, New
    Orleans, Louisiana 70130 U.S.A., Fax: (504) 529-1691, WTC NETWORK:
    WTCNO, Telephone: (504) 529-1601, Eugene J. Schreiber, Managing Director,
    Services: INCIMDCOST.

NEW YORK

World Trade Center New York (R-O), The Port Authority of New York & New
    Jersey, One World Trade Center, Suite 63W, New York, New York 10048
    U.S.A., Telex: 285472 WTNY UR, Cable: WORLDTRADE NEWYORK, Fax:
    (212) 432-0410, TWX: 7105815057, WTC NETWORK: WTCNY, For WTC
    Services: (212) 466-3151, Services: INCEMDGHOST.

NORFOLK

Virginia Port Authority (R-O), 600 World Trade Center, Norfolk, Virginia 23510
    U.S.A., Telex: TWX 710 8811231, Cable: Vast Ports-Norfolk, Fax: (804) 683-

8500, V4TC NETWORK: VffCNF, Telephone: (804) 683-8000, J. Robert Bray, Executive Director, Services: INCEMST.

ORLANDO
Greater Orlando Chamber of Commerce (Af), P.O. Box 1234, Orlando, Florida 32802 U.S.A., Fax: (407) 839-5020, Telephone: (407) 425-1234, Hal Sumrall, Director International Affairs, Services: IEMGOST.

OSAKA
World Trade Center Osaka (R-P), 1-3-20, Nakanoshima, Kita-ku, Osaka, 530, Japan, Fax: (816) 202-6966, Telephone: (816) 208-8969, Masaya Nishio, Mayor, City of Osaka, (NSR).

OSLO
World Trade Center Oslo (R-P), c/o K-Eiendom Oslo og Akershus, H. Heyerdahlsgt. 1, 0160 Oslo 1, Norway, Fax: (472) 426368, Telephone: (472) 485000, Arnt P. Sundli, Director, (NSR).

OTTAWA
World Trade Centre Ottawa (R-P), c/o Suite 1011, 50 O'Connor Street, Ottawa on Canada KIP 6L2, Fax: (613) 232-4806, WTC NETWORK: WTCOT, Telephone: (613) 232-4804, Gregory J. Gorman, President, Services: N. OXNARD, World Trade Center of Oxnard (R-IP), 300 Esplanade Drive, Suite 1020, Oxnard, California 93030 U.S.A., Fax: (805) 988-1862, WrC NETWORK: WTCOX, Telephone: (805) 988-1406, Thomas Rainey, Executive Director, Services: INE.

PANAMA
World Trade Center Panama (R-P), Cacalle 50 y Calle Colombia, Bella Vista, Panama City, or, P.O. Box 6-2432, El Dorado, Panama City, Republic of Panama, Telex: 3516 ECF PG, Fax: (507) 69-6126, WTC NETWORK: WTCPN, Telephone: (507) 69-6124, Guillermo A. Ronderos, President, Services: INT.

PARIS
World Trade Center of Paris (R-O), Chamber of Commerce and Industry, 2 rue de Viarmes, 75001 Paris, France, Telex: 230823 CRFCCIP, Fax: 33(1) 45083851, WTC NETWORK: PARII, Telephone: 33(1) 45.08.35.30, Denis Danset, Director, Services: INECMDGO.

World Trade Center Club, 2, Place de la Defense, CNIT-BP 430, 92053 Paris-La Defense (France), Fax: 33 (1) 47 73 60 04, WTC NETWORK: WTCPA, Telephone: 33(1) 46 92 25 80, Genevieve Fournier, Secretary General, Services: INCEMDGHOST.

PERNAMBUCO
I World Trade Center Pernambuco (R-P), Av. Domingos Ferreira, 2142 Boa Viagem, CEP 51011 Recife Pe, Pernambuco, Brazil, Telex: 81-1945, Telephone: 81-325 2811, Antonio Joao Dourado, (NSR).

PERTH
World Trade Centre Perth Pty. Ltd. (R-P), 88 Thomas Street, Suite 3, West Perth, W.A. 6005, Box 34, Nedlands, W.A. 6008, Australia, Fax: (619) 321-9556, WTC NETWORK: WTCPE, Telephone: (619) 321-9555, Don O'Sullivan, Managing Director, (NSR).

PHILADELPHIA
World Trade Center Philadelphia (R-P), c/o Silver, Harting and Company, 23 North Third Street, Philadelphia, Pennsylvania 19106 U.S.A., Telephone: (215) 629-1444, S. Lance Silver, Partner, (NSR).

PHOENIX
The Phoenix World Trade Center (R-P), Sunbelt Holdings, Inc., 426 N. 44th Street, Suite 375, Phoenix, Arizona 85008 U.S.A., Fax: (602) 267-9114, WTC NETWORK: WTCPH, Telephone: (602) 244-1440, John W. Graham, Executive Vice President, (NSR).

The Arizona World Trade Association (Af), 34 W. Monroe, Suite 900, Phoenix, Arizona 85003 U.S.A., Cable: KERODEN PHX, Telephone: (602) 254-5521, Andrew M. Line, (NSR).

POINTE-A-PITRE
World Trade Center Pointe-a-Pitre (R-IP), Chamber of Commerce and Industry of Pointe-a-Pitre, P.O. Box 64, 97152 Pointe-a-Pitre, Cedex Guadeloupe, F.W.I., Telex: 919780 gl CCI PAP, Fax: 590-902187, WTC NETWORK: WTCPP, Telephone: 590-900808, Georges Marianne, President, Services: NCEGT.

PONCE
The World Trade Center, of Puerto Rico/Ponce (R-P), The Port of Ponce Building-Ponce Playa, P.O. Box 119 Playa Station, Ponce, Puerto Rico 00734-0119, Telex: 3451071, Fax: (809) 836-5142, Telephone: (809) 836-1818/1707, Lucas Valdivieso, Chairman, (NSR).

PORTLAND
World Trade Center Portland (R-O), One World Trade Center, I WTC-Bridge, Suite 250, 121 Southwest Salmon Street, Portland, Oregon 97204 U.S.A., Telex: 446640 WORLDTRADE PDX, Cable: Worldtrade Portland, Fax: (503) 464-8880, WTC NETWORK: WTCPD, Telephone: (503) 464-8888, Charles Allcock, President, Services: INCEMDGHOST, 58, WTCA Members.

PORTO
World Trade Center Porto SARL (R-O), Av. Da Boavista 1269/81, 4100 Porto, Portugal, Telex: 28538 WTCPRT P, Fax (2) 691678, WTC NETWORK: WTCPO, Telephone: (2) 691560, (2) 691660, (2) 691637, (2) 691626, Luisa Abezeeo, Secretary General, Services: INCEMDHOST.

PORT SAID

World Trade Center Port Said (R-P), Arab International Bank, 35 Abdel Khalek
 Sarwat Street, P.O. Box 1563, Cairo, Egypt, Telex: 2079 AIB, Cable:
 ARABINBANK, Telephone: 916233/916244, (NSR).

PROVIDENCE

World Trade Center of Rhode Island, Greater Providence (R-O), P.O. Box 61,
 Bryant College, Smithfield, Rhode Island 02917 U.S.A., Fax: (401) 232-6319,
 WTC NETWORK: WTCRI, Telephone: (401) 232-6400, Priscilla J. Anglo,
 Director, Services: INEMDOST.

RALEIGH-DURHAM

The Research Triangle World Trade Center (R-O), The Imperial Center, 1007
 Slater Road, Suite 200, Mauriceville, North Carolina 27560 U.S.A., or, P.O. Box
 134X7, Research Triangle Park, North Carolina 27709 U.S.A., Fax: (919) 941-
 1917, WTC NETWORK: WTCRT, Telephone: (919) 941-5120, Ruth Turner,
 Managing Director, Services: INEMDHOS.

RIO DE JANEIRO

World Trade Center do Rio de Janeiro (R-IP), Av. Rio Branco 99-20th Floor, 20040
 Rio de Janeiro, Brazil, Telex: 2131299 BMTR BR, 2133798 RPAR BR, Fax: 55 (21)
 262-4036, Telephone: 55 (21) 240-3700/263-2082, Paulo Manoel Protasio,
 President, Services: ICEMDG.

ROTTERDAM

World Trade Center Rotterdam N.V. (R-O), Beursplein 37, P.O. Box 30055, 3001
 DB Rofterdam, The Netherlands, Telex: 23229 BEURS NE, Fax: 10-4054400,
 WTC NETWORK: WTCRO, Telephone: 10-405 4444, WTC Club: 10-405 4100,
 Henk J. Van Engelenburg, Managing Director, Services: INCEMDGHOST.

RUHR VALLEY

World Trade Center Ruhr Valley (R-O), Sparkassenstrasse I, 4650 Gelsenkirchen,
 West Germany, Telex: 824840 RWE D, Fax: 49-209-144285, WTC NETWORK:
 WTCRV, Telephone: 49-209-22097, Rainer M. Buhr, Executive Director,
 Services: INCMGHOST.

ST. LOUIS

The St. Louis World Trade Center (R-P), FAMCO Development, Inc., P.O. Box
 2511, St. Charles, Missouri 63302 U.S.A., VVTC NETWORK: V4TCST,
 Telephone: (314) 946-7890, John Schwarz, President, Services: INEMGHOST.

ST. PAUL

Minnesota World Trade Center, St. Paul (R-O), 400 Minnesota World Trade
 Center, 30 East 7th Street, St. Paul, Minnesota 55101 U.S.A., Telex: 910 2500382
 MNWRLDTRADE UD, Fax: (612) 297-4812, WTC NETWORK: WTCMN,

Telephone: (612) 297-1580, Richard Nolan, President, Services: INCEMDGHOST.

SALZBURG

World Trade Center Salzburg (R-IP), c/o WTC Development Ges.m.b.h., Kohlmarkt 4, A-1010 Vienna, Austria, Fax: (431) 535617X, Telephone: (431) 5356420, Georg Katcz, President, WTC Viennz, Services: H.

SAN ANTONIO

World Trade Center San Antonio (R-O), 118 Broadway, San Antonio, Texas 78205 U.S.A., Fax: (512) 225-5846, WTC NETWORK: WTCSA, Telephone: (512) 225-5877, Josef E. Seiterle, President, Services: INEMGHOST.

SAN FRANCISCO

World Trade Center of San Francisco, Inc. (R-P), 110 Sutter Street, Suite 408, San Francisco, California 94104 U.S.A., Telex: 2106217827 IPSHARP TOR, Fax: (415) 392-1710, WTC NETWORK: WTCSF, Telephone: (415) 392-2705, Stanley Herzstein, President, Services: INEGHOST.

SANTA ANA

World Trade Center Santa Ana (R-O), 801 West Civic Center Drive, Suite 110, Santa Ana, California 92701 U.S.A., Telex: 255472 ACTM UR, Fax: (714) 550-9165, WTC NETWORK: WTCOC, Telephone: (714) 550-1216, Susan Lentz, Executive Director, Services: INEMGOST.

SANTIAGO

World Trade Center Santiago (R-P), Compania Promotora del Comercio International, Huerfanos 1044,13 Fl., Santiago, Chile, Fax: (541) 313-5291, Telephone: (541) 313-1747, Saul Rotsztain, Director, (NSR).

SAO PAULO

Sao Paulo World Trade Center (R-P), Rua Estados Unldos, 1093, CEP 01427-SP Brazil, Telex: 3911122917 SVIM BR, Telephone: 280-4811, Gilberto Bomeny, President, Services: IMDGHOST.

SCHENECTADY

World Trade Center, Schenectady-Capital District (R-P), P.O. Box 1439, Schenectady, New York 12301-1439 U.S.A., Fax: (518) 377-0085, WTC NETWORK: WTCSC, Telephone: (518) 377-4904, Thomas Maggs, Principal Partner, (NSR).

SEATTLE

Seattle World Trade Center (R-P), 1011 Western Avenue, Suite 900, Seattle, Washington 98104 U.S.A., Telex: (MCI/WUI) 650-412 2386 WTCSE, Fax: (206) 464-0125, WTC NETWORK: WTCSE, Telephone: (206) 382-9999, James Baxendale, President, Services: MNDGHOST.

SEOUL

Korea Foreign Trade Association/Korea, World Trade Center, Seoul (R-O), 159-1 Samsuhg-Dong, Kangnam-Ku, Seoul, Korea, Telex: KOTRASO K24265, Cable: KOTRASO SEOUL, Fax: (02) 551 5100, 5200, WTC NETWORK: WTCSL, Telphone: (02) 551 0114/5114/5018, Jung-Nam Choi, Director International Department, Services: INCEMDGHT.

SEVILLA

World Trade Center Sevilla (R-P), Paseo de la Paimera, 12, 41010 Sevilla, Spain, Fax: (341) 22 40 04, Telephone: (341) 4116145, Antonio Trueba, President, (NSR).

SHANGHAI

World Trade Centre Shanghai (R-O), 33 Zhong Shan Dong Yi Lu, Shanghai, P.R.C., Telex: 33290 SCPIT CN, Cable: "COMTRADE" SHANGHAI, Fax: (021) 3291442, Telephone: (021) 3232348/3213850, Lu Guoxiam, Chairman, Services: ICEMDGHOST.

SHENYANG

Shenyang Sub-Council of CCPIT (Af), No 4. Lane 18, Section 2, Heping Street, Liaoning Building Material Hotel, Shenyang, P.R.C., Telex: 80 4090 SSJ CN, Telephone: (8624) 21429/21925, Chen Gong Shi, (NSR).

SHENZHEN

World Trade Centre Shenzhen (R-O), 2/F, Area B, International Trade Center Mansion, Renmin South Road, Shenzhen, 518014 P.R.C., Telex: 420296 ITC CN, Cable: 5012, Fax: 252043, 250140, Telephone: (755) 250140/250141/250142, Xue Tao, Managing Director and Secretary General, Services: ICEMDGHOST.

SINGAPORE

World Trade Centre Singapore (R-O), 1 Maritime Square, No. 09-72, Singapore 0409, Republic of Singapore, Telex: RS 34975 WTCS, Cable "TANJONG" SINGAPORE, Fax: 2744677, WTC NETWORK: WTCSI, Telephone: 3212791 or 3212187, R. Mahendram, Director, Services: INCMDGHOST.

SOFIA

INTREPRED-World Trade Center Sofia (R-O), 16, Bulgaro-Savetska Drujaba Blvd., 1057 Sofia, Bulgaria, Telex: 23072 WTCS BG, Cable: WORLDTRADE SOFIA, Fax: 700006, 708587, WTC NETWORK: WTCSO, Telephone: 71 46 35 46, Haralambi Lambev, Deputy President, Services: INCEMDGHOST.

Bulgarian Chamber of Commerce &, Industry (Af), AL. Stamboliiski Blvd., Sofia, Bulgaria 11A, Telex: 22374, Cable: TORGPALATA, Peter Rousseu, President, Services: IMDGT.

SOUTHAMPTON

World Trade Center Southampton (R-P), c/o World Trade Centre (Holdings) Ltd., 17 Walter Road, Swansea, West Glamorgan, SAI 5NG, United Kingdom, Fax: 0792 648821, Telephone: 0792 473646, Derrick Hughes Morgan, Director, (NSR).

SPLIT

World Trade Center Split (R-P), Institution for Inforinatics & Telecomm., Rudjera Boskovica 22, 58000 Split, Yugoslavia, Telex: X6226178, Fax: (3858) 42474/521351, WTC NETWORK: WTCSP, Telephone: (3858) 561119/561000, Zoran Milic, Director, (NSR).

STOCKHOLM

World Trade Center Stockholm (R-IP), Box 70354, 10724 Stockholm, Sweden, Fax: 46(8) 2106 81, WTC NETWORK: WTCSM, Telephone: 46(8) 700-45-00, Susanne Ihre, President, Services: N.

STRASBOURG

Maison du Commerce International, de Strasbourg (MCIS) (R-O), Immeuble Le Concords, 4 Quai Kelber, F 67056 Strasbourg Cedex, France, Telex: 891 059F, Fax: (88) 75.51.23, WTC NETWORK: WTCSB, Telephone: (88) 32.48.90, Catherine Seegmuller, Executive Director, Services: INCEMDGHOST.

STUTTGART

World Trade Center Stuttgart GmbH (R-P), Neuer Wall 50, 2000 Hamburg 36, Federal Republic of Germany, Fax: (4940) 364882, WTC NETWORK: WTCHH, Telephone: (4940) 372630, Herman H. Schurink, Managing Director, (NSR).

SURABAYA

World Trade Center Surabaya (R-P), Pt. Dhannatimur Centratrada, Wisma Darmo Grande, JL. Mayjen Soengkono (Depan Tvri)., Surabaya 60225, Indonesia, Telex: 33237 DMT DG IA, Fax: (6231) 65475, Telephone: (6231) 66007/65198/65284, Alim Sutresno, Director, (NSR).

SIDNEY

World Trade Centre Sydne (R-P), G.P.O. Box 5130, North Sydney, NSW 2001, Australia, Fax: (612) 909-8803, WTC NETWORK: WTCSY, Telephone: (612) 909-8566, Niel E. Allen, Managing Director, Services: N.

TACOMA

World Trade Center Tacoma (R-O), 3600 Port of Tacoma Road, Suite 209, Tacoma, Washington 98424 U.S.A., Telex: 32-7473 PORT OF TAC, Fax: (206) 383-9474, WTC NETWORK: WTCTA, Telephone: (206) 383-9474, Nancy Peregrine, Executive Director, Services: DMMDGHOST.

TAIPEI

Taipei World Trade Center Co., Ltd. (R-O), 4-8th Floor, CETRA TOWER, 333 Keelung Road, Section 1, Taipei 10548, Taiwan, Telex: 21676 CETRA, Fax: 886 (2) 757-6653, WTC NETWORK: WTCTP, Telephone: 886 (2) 725-5200, Agustine Tingtsu Liu, President, Services: INCEMDGHST.

TAMPA

World Trade Center Tampa (R-P), Taylor Woodrow Property Company (Florida) Inc., One Tampa City Center, Suite 2570, Tampa, Florida 33602 U.S.A., Fax: (813) 229-7120, Telephone: (813) 221-6072, Nick Shackleton, President, (NSR).

TEL-AVIV

World Trade Center Israel, Tel-Aviv (R-O), Industry House, 29 Homered Street, Tel-Aviv, 68125 Israel, Telex: 342651 MAIS IL, Cable: MAIS, Fax: 972 (3) 662026, WTC NETWORK: WTCTV, Telephone: 972 (3) 65 89 02/512 8815, Moshe Nahum, Director, Services: IEMDGHOST.

TIANJIN

World Trade Center Tianjin (R-P), Tianjin Leader (Group) Corp., 3 Xinyuan, Kunming Road, Heping District, 300050 Tianjin, PRC, Telex: 23254 TJEDC CN, Cable: TLGC TIANJIN, Fax: (022) 317471, Telephone: (022) 31 49 03, Ge Zi Ping, Chairman and General Manager, Services: IH.

TIJUANA

World Trade Center Tijuana (R-P), P.O. Box 57, World Trade Center Building, No. 4-1, 2-chome, Hamamatsu-cho, Minato-ku, Tokyo, 105 Japan, Telex: 2422661 WORLDT J, Cable: WORLDTRADE TOKYO, Fax: (03) 436-4368, WTC NETWORK: WTCTO, Telephone: (03) 435-5651, Sensuke Igarashi, Director and Secetary General, Services: INCEMDGHOST.

TOLEDO

Toledo World Trade Center (R-IP), 136 North Summit Street, Toledo, Ohio 43604 U.S.A., WTC NETWORK: WTCTL, Telephone: (419) 255-7226, Services: INCEMOST.

TORONTO

World Trade Centre Toronto (R-O), 60 Harbour Street, Torontol Ontario, Canada M5J 1B7, Telex: 21 06-219666 WORLDTRADE TOR, Cable: WORLDTRADE TORONTO, Fax: (416) 863-4830, WTC NETWORK: WTCTR, Telephone: (416) 863-2001, Gary Reid, Executive Director, Services: INCEMDGHOST.

TRINIDAD AND TOBAGO

World Trade Center Trinidad and Tobago (R-P), Airports Authority of Trinidad and Tobago, Airports Administration Centre, Caroni North Bank Road, Piarco, P.O. Box 1273, Port of Spain, Trinidad, Fax: 809 669-2319, WTC NETWORK:

WTCTT, Telephone: (809) 664-8047/8048/8049 and, 669-2320, Dolores Hendy, Coordinator, Services: INGHMT.

TUCSON

World Trade Center Tucson (R-P), The Hilton East Hotel, 7600 E. Broadway, Suite 232, Tucson, Arizona 85710 U.S.A., Fax: (602) 8X5-8437, WTC NETWORK: WTCTC, Telephone: (602) 885-7866, Peggy C. Browne, President, (NSR).

TUNIS

Tunis World Trade Center (R-P), 6 Avenue Mohamcd Ali Akid, 1003 Tunis, Tunisia, Telex: 14512, WTC NETWORK: WTCTU, Telephone: 271307, Slaheddine El Goulli, President, Director General, (NSR).

VALENCIA

World Trade Center Valencia, S.A. (R-P), Av. De Las Ferias, 2, 46035, Valencia, Spain, Telex: MN 61079 TOFE E, Cable: VALTRADE, WTC NETWORK: WTCVL, Telephone: 6364 5483, Satumino Beltran, Secretary General, Services: IMHOST.

VANCOUVER

World Trade Centre Vancouver (R-O), The Vancouver Board of Trade, 999 Canada Place, Suite 400, Vancouver, B.C. Canada V6C 3CI, Telex: CA 062 17827 IP SHARP TOR, Fax: 604 681 0437, WTC NETWORK: WTCVN, Telephone: (604) 681-2111, Darcy Rezac, Managing Director, Services: INCEMDGHOST.

VIENNA

World Trade Center Vienna-Airport (R-O), c/o Katcz & Corvin GmbH, Kohlmarkt 4, A-1300 Wien-Flughafen, Austria, Telex: 11 45 49, Fax: 43 (1) 7770-6017/6027, WTC NETWORK: WTCVA, Telephone: 43 (1) 7770-6000, Georg Katcz President, Services: INCEMDGOST.

WARSAW

World Trade Center Warsaw (R-P), c/o Kurt Thorsen Totalentreprise A/S, World Trade Center Aarhus, Dalgas Avenue 42, Aarhus, Denmark 8000, Fax: 45 (86)116990, WTC NETWORK: WTCAA, Telephone: 45 (86) 116900, Ebb Johansen, Managing Director, (NSR).

WASHINGTON, DC

World Trade Center Washington, DC (R-O), 1101 King Street, Suite 700, Alexandria, Virginia 22314 U.S.A., Telex: 5106004086 WTC WASH, WTC NETWORK: WTCWA, Telephone: (703) 684-6630, Richard C. Anderson, President, Services: INCEMGHOST.

WICHITA
World Trade Center Wichita (R-O), EPIC Center, 301 North Main, Suite 1860, Wichita, Kansas 67202 U.S.A., Fax: (316) 291-8475, WTC NETWORK: WTCWC, Telephone: (316) 291-8475, Elliott Wirnberly, President, Services: INEMGHOST.

WILMINGTON, DE
World Trade Center, Delaware, Inc., Wilmington (R-P), Dupont Bldg., Suite 1022, P.O. Box 709, Wilmington, Delaware 19899 U.S.A., Telex: 905015, Fax: (302) 656 7905/08, R. Michael Rice, Executive Director, Services: IENMHT.

WILMINGTON, NC
World Trade Center Wilmington (R-O), Greater Wilmington Chamber of Commerce, P.O. Box 330, Wilmington, North Carolina 28402 U.S.A., Fax: (919) 763-0106, WTC NETWORK: WTCWL, Telephone: (919) 762-3525, Tracey K. Frank, WTC Coordinator, Services: INEMDST.

WINNIPEG
World Trade Center Winnipeg (R-P), c/o W.T.C. World Trade Centers of Canada Ltd., 1191 Mountain Street, Montreal, Canada H3G 1Z2, Fax: (514) 866-0668, WTC NETWORK: WTCOT, Telephone: (514) 866-1352, J. Rodolphe Rousseau, President, (NSR).

XI'AN
World Trade Center Club Xi'an (Af), China Council for the Promotion of International Trade, Shaanxi Sub-Council, Xinchengnei Xi'an, 710004 P.R.C., Telex: 71249 SXCIC CN, Cable: 6345 (XI'AN), Fax: (29) 791461, Telephone: (29) 22206, 716345, Zeng Xian Wu, President, (NSR).

ZAGREB
World Trade Center Zagreb (R-P), Zagreb Fair, Avenija Borisa Kidrica 2, 41020 Zagreb, Yugoslavia, Telex: 21385 YUZVG, Fax: 520-643, Telephone: 511-605, Vera Soldan, General Manager, (NSR).

ZURICH
World Trade Center Zurich (R-P), c/o Spaltenstein Immobilien AG, Attn: Ms. M. Zehnder, Siewerdstrasse 8, CH-8050 Zurich, Switzerland, Telex: 822621 SMB CH, Fax: 41 (1) 3161394, Telephone: 41 (1) 316 1333, Marianne Zehnder, Marketing Assistant, (NSR).

INTERNATIONAL TRADE ADMINISTRATION
U.S. and Foreign Commercial Service Overseas Posts

ALGERIA
American Embassy
Algiers
SCO Andrew Tangalos
Tel: 011-213-2-60-18-63
Fax: 011-213-2-60-18-63
U.S. Dept of State (Algiers)
Washington, D.C. 20521-6030

ARGENTINA
American Embassy
Buenos Aires
SCO Ralph Fermoselle
Tel: 011-54-1-773-1063
Fax: 011-54-1-775-6040
Unit 4326
APO AA 34034

AUSTRALIA
American Consulate
General
Sydney
SCO Michael Hand
Tel: 011-61-2-261-9200
Fax: 011-61-2-261-8148
Unit 11024
APO AP 96554-0002

American Consulate
Brisbane
FCSN Keith Sloggett
Tel: 011-61-7-831-1345
Fax: 011-61-7-832-6247
Unit 11018
APO AP 96553-0002

American Consulate General
Melbourne
FCSO Daniel Young
Tel: 011-61-3-526-5900
Fax: 011-61-3-510-4660
Unit 11011
APO AP 96551-0002

American Consulate General
Perth
FCSN Marion Shingler
Tel: 011-61-9-221-1177
Fax: 011-61-9-325-3569
Unit 11021
APO AP 96553-0002

AUSTRIA
American Embassy
Vienna
SCO Benjamin Brown
Tel: 011-43-222-31-55-11
Fax: 011-43-222-34-12-61
APO AE 09108

BARBADOS
American Embassy
Bridgetown
SCO Richard Ades (contact
via Miami D.O.)
Tel: 1-809-436-4950
Fax: 1-809-426-2275
Box B
FPO AA 34054

BELGIUM
American Embassy
Brussels
SCO Jerry Mitchell
Tel: 011-32-2-513-3830
Fax: 011-32-2-512-6653
PSC 82 Box 002
APO AE 09724-1015

US Mission to the
European Communities
Brussels
SCO James Blow
Tel: 011-32-2-513-3830
Fax: 011-32-2-513-1228
PSC 82 Box 002
APO AE 09724

BRAZIL
American Embassy
Brasilia
SCO Kevin Brennan
Tel: 011-55-61-223-0120
Fax: 011-55-61-225-3981
Unit 3502
APO AA 34030

American Consular Agency
Belem
FCSN Raymundo Teixiera
Tel: 011-55-91-223-0800
Fax: 011-55-91-223-0413
Unit 3500
APO AA 34030

American Consular Agency
Belo Horizonte
FCSN Jose Mauricio de
Vasconcelos
Tel: 011-55-31-335-3250
Fax: 011-55-31-335-3054
Unit 3505
APO AA 34030

American Consulate General
Rio De Janeiro
FCSO Walter Hage
Tel: 011-55-21-292-7117
Fax: 011-55-21-240-9738
APO AA 34030

American Consulate General
Sao Paulo
FCSO Arthur Alexander
Tel: 011-55-11-853-2011
Fax: 011-55-11-853-2744
APO AA 34030

CAMEROON
American Consulate
Douala
FCSN Jean Sumo
Tel: 011-237-425-331
Fax: 011-237-427-790
U.S. Dept. of State (Douala)
Washington, D.C. 20251-2530

CANADA
American Embassy
Ottawa
SCO Robert Marro
Tel: 1-613-238-5335
Fax: 1-613-233-8511
P.O. Box 5000
Ogdensburg, N.Y. 13669

American Consulate General
Calgary
FCSO Randall Labounty
Tel: 1-403-265-2116
Fax: 1-403-264-6630
Suite 1050
615 Macleod Trail, SE.
Calgary, Alberta, Canada
T2G 4T8

American Consulate General
Halifax
FCSN Richard Vinson
Tel: 1-902-429-2482
Fax: 1-902-423-6861
Suite 900, Cogswell Tower
Halifax, Nova Scotia, Canada
B3J 3K1

American Consulate General
Montreal
FCSO Geoffrey Walser
Tel: 1-514-398-9695
Fax: 1-514-398-0711
P.O. Box 847
Champlain, N.Y. 12919-0847

American Consulate General
Toronto
FCSO Dan Wilson
Tel: 1-416-595-5413
Fax: 1-416-595-5419
P.O. Box 135
Lewiston, N.Y. 14092

American Consulate General
Vancouver
FCSO Stephen Wasylko
Tel: 1-604-685-3382
Fax: 1-604-685-5285
P.O. Box 5002
Point Roberts, Wash. 98281-5002

CHILE
American Embassy
Santiago
SCO Ricardo Villalobos
Tel: 011-56-2-671-0133
Fax: 011-56-2-697-2051
Unit 4111
APO AA 34033

CHINA
American Embassy
Beijing
SCO Tim Stratford
Tel: 011-86-1-532-3831
Fax: 011-86-1-532-3297

PSC 461 Box 50
FPO AP 96521-0002

American Consulate General
Guangzhou
FCSO Dennis Barnes
Tel: 011-86-20-677-842
Fax: 011-86-20-666-409
PSC 461 Box 100
FPO AP 96521-0002

American Consulate General
Shanghai
FCSO Nora Sun
Tel: 011-86-21-433-2492
Fax: 011-86-21-433-1576
PSC 461 Box 200
FPO AP 96521-0002

American Consulate General
Shenyang
FCSO (vacant)
Tel: 011-86-24-220-057
Fax: 011-86-24-290-074
PSC 461 Box 45
FPO AP 96521-0002

COLOMBIA
American Embassy
Bogota
SCO Arthur Trezise
Tel: 011-57-1-232-6550
Fax: 011-57-1-285-7945
Unit 5120
APO AA 34038

COSTA RICA
American Embassy
San Jose
SCO Judith Henderson
Tel: 011-506-20-3939
Fax: 011-506-31-4783
Unit 2508
APO AA 34020

COTE D'IVOIRE
American Embassy
Abidjan
SCO Catherine Houghton
Tel: 011-225-21-4616
Fax: 011-225-22-3259
U.S. Dept of State (Abidjan)
Washington, D.C. 20521-2010

CZECHOSLOVAKIA
American Embassy
Prague
SCO Robert Shipley
Tel: 011-42-2-536-641 or 532-470
Fax: 011-42-2-532-457   or
537-534
Unit 25402
APO AE 09213-5630

American Consulate General
Bratislava (Commercial Section
to open spring 1992)
FCSN

INTERNATIONAL TRADE ADMINISTRATION
U.S. and Foreign Commercial Service Overseas Posts

DENMARK
American Embassy
Copenhagen
SCO Stephen Helgesen
Tel: 011-45-31-42-31-44
Fax: 011-45-31-42-01-75
APO AE 09176

DOMINICAN REPUBLIC
American Embassy
Santo Domingo
SCO Richard Ades (contact via Miami D.O.)
Tel: 1-809-541-2171
Fax: 1-809-688-4838
Unit 5515
APO AA 34041

ECUADOR
American Embassy
Quito
SCO Jere Dabbs
Tel: 011-593-2-561-404
Fax: 011-593-2-504-550
Unit 5334
APO AA 34039-3420

American Consulate General
Guayaquil
FCSN Francisco Von Buchwald
Tel: 011-593-4-323-570
Fax: 011-593-4-324-558
APO AA 34039

EGYPT
American Embassy
Cairo
SCO Norman Glick
Tel: 011-20-2-354-1583
Fax: 011-20-2-355-8368
Unit 64900 Box 11
FPO AE 09839-4900

American Consulate General
Alexandria
FCSN Hanna Abdelnour
Tel: 011-20-3-482-1911
Fax: 011-20-3-482-9199
Unit 64904
APO AE 09839-4904

FINLAND
American Embassy
Helsinki
SCO Maria Andrews
Tel: 011-358-0-171-821
Fax: 011-358-0-635-332
APO AE 09723

FRANCE
American Embassy
Paris
SCO Melvin Searls
Tel: 011-33-1-4296-1202
Fax: 011-33-1-4266-4827
APO AE 09777

US Mission to the OECD

Paris
SCO Robyn Layton
Tel: 011-33-1-4524-7437
Fax: 011-33-1-4524-7410
APO AE 09777

American Consulate General
Bordeaux
FCSN (vacant)
Tel: 011-33-56-52-65-95
Fax: 011-33-56-51-60-42
APO AE 09777

American Consulate General
Lyon
FCSN Alain Beullard
Tel: 011-33-78-24-68-49
Fax: N/A
APO AE 09777

American Consulate General
Marseille
FCSN Igor Lepine
Tel: 011-33-91-54-92-00
Fax: N/A
APO AE 09777

US Commercial Office
Nice
FCSN Reine Joguet
Tel: 011-33-93-88-89-55
Fax: N/A
APO AE 09777

American Consulate General
Strasbourg
FCSN Jacqueline Munzlinger
Tel: 011-33-88-35-31-04
Fax: N/A
APO AE 09777

GERMANY
American Embassy
Bonn
SCO John Bligh
Tel: 011-49-228-339-2895
Fax: 011-49-228-334-649
Unit 21701 Box 370
APO AE 09080

US Embassy Office
Berlin
FCSO James Joy
Tel: 011-49-30-251-0244
Fax: 011-49-30-251-0246
APO AE 09235

US Commercial Office
Duesseldorf
FCSN Barbara Ernst
Tel: 011-49-211-596-798
Fax: 011-49-211-594-897
c/o Amembassy Bonn
Unit 21701 Box 370
APO AE 09080

American Consulate General
Frankfurt

FCSO Donald Businger
Tel: 011-49-69-7535-2453
Fax: 011-49-69-748-204
APO AE 09213

Amercian Consulate General
Hamburg
FCSO Hans Amrhein
Tel: 011-49-40-4117-1304
Fax: 011-49-40-410-6598
APO AE 09215-0002

American Consulate General
Munich
FCSO Edward Ruse
Tel: 011-49-89-2888-748
Fax: 011-49-89-285-261
APO AE 09108

American Consulate General
Stuttgart
FCSO Camille Sailer
Tel: 011-49-711-246-513
Fax: 011-49-711-236-4350
APO AE 09154

GREECE
American Embassy
Athens
SCO John Priamou
Tel: 011-30-1-723-9705
Fax: 011-30-1-721-8660
PSC 108 Box 30
APO AE 09842

GUATEMALA
American Embassy
Guatemala
SCO Robert Fraser
Tel: 011-502-2-348-479
Fax: 011-502-2-317-373
Unit 3306
APO AA 34024

HONDURAS
American Embassy
Tegucigalpa
SCO Eric Weaver
Tel: 011-504-32-3120
Fax: 011-504-32-0027
Unit 2923
APO AA 34022

HONG KONG
American Consulate General
Hong Kong
SCO Thomas L. Boam
Tel: 011-852-521-1467
Fax: 011-852-845-9800
PSC 464 Box 30
FPO AP 96522-0002

HUNGARY
American Embassy
Budapest
SCO Gary Gallagher
Tel: 011-36-1-122-8600

Fax: 011-36-1-142-2529
APO AE 09213-5270

INDIA
American Embassy
New Delhi
SCO James Moorhouse
Tel: 011-91-11-600-651
Fax: 011-91-11-687-2391
U.S. Dept. of State (New Delhi)
Washington, D.C. 20521-9000

American Consulate General
Bombay
FCSO Dorothy Lutter
Tel: 011-91-22-828-0571
Fax: 011-91-22-822-0350
U.S. Dept. of State (Bombay)
Washington, D.C. 20521-6240

American Consulate General
Calcutta
FCSN Nargiz Chatterjee
Tel: 011-91-33-44-3611
Fax: 011-91-33-28-3823
U.S. Dept. of State (Calcutta)
Washington, D.C. 20521-6250

American Consulate General
Madras
FCSO Rajendra Dheer
Tel: 011-91-44-475-947
Fax: 011-91-44-825-0240
U.S. Dept. of State (Madras)
Washington, D.C. 20521-6260

INDONESIA
American Embassy
Jakarta
SCO Theodore Villinski
Tel: 011-62-21-360-360
Fax: 011-62-21-385-1632
Box 1
APO AP 96520

American Consulate General
Medan
FCSN Zulhava Luthfi
Tel: 011-62-61-322-200
Fax: N/A
APO AP 96520

American Consulate General
Surabaya
FCSN Midji Kwee
Tel: 011-62-31-67100
Fax: N/A
APO AP 96520

IRELAND
American Embassy
Dublin
SCO Gene Harris
Tel: 011-353-1-288-4569
Fax: 011-353-1-608-469
U.S. Dept. of State (Dublin)
Washington, D.C. 20521-5290

INTERNATIONAL TRADE ADMINISTRATION
U.S. and Foreign Commercial Service Overseas Posts

ISRAEL
American Embassy
Tel Aviv
SCO Mike Mercurio
Tel: 011-972-3-654-338
Fax: 011-972-3-658-033
PSC 98 Box 100
APO AE 09830

ITALY
American Embassy
Rome
SCO Emilio Iodice
Tel: 011-39-6-4674-2202
Fax: 011-39-6-4674-2113
PSC 59
APO AE 09624

American Consulate General
Florence
FCSN (vacant)
Tel: 011-39-55-211-676
Fax: 011-39-55-283-780
PSC 59 Box F
APO AE 09624

American Consulate General
Genoa
FCSN Erminia Lezzi
Tel: 011-39-10-282-741
Fax: 011-39-10-290-027
PSC 59 Box G
APO AE 09624

American Consulate General
Milan
FCSO Peter Alois
Tel: 011-39-2-498-2241
Fax: 011-39-2-481-4161
PSC 59 Box M
APO AE 09624

American Consulate General
Naples
FCSN Christiano Sartorio
Tel: 011-39-81-761-1592
Fax: 011-39-81-761-1869
PSC 59 Box N
FPO AE 09624

JAMAICA
American Embassy
Kingston
SCO Richard Ades (contact via
Miami D.O.)
Tel: 1-809-929-4850
Fax: 1-809-929-3637
U.S. Dept. of State (Kingston)
Washington, D.C. 20521-3210

JAPAN
American Embassy
Tokyo
SCO George Mu
Tel: 011-81-3-3224-5000
Fax: 011-81-3-3589-4235
Unit 45004 Box 204
APO AP 96337-0001

American Consulate
Fukuoka
FCSN Yoshihiro Yamamoto
Tel: 011-81-92-751-9331
Fax: 011-81-92-271-3922
Box 10
FPO AP 98766

Representative Office
Nagoya
FCSO Todd Thurwachter
Tel: 011-81-52-203-4011
Fax: 011-81-52-201-4612
c/o U.S. Embassy Tokyo
Unit 45004, Box 280
APO AP 96337-0001

American Consulate General
Osaka-Kobe
FCSO Patrick Santillo
Tel: 011-81-6-315-5953
Fax: 011-81-6-361-5978
Unit 45004 Box 239
APO AP 96337

American Consulate General
Sapporo
FCSN Kenji Itaya
Tel: 011-81-11-641-1115
Fax: 011-81-11-641-0911
APO AP 96503

KENYA
American Embassy
Nairobi
SCO Richard Benson
Tel: 011-254-2-334-141
Fax: 011-254-2-340-838
Unit 64100 Box 51
APO AE 09831-4100

KOREA
American Embassy
Seoul
SCO Peter Frederick
Tel: 011-82-2-732-2601
Fax: 011-82-2-739-1628
Unit 15550
APO AP 96205-0001

KUWAIT
American Embassy
Kuwait
SCO Robert Connan
Tel: 011-965-242-4151
or 244-8073
Fax: 011-965-244-7692
Unit 69000 Box 10
APO AE 09880-9000

MALAYSIA
American Embassy
Kuala Lumpur
SCO Paul Walters
Tel: 011-60-3-248-9011
Fax: 011-60-3-242-1866
APO AP 96535-5000

MEXICO
American Embassy
Mexico City
SCO Roger Wallace
Tel: 011-52-5-211-0042
Fax: 011-52-5-207-8938
PO Box 3087
Laredo, Tex. 78044-3087

American Consulate General
Guadalajara
FCSO Americo Tadeu
Tel: 011-52-36-25-0321
Fax: 011-52-36-26-3576
PO Box 3088
Laredo, Tex. 78044-3088

American Consulate General
Monterrey
FCSO Dawn Cooper-Bahar
Tel: 011-52-83-452-120
Fax: 011-52-83-42-5172
PO Box 3098
Laredo, Tex. 78044-3098

MOROCCO
American Consulate General
Casablanca
SCO Sam Starrett
Tel: 011-212-26-45-50
Fax: 011-212-22-02-59
PSC 74 Box 024
APO AE 09718

American Embassy
Rabat
FCSN Asma Daimoussi
Tel: 011-212-7-622-65
Fax: 011-212-7-656-61
APO AE 09718

NETHERLANDS
American Embassy
The Hague
SCO Michael Hegedus
Tel: 011-31-70-310-9417
Fax: 011-31-70-363-2985
PSC 71 Box 1000
APO AE 09715

American Consulate General
Amsterdam
FCSO Bert Engelhardt
Tel: 011-31-20-664-8111
Fax: 011-31-20-675-2856
APO AE 09159

NEW ZEALAND
American Consulate General
Auckland
SCO Bobette Orr
Tel: 011-64-9-303-2038
Fax: 011-64-9-366-0870
PSC 467 Box 99
FPO AP 96531-1099

American Embassy

Wellington
FCSN Janet Coulthart
Tel: 011-64-4-722-068
Fax: 011-64-4-781-701
PSC 467 Box 1
FPO AP 96531-1001

NIGERIA
American Embassy
Lagos
SCO Frederic Gaynor
Tel: 011-234-1-616-477
Fax: 011-234-1-619-856
U.S. Dept. of State (Lagos)
Washington, D.C. 20521-8300

American Consulate General
Kaduna
FCSN Mathias Mgbeze
Tel: 011-234-62-201-070
Fax: N/A
U.S. Dept. of State (Kaduna)
Washington, D.C. 20521-2260

NORWAY
American Embassy
Oslo
SCO Scott Bozek
Tel: 011-47-2-44-85-50
Fax: 011-47-2-55-88-03
PSC 69 Box 0200
APO AE 09707

PAKISTAN
American Consulate General
Karachi
SCO George Kachmar
Tel: 011-92-21-518-180
Fax: 011-92-21-568-1381
Unit 62400 Box No 137
APO AE 09814-2400

American Consulate General
Lahore
FCSN Shalla Malik
Tel: 011-92-42-870-221
Fax: N/A
Unit 62216
APO AE 09812-2216

PANAMA
American Embassy
Panama
SCO Carlos Poza
Tel: 011-507-27-1777
Fax: 011-507-27-1713
Unit 0945
APO AA 34002

PERU
American Embassy
Lima
SCO Richard Lenahan
Tel: 011-51-14-33-0555
Fax: 011-51-14-33-4687
Unit 3780
APO AA 34031

INTERNATIONAL TRADE ADMINISTRATION
U.S. and Foreign Commercial Service Overseas Posts

PHILIPPINES
American Embassy
Manila
SCO Jonathan Bensky
Tel: 011-63-2-818-6674
Fax: 011-63-2-818-2684
APO AP 96440

POLAND
American Embassy
Warsaw
SCO Joan Edwards
Tel: 011-48-22-21-45-15
Fax: 011-48-22-21-63-27
APO AE 09213-5010

PORTUGAL
American Embassy
Lisbon
SCO Miguel Pardo de Zela
Tel: 011-351-1-726-6600
Fax: 011-351-1-726-8914
PSC 83 Box FCS
APO AE 09726

American Consulate
Oporto
FCSN Adolfo Coutinho
Tel: 011-351-2-63094
Fax: 011-351-2-600-2737
APO AE 09726

ROMANIA
American Embassy
Bucharest
SCO Kay Kuhlman
Tel: 011-40-0-10-40-40
Fax: 011-40-0-11-84-47
APO AE 09213-5260

SAUDI ARABIA
American Embassy
Riyadh
SCO Dirck Teller
Tel: 011-966-1-488-3800
Fax: 011-966-1-488-3237
Unit 61307
APO AE 09038-1307

American Consulate General
Dhahran
FCSO Danny Devito
Tel: 011-966-3-891-3200
Fax: 011-966-3-891-8332
Unit 66803
APO AE 09858-6803

American Consulate General
Jeddah
FCSO Mike Frisby
Tel: 011-966-2-667-0040
Fax: 011-966-2-665-8106
Unit 62112
APO AE 09811-2112

SINGAPORE
American Embassy
Singapore

SCO George Ruffner
Tel: 011-65-338-9722
Fax: 011-65-338-5010
FPO AP 96534-0006

SOUTH AFRICA
American Consulate General
Johannesburg
SCO L. Richard Jackson
Tel: 011-27-11-331-3937
Fax: 011-27-11-331-6178
U.S. Dept. of State
(Johannesburg)
Washington, D.C. 20521-2500

American Consulate General
Cape Town
FCSN Sylvia Frowde
Tel: 011-27-21-21-4280
Fax: 011-27-21-254-151
U.S. Dept. of State (Cape Town)
Washington, DC 20521-2480

SPAIN
American Embassy
Madrid
SCO Robert Kohn
Tel: 011-34-1-577-4000
Fax: 011-34-1-575-8655
PSC 61 Box 0021
APO AE 09642

American Consulate General
Barcelona
FCSO Ralph Griffin
Tel: 011-34-3-319-9550
Fax: 011-34-3-319-5621
PSC 64
APO AE 09646

SWEDEN
American Embassy
Stockholm
SCO Harrison Sherwood
Tel: 011-46-8-783-5346
Fax: 011-46-8-660-9181
U.S. Dept. of State (Stockholm)
Washington, D.C. 20521-5750

SWITZERLAND
American Embassy
Bern
SCO Arthur Reichenbach
Tel: 011-41-31-43-73-41
Fax: 011-41-31-43-73-36
U.S. Dept. of State (Bern)
Washington, D.C. 20521-5110

US Mission to GATT
Geneva
SCO Andrew Grossman
Tel: 011-41-22-749-5281
Fax: 011-41-22-749-4885
U.S. Dept. of State (Geneva)
Washington, DC 20521-5120

American Consulate General
Zurich

FCSN Paul Frei
Tel: 011-41-1-552-070
Fax: 011-41-1-383-9814
U.S. Dept. of State (Zurich)
Washington, D.C. 20521-5130

THAILAND
American Embassy
Bangkok
SCO Herbert Cochran
Tel: 011-66-2-253-4920
Fax: 011-66-2-255-2915
APO AP 96546

**TRINIDAD &
TOBAGO**
American Embassy
Port of Spain
SCO Richard Ades (contact
via Miami D.O.)
Tel: 1-809-622-6371
Fax: 1-809-622-9583
U.S. Dept. of State (Port
of Spain)
Washington, D.C. 20521-3410

TURKEY
American Embassy
Ankara
SCO Dave Katz
Tel: 011-90-4-126-5470
Fax: 011-90-4-167-1366
PSC 93 Box 5000
APO AE 09823

American Consulate General
Istanbul
FCSO Russell Smith
Tel: 011-90-1-151-3602
Fax: 011-90-1-152-2417
PSC 97 Box 0002
APO AE 09827-0002

American Consulate General
Izmir
FCSN Berrin Erturk
Tel: 011-90-51-149-426
Fax: 011-90-51-130-493
APO AE 09821

**UNITED ARAB
EMIRATES**
American Consulate General
Dubai
SCO Paul Scogna
Tel: 011-971-4-378-584
Fax: 011-971-4-375-121
U.S. Department of State (Dubai)
Washington, D.C. 20521-6020

American Embassy
Abu Dhabi
FCSO Sam Dhir
Tel: 011-971-2-345-545
Fax: 011-971-2-331-374
U.S. Dept. of State (Abu Dhabi)
Washington, D.C. 20521-6010

UNITED KINGDOM
American Embassy
London
SCO Kenneth Moorefield
Tel: 011-44-71-499-9000
Fax: 011-44-71-491-4022
PSC 801 Box 33
FPO AE 09498-4033

U.S.S.R.
American Embassy
Moscow
SCO James May
Tel: 011-7-095-255-4848
Fax: 011-7-095-230-2101
APO AE 09721

American Consulate General
St. Petersburg
FCSO Douglas Wake
Tel: 011-7-812-274-8235
Fax: N/A
APO AE 09723

VENEZUELA
American Embassy
Caracas
SCO Bob Taft
Tel: 011-58-2-285-2222
Fax: 011-58-2-285-0336
Unit 4958
APO AA 34037

YUGOSLAVIA
American Embassy
Belgrade
SCO Peter Noble
Tel: 011-38-11-645-655
Fax: 011-38-11-645-096
APO AE 09213-5070

American Consulate General
Zagreb
FCSN Djuro Njers
Tel: 011-38-41-444-800
Fax: 011-38-41-440-235
APO AE 09213-5080

TAIWAN
Unofficial, commercial, and
other relations with Taiwan are
conducted through an unofficial instrumentality, the American Institute in Taiwan (AIT),
which has offices in Taipei and
Kaoshiung. Contact AIT at
American Trade Center, Room
3207, International Trade
Building, Taipei World Trade
Center, 333 Keelung Road,
Section 1, Taipei 10548 Taiwan, tel. 886-2-7201550; telex
23890 U.S. Trade; fax
886-2-7577162.

POWER OF ATTORNEY

The Department of the Treasury
Bureau of Customs
8.19, 17.2, C.R.; 8.19, C.M.

Check appropriate box:
☐ Individual
☐ Partnership
☐ Corporation
☐ Sole Proprietorship

KNOW ALL MEN BY THESE PRESENTS: That, _____

(Full Name of person, partnership, or corporation, or sole proprietorship (identify))

a corporation doing business under the laws of the State of _____ or a

doing business as _____ residing at _____

having an office and place of business at _____ , hereby constitutes and appoints each of the following persons

"F. W. Myers & Co., Inc., and Frank P. Dow Division of F. W. Myers & Co., Inc. through any of its licensed officers and any employees specifically authorized to act for the foregoing by power of attorney filed with the District Director of Customs. If a non-resident corporation, we further authorize for foregoing to accept service of process and for the appointment of sub-agent or sub-agents. If a resident corporation, we further authorize any of the foregoing to appoint as our agent, such other broker(s) as may be required. Such agent(s) shall be authorized to accept service of process in our behalf."

as a true and lawful agent and attorney of the grantor named above for and in the name, place, and stead of said grantor from this date and in Customs District _____ all and in no other name, to make, endorse, sign, declare, or swear to any entry, withdrawal, declaration, certificate, bill of lading, or other document required by law or regulation in connection with the importation, transportation, or exportation of any merchandise shipped or consigned by or to said grantor; to perform any act or condition which may be required by law or regulation in connection with such merchandise; to receive any merchandise deliverable to said grantor;

To make endorsements on bills of lading conferring authority to make entry and collect drawback, and to make, sign, declare, or swear to any statement, supplemental statement, schedule, supplemental schedule, certificate of delivery, certificate of manufacture, certificate of manufacture and delivery, contract manufacturing records, declaration of proprietor on drawback entry, declaration of exporter on drawback entry, or any other affidavit or document which may be required by law or regulation for drawback purposes, regardless of whether such bill of lading, sworn statement, schedule, certificate, abstract, declaration, or other affidavit or document is intended for filing in said district or in any other customs district;

To sign, seal, and deliver for and as the act of said grantor any bond required by law or regulation in connection with the entry or withdrawal of imported merchandise or merchandise exported with or without benefit of drawback, or in connection with the entry, clearance, lading, unlading or navigation of any vessel or other means of conveyance owned or operated by said grantor, and any and all bonds which may be voluntarily given and accepted under applicable laws and regulations, consignee's

and owner's declarations provided for in section 485, Tariff Act of 1930, as amended, or affidavits in connection with the entry of merchandise;

To sign and swear to any document and to perform any act that may be necessary or required by law or regulation in connection with the entering, clearing, lading, unlading, or operation of any vessel or other means of conveyance owned or operated by said grantor;

To authorize other Customs Brokers to act as my agent; to receive, endorse and collect checks issued for Customs duty refunds in a grantor's name drawn on the Treasurer of the United States; if the grantor is a nonresident of the United States, to accept service of process on behalf of the grantor.

And generally to transact at the customhouses in said district any and all Customs business, including making, signing, and filing of protests under section 514 of the Tariff Act of 1930, in which said grantor is or may be concerned or interested and which may properly be transacted or performed by any agent and attorney, giving to said agent and attorney full power and authority to do anything whatever requisite and necessary to be done in the premises as fully as said grantor could do if present and acting, hereby ratifying and confirming all that the said agent and attorney shall lawfully do by virtue of these presents; the foregoing power of attorney to remain in full force and effect until the _____ day of _____ , 19___ , or until notice of revocation in writing is duly given to and received by the District Director of Customs of the district aforesaid. If the donor of this power of attorney is a partnership, the said power shall in no case have any force or effect after the expiration of 2 years from the date of its receipt in the office of the District Director of Customs of the said district.

IN WITNESS WHEREOF, the said _____

has caused these presents to be sealed and signed: (Signature) _____

(Capacity) _____ (Date) _____

WITNESS _____

(Corporate seal) * (Optional)

Customs Form 5291 (10-07-80)
M-I-80

Certification on reverse must be made in all cases.

(SEE OVER)

247

INDIVIDUAL OR PARTNERSHIP CERTIFICATION   *(Optional)

CITY _____

COUNTY _____ SS.

STATE _____

On this _____ day of _____, 19 _____, personally appeared before me _____, personally known or sufficiently identified to me, who certifies that

residing at _____

_____ (is) (are) the individual(s) who executed the foregoing instrument and acknowledge it to be _____ free act and deed.

_____

_____
                                    (Notary Public)

CORPORATE CERTIFICATION

(To be made by an officer other than the one who executes the power of attorney)

I, _____, certify that I am the _____

of _____, organized under the laws of the State of _____

that _____, who signed this power of attorney on behalf of the donor, is the _____

of said corporation; and that said power of attorney was duly signed, sealed, and attested for and in behalf of said corporation by authority of its governing body as the

same appears in a resolution of the Board of Directors passed at a regular meeting held on the _____ day of _____, now in my possession or custody. I further

certify that the resolution is in accordance with the articles of incorporation and bylaws of said corporation.

IN WITNESS WHEREOF, I have hereunto set my hand and affixed the seal of said corporation, at the City of _____ this _____ day of

_____, 19 _____.

_____
(Signature)

_____
(Date)

If the corporation has no corporate seal, the fact shall be stated, in which case a scroll or adhesive shall appear in the appropriate, designated place.

Customs powers of attorney of residents (including resident corporations) shall be without power of substitution except for the purpose of executing shipper's export

declarations. However, a power of attorney executed in favor of a licensed customhouse broker may specify that the power of attorney is granted to the customhouse

broker to act through any of its licensed officers or any employee specifically authorized to act for such customhouse broker by power of attorney.

If you are the importer of record, payment to the broker will not relieve you of liability for Customs charges in the event the charges are not paid by the broker.

Therefore, if you pay by check, Customs charges may be paid with a separate check payable to the "U.S. Customs Service."

Importers who wish to utilize this procedure must contact our office in advance to arrange timely receipt of duty checks.

All transactions subject to the terms and conditions approved by the National Customs Brokers and Forwarders Association of America, Inc.

*NOTE: The corporate seal may be omitted. Customs does not require completion of a certification. The grantor has the option of executing the certification or omitting it.

GPO 1970 OL-374-079
GPO 945-705

FORM NO. S-NA-002-0485-RP

DEPARTMENT OF THE TREASURY
UNITED STATES CUSTOMS SERVICE

Approved through 4/30/89
OMS No. 1515-0164

U.S. - CANADA FREE TRADE AGREEMENT
EXPORTER'S CERTIFICATE OF ORIGIN

19 CFR 10.307(d)

1. GOODS CONSIGNED FROM (Exporter's business name, address, country, tax identification number)	2. IF BLANKET CERTIFICATION
	EFFECTIVE DATE
	EXPIRATION DATE
3. GOODS CONSIGNED TO (Consignee's name, address, country)	4. PRODUCER'S NAME, ADDRESS, COUNTRY, TAX IDENTIFICATION NUMBER (if different from exporter)

5. ORIGIN CRITERIA FOR GOODS COVERED BY THIS CERTIFICATE.

A. Wholly produced or obtained in Canada or the United States; or

B. The goods have been transformed in the United States or Canada so as to be subject:
   1) to change in tariff classification as described in the Rules of Annex 301.2; or
   2) to a change in tariff classification as described in the Rules of Annex 301.2 and the value of originating materials plus the direct cost of processing in Canada or the United States is not less than 50 percent or, as required by Section VI Rule 15 of Annex 301.2, 70 percent of the value of exported goods; or
   3) to Rule 5, Section XII of Annex 301.2; or

C. No change in tariff classification because goods and parts are provided for in the same tariff subheading or goods were imported in unassembled or disassembled form and were classified pursuant to General Rule of Interpretation 2a) of the Harmonized System, and the value of originating materials plus the direct cost of assembly in Canada or the United States is not less than 50 percent of the value of exported goods.

6. SPECIAL DECLARATION FOR TEXTILE PRODUCTS SUBJECT TO TARIFF RATE QUOTA:

A. Apparel goods cut and sewn in Canada or the United States from fabric produced or obtained in a third country.

B. Non-wool fabric and non-wool made-up textile articles, woven or knitted in Canada from yarn produced or obtained in a third country.

7. Origin Criterion (See Fields 5 or 6)	8. Description of Goods	Tariff Classification (To Six Digits)	9. Gross Weight or Other Quantity	10. Invoice Number(s) & Date(s)

11. CERTIFICATION OR ORIGIN

I certify that the information and statements herein are correct, that all the goods were produced in Canada or the United States, that they comply with the origin requirements specified for those goods in the United States-Canada Free Trade Agreement, and that further processing or assembly in a third country has not occurred subsequent to processing or assembly in Canada or the United States.

I agree to maintain, and present upon request, the documentation to support this certification and, if this is a blanket certification, to inform the importer or other appropriate party of any change that would affect the validity of this certification.

This certificate consists of _____ pages.

PLACE AND DATE	AUTHORIZED SIGNATURE	TITLE

REORDER NO. G-084-1288

Customs Form 353 (120188)

INFORMATION FOR THE
COMPLETION OF THE
EXPORTER'S CERTIFICATE OF ORIGIN

Paperwork Reduction Act Notice: The Paperwork Reduction Act of 1980 says we must tell you why we are collecting this information, how we will use it and whether you have to give it to us. We ask for the information to carry out the terms of Annex 406 of the U.S./Canadian Free Trade Agreement and the Statement of Administrative Action for the implementing legislation (P.L. 100-449). Annex 406 requires that, upon request, an importer must provide the Customs Administration of the Party (U.S./Canada) with proof of the exporter's written certification of the origin of the goods. The exporter's certification, provided for in the Agreement, is essential to substantiate compliance with the rules of origin under the Agreement. You are required to give us this information.

Statement Required by 5 CFR 1320.21: The estimated average burden associated with this collection of information is 20 minutes per respondent or recordkeeper depending on individual circumstances. Comments concerning the accuracy of this burden estimate and suggestions for reducing this burden should be directed to U.S. Customs Service, Paperwork Management Branch, Washington, DC 20229, and to the Office of Information and Regulatory Affairs, Office of Management and Budget, Washington, DC 20503, attention Desk Officer for U.S. Customs Service.

FIELD

1. Complete with the full legal name, address, country and tax identification number.

2. Complete with the effective and expiration dates (Maximum 6 months),[1] if this certificate is to cover multiple FTA qualified shipments to the same importer. NOTE: it is the exporter's responsibility to notify everyone to whom a blanket certificate is issued if changes occur in materials, costs, or production sites that would materially affect the accuracy or validity of the certification during the period. Failure to do so could make the exporter subject to penalties.

3. Complete with the consignee's full legal name, address, and country, or importer of record.

4. Complete with the full legal name, address, country and if known, the tax identification number. This field is to be completed **only** if the exporter is **not** the producer of the goods. If more than one producer's goods are included in a single or blanket certificate, attach a numbered list of the additional producers, indicate the appropriate producer's number in parenthesis after the origin criteria in Field 7.

5. Fields 5 and 6 reflect the various origin criteria by which exported goods may be eligible for FTA treatment, and are to be identified in Field 7 for each corresponding item listed in Field 8.

5.A. Indicate this criterion if the goods are wholly produced or obtained in Canada or U.S. as defined in Article 304 of the Agreement.

5.B.1. Requires that a change in the tariff classification take place along with any other requirements, other than value-added, as described in the Rules of Annex 301.2 of the Agreement.

5.B.2. Also requires that a change in tariff classification take place. Additionally, it requires that the value of domestic materials and direct cost of processing, as described in the Rules of Annex 301.2, be either 50 or 70 percent, as specified in the Rules of Annex 301.2, of the value of the exported good.[2]

5.B.3. This field does not require that a change in tariff classification take place but other requirements as described in the Rules of Annex 301.2, other than value-added, be met.[2]

5.C. This criterion does not require that a change in tariff classification take place but requires that the value of domestic materials and direct cost of assesmbly is not less than 50 percent of the value of exported goods. The provisions of this criterion are in accordance with paragraphs 3, 4, and 5 of the Interpretation of Annex 301.2 of the Agreement. The imported components from which the goods were produced in Canada must have constituted an unassembled or disasembled article as per the General Rule of interpretation 2 (a) of the Harmonized System, or the tariff subheading for the imported components must have provided for both the goods and their parts.

6. The special declarations for textile products are identified for use in Field 7.

7. Indicate the origin criterion selected from Fields 5 or 6 for each corresponding item listed in Field 8. If more than one article for export is covered by this certificate, the origin criterion for each is required. If necessary, a continuation sheet may be used to list the articles for export and their respective criteria. If more than one producer (Field 4) is identified, indicate next to the criteria the producer number assigned; e.g. 5.A.(3).

8. Fully describe the goods. If more than one article for export is covered by this certificate, a complete description of each article is required. The tariff classification, to six digits, of each article for export is required beside each description.

9. Indicate the gross weight or other pertinent qualities, as described on the invoice(s) or purchase order, of each good listed in Field 8, if this is a blanket certificate, indicate the contracted for weight or other quantity anticipated or contracted for during the blanket certification period, if known.

10. Indicate the invoice number(s) and date(s) for each item being shipped. If this is a blanket certificate, this field need not be completed.

11. Self-explanatory. The number of pages the certificate comprises must be indicated. NOTE: Unless the place, date, signature and title of the exporter appear on the space provided, this document will be considered invalid.

Note: Where the certificate or instructions makes reference to "Canada or the United States" or "domestic", this is to be interpreted as meaning either Canada or the United States or both.

[1] Canada will accept blanket exporter certificates with a validity period of twelve months; the United States will accept a validity period of six months.

[2] Canada requires the exporter to indicate the specific rule which the goods qualify; the United States simply requires an indication of the criterion.

SAMPLE CONFIRMING BANK COVER LETTER

BayBank Boston

SWIFT Address: BAYB US 33
Telex Address: 921840
Answerback: BayBank BSN

MAIL TO

High Technology Export, Inc.
Industrial Park Road
Cambridge, MA   02138

Our Reference	XC-14672
Correspondent's L/C No.	24688
Amount	$25,000.00

Gentlemen:

This letter is an integral part of the above referenced credit. Please be guided by the clauses marked "X".

1. (x) At the request of our correspondent we enclose herewith the original Letter of Credit mentioned above issued in your favor.

2. ( ) This Letter of Credit is being forwarded to you at the request of our correspondent and conveys no engagement by us.

3. (x) At the request of our correspondent, we confirm this Credit and any subsequent amendments thereto (unless otherwise specified) and thereby undertake that all drafts drawn in accordance with the terms thereof will be duly honored on presentation.

4. ( ) At the request of our correspondent, we enclose amendment to their Letter of Credit established in your favor. Please acknowledge your agreement by signing and returning to us the attached copy of this Letter.

5. ( ) We are in receipt of a telegraphic advice from our correspondent, which reads as follows:

IMPORTANT: Telegraphic advices are subject to errors in transmission and it is understood that such advices forwarded to you are subject to change unless otherwise specified above. Documents presented must comply exactly with conditions described in credit.

This credit is subject to the Uniform Customs and Practice for Documentary Credits (1974 Revision) International Chamber of Commerce Publication 290.

Very truly yours,

_____ _____
Authorized Signature   Date

Irrevocable Documentary Letter of Credit

FIRST BANK OF TAIWAN
10 CHUNG KUNG ROAD
KEELUNG, TAIWAN

☐ This credit was pre-advised telegraphically

SAMPLE EXPORT LETTER OF CREDIT

Credit Number: Of Issuing Bank	Of Advising Bank	Date
LC 24683		June 29, 1987

Advising Bank	Applicant
BayBank Boston, N.A. 175 Federal Street Boston, MA 02110	Overseas Import Company P. O. Box 378, 3 Park Road Keelung, Taiwan

Beneficiary	Amount
High Technology Export, Inc. Industrial Park Road Cambridge, MA 02138	$25,000 (Twenty-five thousand and 00/100 U. S. Dollars) Latest date for negotiation August 31, 1987

We hereby issue this documentary letter of credit in your favor which is available for negotiation of your draft at:
SIGHT

drawn on First Bank of Taiwan bearing the clause "Drawn under Letter of Credit No. 24683, dated June 29, 1987 accompanied by the following documents.

1. Commercial Invoice, CIF Keelung, Taiwan, 1 original and 4 copies
2. Insurance Certificate
3. Inspection Certificate signed by Bureau Veritas
4. Full set Clean on Board Ocean Bill of Lading made out to order and blank endorsed notify buyer, marked Freight Paid, dated no later than August 8, 1987, plus 3 non-negotiable copies

Covering 100% of invoice value of 10 digital telecommunications test instruments, Model #874, as per pro forma invoice #4326, dated June 4, 1987

Shipment from Boston to Keelung, Taiwan	Partial shipments are not permitted. Transshipments are permitted.

All charges except ours are for beneficiary's account. We suggest negotiating bank forward us all documents in one mailing.

WE UNDERTAKE THAT DRAFTS DRAWN AND PRESENTED IN CONFORMITY WITH THE TERMS OF THIS CREDIT WILL BE DULY HONOURED.

INSTRUCTIONS TO THE NEGOTIATING BANK
The amount of each drawing must be endorsed on the reverse hereof.
Drafts accompanied by a certificate from the negotiating bank that all terms and conditions of this credit have been complied with, are to be forwarded to the drawee bank.

INSTRUCTIONS TO THE ADVISING BANK
Please complete and forward to beneficiary the attached original advice without adding your confirmation.

Authorized Signature

Remarks, Place, Date, Name and Signature of Advising Bank

BayBank Boston, N.A.
175 Federal Street
Boston, MA 02110

Form No.

This credit is subject to the Uniform Customs and Practice for Documentary Credits (1974 Revision), International Chamber of Commerce Publication ...

To: ⌐   ⌐

BayBank Boston, N.A.
International Department
175 Federal Street
Boston, Massachusetts 02110, U.S.A.
SWIFT Address: BAYB US 33, Telex 921840

⌐   ⌐

☐ Please enter for collection as if received
direct from *BayBank Boston, N.A.*

☐ We enclose for collection

Date: _____

REFERENCE NUMBER
D 17527

the attached draft with documents described below,
subject to the Uniform Rules for Collections I.C.C. Pub. No. 322.

COMMODITY

DATE OF DRAFT	DRAFT NUMBER	TENOR	AMOUNT	PER S/S

Drawee: _____

Drawer: _____

DRAFTS ORIG. DUP.	NEGOTIABLE BILLS OF LADING ORIG. DUP. TRIP	NON-NEGO. B/L	CONSULAR INVOICES	INSURANCE CTFS. ORIG. DUP.	INVOICES ORIG. DUPL. TRIP	INSP. CERTIF	WEIGHT CERTIF.	CERTIF. OF ORIGIN	PARCEL POST RECEIPTS	MISCELLANEOUS

	DRAWEE'S EXPENSE	DRAWER'S EXPENSE	
MAIL DOCUMENTS	DRAWEE'S EXPENSE	DRAWER'S EXPENSE	IN CASE OF NEED, REFER TO: (IF AGENT, SPECIFY HIS AUTHORITY)
DELIVER DOCUMENTS AGAINST	ACCEPTANCE	PAYMENT	NAME:
PRESENT ON ARRIVAL OF VESSEL(S) CARRYING GOODS			ADDRESS:
PROTEST	NON-ACCEPTANCE	NON-PAYMENT	
NO PROTEST			WHO IS AUTHORIZED TO GIVE INSTRUCTIONS WHICH MAY BE FOLLOWED:

SPECIAL NOTICE: ADVISE BY:

OF: ☐ NON-ACCEPTANCE ☐ ACCEPTANCE   AIR MAIL NON-PAYMENT   CABLE PAYMENT

☐ IN EVERY RESPECT ☐ WITH THE EXCEPTION OF:

☐ WHO IS AUTHORIZED TO OBTAIN HONORING OF DRAFT AS DRAWN ONLY.

	DRAWEE'S EXPENSE	DRAWER'S EXPENSE
INCUR NO CABLE EXPENSE		
FOREIGN BANK CHARGE	DRAWEE'S EXPENSE	DRAWER'S EXPENSE
YOUR CHARGES	DRAWEE'S EXPENSE	DRAWER'S EXPENSE
DO NOT WAIVE CHARGES		
WAIVE CHARGES IF REFUSED BY DRAWEE		
REMIT PROCEEDS BY AIR MAIL	DRAWEE'S EXPENSE	DRAWER'S EXPENSE
REMIT PROCEEDS BY CABLE	DRAWEE'S EXPENSE	DRAWER'S EXPENSE

Special Instructions:

INTEREST TO BE COLLECTED AT _____ % PER ANNUM FROM DATE OF ISSUE UNTIL APPROXIMATE DATE OF ARRIVAL OF COVER IN

INTEREST TO BE COLLECTED AT _____ % PER ANNUM FOR ANY DELAY IN PAYMENT.

IN THE EVENT U.S. DOLLAR COVER IS NOT IMMEDIATELY OBTAINABLE A PROVISIONAL DEPOSIT IN LOCAL CURRENCY MAY BE ACCEPTED UNDER DRAWEE'S WRITTEN OBLIGATION TO ASSUME ALL EXCHANGE RISKS.

Remit Proceeds to us
☐ By Check   ☐ By Crediting Our Account.

Firm: _____

_____
OFFICER AND TITLE — AUTHORIZED SIGNATURE REQUIRED

$ _____ *Boston, Massachusetts* _____ No. _____
Amount   *Date*

_____ *Pay to the order of*

BayBank Boston, N.A.

_____ *Dollars*

Value received and charge the same to the account of

To _____

_____

Authorized Signature

EXPORT QUOTATION WORKSHEET

UNITRAK®

DATE _____ REF/PRO FORMA INVOICE NO. _____

COMMODITY _____ EXPECTED SHIP DATE _____

CUSTOMER _____ PACKED DIMENSIONS _____

COUNTRY _____ PACKED WEIGHT _____

PAYMENT TERMS _____ PACKED CUBE _____

PRODUCTS TO BE SHIPPED FROM _____

TO _____

SELLING PRICE OF GOODS: $ _____

SPECIAL EXPORT PACKING:

$ _____ quoted by _____

$ _____ quoted by _____

$ _____ quoted by _____ $ _____

INLAND FREIGHT:

$ _____ quoted by _____

$ _____ quoted by _____

$ _____ quoted by _____ $ _____

Inland freight includes the following charges:

☐ unloading   ☐ pier delivery   ☐ terminal   ☐ . _____

OCEAN FREIGHT			AIR FREIGHT		
	quoted by	tariff item		quoted by	spec code
$ _____	_____	# ____	$ _____	_____	# ____
$ _____	_____	# ____	$ _____	_____	# ____
$ _____	_____	# ____	$ _____	_____	# ____

Ocean freight includes the following surcharges:

☐ Port congestion   ☐ Heavy lift

☐ Currency adjustment   ☐ Bunker

☐ Container rental   ☐ Wharfage

☐ _____   ☐ _____

☐ INSURANCE   ☐ includes war risk

rate: _____ per $100 or $ _____

TOTAL OCEAN CHARGES $ _____

notes:

Air freight includes the following surcharges:

☐ Fuel adjustment

☐ Container stuffing

☐ _____

☐ INSURANCE   ☐ includes war risk

rate: _____ per $100 or $ _____

TOTAL AIR CHARGES $ _____ $ _____

notes:

FORWARDING FEES: $ _____

Includes: ☐ Courier Fees   ☐ Certification Fees   ☐ Banking Fees   ☐ _____

CONSULAR LEGALIZATION FEES: $ _____

INSPECTION FEES: $ _____

DIRECT BANK CHARGES: $ _____

OTHER CHARGES: _____ $ _____

_____ $ _____

TOTAL: ☐ FOB _____   ☐ C&F _____

☐ FAS _____   ☐ CIF _____ $ _____

PROFORMA INVOICE/EXPORT ORDER

UNITRAK®

SHIPPER:	IN-HOUSE ORDER NO. — DATE
	PRO FORMA INVOICE NO. — DATE
CUSTOMER:	COMMERCIAL INVOICE NO. — DATE
	CUSTOMER PURCHASE ORDER NO. — DATE
	CUSTOMER ACCOUNT NO.
SHIP TO (If different than Customer):	PURCHASER'S NAME — TITLE
	SHIP VIA — EST. SHIP DATE
NOTIFY (Intermediate Consignee):	TELEPHONE NO.
	TELEX/FAX/CABLE NO.

PART NUMBER	UNIT OF MEASURE	QUANTITY	DESCRIPTION	UNIT PRICE	TOTAL PRICE

SPECIAL INSTRUCTIONS:

ADDITIONAL CHARGES

FREIGHT ☐ Ocean ☐ Air _____

CONSULAR/LEGALIZATION _____

INSPECTION/CERTIFICATION _____

SPECIAL PACKING _____

_____ _____

_____ _____

TERMS OF PAYMENT

☐ LETTER OF CREDIT Bank _____

☐ DRAFT Terms _____

☐ OPEN ACCOUNT Terms _____

☐ OTHER _____

CURRENCY OF PAYMENT _____

PROFORMA INVOICE

DIRECT COLLECTION

BANK OF NEW ENGLAND, N.A.

INTERNATIONAL DIVISION
BOSTON, MASSACHUSETTS, U.S.A.
Direct Collection Form
TELEX 940191   CABLE BKNE INT, BSN
SWIFT: BNEW US 33

ATTACH THIS COPY TO SHIPPING DOCUMENTS

Via Airmail To —

DATE_____

REFER TO COLLECTION

No. DICOL 32953

We enclose the following draft and documents for collection in accordance with the instructions shown below. Please accept this collection FOR ACCOUNT OF **BANK OF NEW ENGLAND, N.A.** as if received directly from them and SEND PAYMENT, ALL REPORTS, AND YOUR ACKNOWLEDGEMENT TO **BANK OF NEW ENGLAND, N.A., ATTN. INTERNATIONAL DIVISION COLLECTION DEPARTMENT, P.O. BOX 2197, BOSTON, MASS 02106,** MENTIONING THE COLLECTION NO. SHOWN ABOVE SUBJECT TO UNIFORM RULES FOR THE COLLECTION OF COMMERCIAL PAPER (1979 REVISION) INTERNATIONAL CHAMBER OF COMMERCE, BROCHURE NO. 322 AS AMENDED.

DRAWER'S REFERENCE NUMBER	DATE OF DRAFT	TENOR	AMOUNT

DRAWER AND ADDRESS	DRAWEE AND ADDRESS

BILL OF LADING ORIG	DUP	PARCEL POST RECEIPTS	INSUR. CERT'S.	INVOICES	CONSULAR INVOICES	PACKING LISTS	WEIGHT CERT'S.	CERT'S. OF ORIGIN	OTHER DOCUMENTS

DELIVER DOCUMENTS AGAINST	ACCEPTANCE	PAYMENT	ALL CHARGES INCLUDING STAMPS, EXCHANGE, TAXES, ETC. FOR DRAWEE'S ACCOUNT PLUS BANK OF NEW ENGLAND, N.A. CHARGE OF
ADVISE BY CABLE	NON-ACCEPTANCE	NON-PAYMENT	
REMIT PROCEEDS BY CABLE	DRAWEE'S EXPENSE	DRAWER'S EXPENSE	
REMIT PROCEEDS BY AIRMAIL			WAIVE CHARGES IF REFUSED
PROTEST	NON-ACCEPTANCE	NON-PAYMENT	DO NOT WAIVE CHARGES
DO NOT PROTEST			HOLD FOR ARRIVAL OF MERCHANDISE

IF DOLLAR EXCHANGE IS NOT IMMEDIATELY AVAILABLE AT MATURITY (OR ON PRESENTATION IF DRAWN AT SIGHT) AND IT IS NECESSARY TO PROVISIONALLY ACCEPT LOCAL CURRENCY PENDING AVAILABILITY OF DOLLAR EXCHANGE, IT MUST BE DISTINCTLY UNDERSTOOD THAT THE DRAWEE SHALL REMAIN LIABLE FOR ALL EXCHANGE DIFFERENCES. AT TIME OF DEPOSIT OF LOCAL CURRENCY OBTAIN FROM DRAWEES THEIR WRITTEN UNDERTAKING TO BE RESPONSIBLE FOR ANY EXCHANGE DIFFERENCES. THE DRAFT MUST NOT BE SURRENDERED TO DRAWEES UNTIL PAYMENT FOR FACE AMOUNT IN U.S. DOLLAR EXCHANGE.

ALLOW A DISCOUNT OF	IF PAID
COLLECT INTEREST AT THE RATE OF	% FROM

IN CASE OF NEED REFER TO		WHO IS EMPOWERED BY US: TO ACT FULLY ON OUR BEHALF I.E. AUTHORIZE REDUCTIONS, EXTENSIONS, FREE DELIVERY, WAIVING OF PROTESTS ETC.	WHO MAY ASSIST IN OBTAINING ACCEPTANCE OR PAYMENT OF DRAFT, AS DRAWN, BUT IS NOT TO ALTER ITS TERMS IN ANY WAY.

SPECIAL INSTRUCTIONS: IF YOU DO NOT MAINTAIN AN ACCOUNT WITH US, PAY BE TELEX TO CONNECTICUT BANK INTERNATIONAL, NEW YORK FOR CREDIT TO BANK OF NEW ENGLAND, BOSTON, QUOTING OUR DICOL REFERENCE.

FROM_____
(DRAWER'S NAME)

_____
AUTHORIZED SIGNATURE

$_____   DATE_____NO._____

DAYS AFTER   of this SOLE BILL OF EXCHANGE

pay   to   the   order   of   BANK   OF   NEW   ENGLAND,   N.A.

Value received and charge the same to account of _____

To_____

_____

FORM **7525-V** (1-1-88)   **SHIPPER'S EXPORT DECLARATION**   OMB No. 0607-0018

1a. EXPORTER *(Name and address including ZIP code)*

ZIP CODE

2. DATE OF EXPORTATION

3. BILL OF LADING/AIR WAYBILL NO.

b. EXPORTER'S EIN (IRS) NUMBER

c. PARTIES TO TRANSACTION

☐ Related   ☐ Non-related

4a. ULTIMATE CONSIGNEE

b. INTERMEDIATE CONSIGNEE

5. FORWARDING AGENT

6. POINT (STATE) OF ORIGIN OR FTZ NO.

7. COUNTRY OF ULTIMATE DESTINATION

8. LOADING PIER *(Vessel Only)*

9. MODE OF TRANSPORT *(Specify)*

10. EXPORTING CARRIER

11. PORT OF EXPORT

12. PORT OF UNLOADING *(Vessel and Air Only)*

13. CONTAINERIZED *(Vessel only)*

☐ Yes   ☐ No

14. SCHEDULE B DESCRIPTION OF COMMODITIES, *(Use columns 17-19)*

15. MARKS, NOS., AND KINDS OF PACKAGES

VALUE (U.S. dollars, omit cents) *(Selling price or cost if not sold)*

D/F (16)	SCHEDULE B NUMBER (17)	CHECK DIGIT	QUANTITY – SCHEDULE B UNIT(S) (18)	SHIPPING WEIGHT *(Kilos)* (19)	(20)

21. VALIDATED LICENSE NO./GENERAL LICENSE SYMBOL

22. ECCN *(When required)*

23. Duly authorized officer or employee

The exporter authorizes the forwarder named above to act as forwarding agent for export control and customs purposes.

24. I certify that all statements made and all information contained herein are true and correct and that I have read and understand the instructions for preparation of this document, set forth in the "**Correct Way to Fill Out the Shipper's Export Declaration.**" I understand that civil and criminal penalties, including forfeiture and sale, may be imposed for making false or fraudulent statements herein, failing to provide the requested information or for violation of U.S. laws on exportation (13 U.S.C. Sec. 305; 22 U.S.C. Sec. 401; 18 U.S.C. Sec. 1001; 50 U.S.C. App. 2410).

Signature

Title

Date

Confidential - For use solely for official purposes authorized by the Secretary of Commerce (13 U.S.C. 301 (g)).

Export shipments are subject to inspection by U.S. Customs Service and/or Office of Export Enforcement.

25. AUTHENTICATION *(When required)*

The "**Correct Way to Fill Out the Shipper's Export Declaration**" is available from the Bureau of the Census, Washington, D.C. 20230.

SHIPPER'S LETTER OF INSTRUCTIONS

1a. EXPORTER *(Name and address including ZIP code)*

ZIP CODE

b. EXPORTER'S EIN (IRS) NO.

c. PARTIES TO TRANSACTION
☐ Related ☐ Non-related

4a. ULTIMATE CONSIGNEE

b. INTERMEDIATE CONSIGNEE

5. FORWARDING AGENT

Myers Airspeed • Myers Maritime (FMC 710-R) divisions of F.W. MYERS & CO., INC.

8. LOADING PIER *(Vessel only)*	**9. MODE OF TRANSPORT** *(Specify)*
10. EXPORTING CARRIER	**11. PORT OF EXPORT**
12. PORT OF UNLOADING *(Vessel and air only)*	**13. CONTAINERIZED** *(Vessel only)* ☐ Yes ☐ No

SHIPPER REQUESTS INSURANCE ☐ No ☐ Yes $

SHIPPER: PLEASE BE SURE TO COMPLETE ALL BLUE SHADED AREAS.

☐ ☐
MYERS AIRSPEED • MYERS MARITIME (FMC 710-R)
divisions of
F.W. MYERS & CO., INC.

SHIPPER MUST CHECK

☐ PREPAID ☐ COLLECT C.O.D. $_____

☐ AIR ☐ OCEAN ☐ CONSOLIDATE ☐ DIRECT

SHIPPER'S INSTRUCTIONS IN CASE OF INABILITY TO DELIVER CONSIGNMENT

AS ASSIGNED ☐ ABANDON ☐ RETURN TO SHIPPER

☐ DELIVER TO

14. SCHEDULE B DESCRIPTION OF COMMODITIES,
15. MARKS, NOS., AND KINDS OF PACKAGES } *(Use columns 17—19)*

D/F (16)	SCHEDULE B NUMBER (17)	CHECK DIGIT	QUANTITY – SCHEDULE B UNIT(S) (18)	SHIPPING WEIGHT (Kilos) (19)

SHIPPER'S REF. NO. | **DATE**

SHIPPER NOTE:

IF YOU ARE UNCERTAIN OF THE SCHEDULE B COMMODITY NO. DO NOT TYPE IT IN – WE WILL COMPLETE WHEN PROCESSING THE 7525V.

WE HAVE FORWARDED TO YOU, THE SHIPMENT DESCRIBED BELOW VIA:

☐ YOUR TRUCK, OR

☐ OTHER CARRIER (LISTED BELOW)

TRUCK LINE NAME_____

_____

RECEIPT (PRO) NUMBER____

_____

DECLARED VALUE FOR CARRIAGE
$

VALUE (U.S. dollars, omit cents)
(Selling price or cost if not sold)
(20)

21. VALIDATED LICENSE NO./GENERAL LICENSE SYMBOL

22. ECCN *(When required)*

PLEASE SIGN THE FIRST EXPORT DECLARATION IN BOX 23 WITH PEN AND INK.

23. Duly authorized officer or employee

The exporter authorizes the forwarder named above to act as forwarding agent for export control and customs purposes.

DOCUMENTS ENCLOSED:

24. I certify that all statements made and all information contained herein are true and correct and that I have read and understand the instructions for preparation of this document, set forth in the "**Correct Way to Fill Out the Shipper's Export Declaration.**" I understand that civil and criminal penalties, including forfeiture and sale, may be imposed for making false or fraudulent statements herein, failing to provide the requested information or for violation of U.S. laws on exportation (13 U.S.C. Sec. 305; 22 U.S.C. Sec. 401; 18 U.S.C. Sec. 1001; 50 U.S.C. App. 2410).

Signature

Confidential - For use solely for official purposes authorized by the Secretary of Commerce (13 U.S.C. 301 (g).

Title

Export shipments are subject to inspection by U.S. Customs Service and/or Office of Export Enforcement.

Date

25. AUTHENTICATION *(When required)*

SPECIAL INSTRUCTIONS:

NOTE: The Shipper or his Authorized Agent hereby authorizes the above named Company, in his name and on his behalf, to prepare any export documents, to sign and accept any documents relating to said shipment and forward this shipment in accordance with the conditions of carriage and the tariffs of the carriers employed. The shipper guarantees payment of all collect charges in the event the consignee refuses payment. Hereunder the sole responsibility of the Company is to use reasonable care in the selection of carriers, forwarders, agents and others to whom it may entrust the shipment.

COMMERCIAL INVOICE

SHIPPER/EXPORTER	

COMMERCIAL INVOICE NO.	DATE

CUSTOMER PURCHASE ORDER NO.	

COUNTRY OF ORIGIN	DATE OF EXPORT

CONSIGNEE

TERMS OF PAYMENT

NOTIFY: INTERMEDIATE CONSIGNEE

EXPORT REFERENCES

QUANTITY	DESCRIPTION OF MERCHANDISE	UNIT PRICE	TOTAL VALUE

PACKAGE MARKS:

MISC. CHARGES (Packing, Insurance, etc.)

INVOICE TOTAL

CERTIFICATIONS

_____

AUTHORIZED SIGNATURE

PACKING LIST

Shipper: ....19........

                                  Place and Date of Shipment

                          Reference No. _____

Consignee:

Under your Order No...the material listed below

                via

Shipment consists of:	Marks
........Cases............Packages	
........Crates............Cartons	
........Bbls.............Drums	
........Reels..........................	

*LEGAL WEIGHT IS WEIGHT OF ARTICLE PLUS PAPER, BOX, BOTTLE, ETC., CONTAINING THE ARTICLE AS USUALLY CARRIED IN STOCK.

Pkg No.	GROSS WEIGHT EACH	*LEGAL WEIGHT EACH	NET WEIGHT EACH	HEIGHT	WIDTH	LENGTH	QUANTITY	CLEARLY STATE CONTENTS OF EACH PACKAGE
	WEIGHTS IN LBS. or KILOS			DIMENSIONS				

Form 35-585 ©, 1986 *UNZ&CO* 190 Baldwin Ave., Jersey City, NJ 07306 • (800) 631-3098 • (201) 795-5400

(SPACES IMMEDIATELY BELOW ARE FOR SHIPPERS MEMORANDA—NOT PART OF DOCK RECEIPT)

DELIVERING CARRIER TO STEAMER:

CAR NUMBER—REFERENCE

FORWARDING AGENT—REFERENCES

EXPORT DEC. No.

DOCK RECEIPT
NON-NEGOTIABLE

SHIPPER

| SHIP | VOYAGE NO. | FLAG | PIER | PORT OF LOADING |

FOR. PORT OF DISCHARGE *(Where goods are to be delivered to consignee or on-carrier)*   For TRANSSHIPMENT TO *(If goods are to be transshipped or forwarded at port of discharge)*

PARTICULARS FURNISHED BY SHIPPER OF GOODS

MARKS AND NUMBERS	No. of PKGS.	DESCRIPTION OF PACKAGES AND GOODS	MEASURE-MENT	GROSS WEIGHT

DIMENSIONS AND WEIGHTS OF PACKAGES TO BE SHOWN ON REVERSE SIDE

DELIVERED BY:

RECEIVED THE ABOVE DESCRIBED MERCHANDISE FOR SHIPMENT AS INDICATED HEREON, SUBJECT TO ALL CONDITIONS OF THE UNDERSIGNED'S USUAL FORM OF DOCK RECEIPT AND BILL OF LADING. COPIES OF THE UNDERSIGNED'S USUAL FORM OF DOCK RECEIPT AND BILL OF LADING MAY BE OBTAINED FROM THE MASTER OF THE VESSEL, OR THE VESSEL'S AGENT

LIGHTER }
TRUCK } ....

ARRIVED— DATE .... TIME ....

UNLOADED— DATE .... TIME ....

AGENT FOR MASTER

CHECKED BY ....

BY ....
RECEIVING CLERK

PLACED IN SHIP ON DOCK LOCATION ....

DATE ....

SHIPPERS ARE REQUESTED TO FILL OUT AS BELOW
WHICH WILL ENABLE US TO VERIFY CORRECTNESS OF SAME AND AVOID ALL DISPUTES
EXCEPT IF ANY ONE PACKAGE WEIGHS 4,480 LBS. OR OVER, THEN
WEIGHT MUST BE MENTIONED SEPARATELY.

MARKS	No. of Pkge.	MEASUREMENTS						TOTAL Cubic Ft.		Gross Weight
		Length		Breadth		Depth				
		Ft.	In.	Ft.	In.	Ft.	In.	Ft.	In.	
Totals										

DELIVERING CARRIER TO STEAMER:	CAR NUMBER—REFERENCE
FORWARDING AGENT—REFERENCES	EXPORT DEC. No.

BILL OF LADING
(Conditions Continued from Reverse Side Hereof)

SHIPPER...

CONSIGNEE: ORDER OF...

ADDRESS ARRIVAL NOTICE TO	ALSO NOTIFY

SHIP	VOYAGE NO.	FLAG	PIER	PORT OF LOADING

FOR. PORT OF DISCHARGE (*Where goods are to be delivered to consignee or on-carrier*) | For TRANSSHIPMENT to (*If goods are to be transshipped or forwarded at port of discharge*)

PARTICULARS FURNISHED BY SHIPPER OF GOODS

MARKS AND NUMBERS	No. of PKGS.	DESCRIPTION OF PACKAGES AND GOODS	MEASURE-MENT	GROSS WEIGHT

FREIGHT PAYABLE IN

..................@.............PER 2240 LBS......$................		
..................@.............PER 100 LB........$................		
....FT.......IN. @.............PER 40 CU. FT.....$................		
....FT.......IN. @....PER CU. FT........$................		
....$................		
....$................		
....$................		
....$................		
TOTAL.........$................		

(CONDITIONS CONTINUED FROM REVERSE SIDE HEREOF)

IN WITNESS WHEREOF, THERE HAVE BEEN EXECUTED........
BILLS OF LADING, ALL OF THE SAME TENOR AND DATE, ONE OF WHICH
BEING ACCOMPLISHED, THE OTHERS TO STAND VOID.

BY...
FOR THE MASTER

ISSUED AT...
(DATE)

B/L No...

Form 35-084 ©, 1986 UNZ&CO 190 Baldwin Ave., Jersey City, NJ 07306 • (800) 631-3098 • (201) 795-5400

House Air Waybill Number

Shippers Name and Address | Shippers account Number

Not negotiable

Air Waybill
(Air Consignment note)
Issued by

Copies 1, 2 and 3 of this Air Waybill are originals and have the same validity

Consignee's Name and Address | Consignee's account Number

It is agreed that the goods described herein are accepted in apparent good order and condition (except as noted) for carriage SUBJECT TO THE CONDITIONS OF CONTRACT ON THE REVERSE HEREOF. THE SHIPPER'S ATTENTION IS DRAWN TO THE NOTICE CONCERNING CARRIERS' LIMITATION OF LIABILITY. Shipper may increase such limitation of liability by declaring a higher value for carriage and paying a supplemental charge if required.

These commodities licensed by the United States for ultimate destination

Diversion contrary to

United States law prohibited.

Airport of Departure (Addr. of first Carrier) and requested Routing

to	By first Carrier \ Routing and Destination /	Air Waybill Number	Currency	CHGS Code	WT/VAL PPD COLL	Other PPD COLL	Declared Value for Carriage	Declared Value for Customs

Airport of Destination	Flight/Date	For Carrier Use only / Flight/Date	Amount of Insurance	INSURANCE: If Carrier offers insurance and such insurance is requested in accordance with conditions on reverse hereof, indicate amount to be insured in figures in box marked "amount of insurance".

Handling Information

No. of Pieces RCP	Gross Weight	kg lb	Rate Class / Commodity Item No.	Chargeable Weight	Rate / Charge	Total	Nature and Quantity of Goods (incl. Dimensions or Volume)

Prepaid	Weight Charge	Collect	Other Charges
	Valuation Charge		
	Tax		
	Total other Charges Due Agent		Shipper certifies that the particulars on the face hereof are correct and that insofar as any part of the consignment contains dangerous goods, such part is properly described by name and is in proper condition for carriage by air according to the applicable Dangerous Goods Regulations.
	Total other Charges Due Carrier		
Total prepaid	Total collect		.... Signature of Shipper or his Agent
Currency Conversion Rates	cc charges in Dest. Currency		

Executed on (Date) at (Place) Signature of Issuing Carrier or its Agent

Form 16-810 ©, 1986 UNZ&CO 190 Baldwin Ave., Jersey City, NJ 07306 • (800) 631-3098 • (201) 795-5400

House Air Waybill Number

ORIGINAL 3 — FOR SHIPPER

INSURANCE CERTIFICATE

EXPORTER (Principal or seller-licensee and address including ZIP Code)		DOCUMENT NUMBER	B/L OR AWB NUMBER
		EXPORT REFERENCES	
	ZIP CODE		

CONSIGNED TO	FORWARDING AGENT (Name and address—references)
	POINT (STATE) OF ORIGIN OR FTZ NUMBER

NOTIFY PARTY/INTERMEDIATE CONSIGNEE (Name and address)	DOMESTIC ROUTING/EXPORT INSTRUCTIONS

PRE-CARRIAGE BY	PLACE OF RECEIPT BY PRE-CARRIER	
EXPORTING CARRIER	PORT OF LOADING/EXPORT	LOADING PIER/TERMINAL
FOREIGN PORT OF UNLOADING (Vessel and air only)	PLACE OF DELIVERY BY ON-CARRIER	TYPE OF MOVE	CONTAINERIZED (Vessel only) ☐ Yes ☐ No

MARKS AND NUMBERS	NUMBER OF PACKAGES	DESCRIPTION OF COMMODITIES in Schedule B detail	GROSS WEIGHT (Kilos)	MEASUREMENT	D OR F

DATE OF POLICY	SUM INSURED $	AMOUNT IN WORDS	DOLLARS

SPECIAL TERMS AND CONDITIONS: SHIPMENTS ON DECK or AIR CARGO when Insured Under this Policy are subject to terms and conditions specified on the reverse side hereof. SHIPMENTS SUBJECT TO AN "UNDER DECK" BILL OF LADING are Insured:-

THIS INSURANCE IS ALSO SUBJECT TO THE FOLLOWING AMERICAN INSTITUTE CLAUSES CURRENT ON THE DATE OF ISSUANCE OF THIS POLICY: **MARINE EXTENSION CLAUSES** **S.R. & C.C. ENDORSEMENT** **WAR RISK INSURANCE**	WHEN GOODS ARE SO DESTINED THIS INSURANCE IS SUBJECT TO:- **SOUTH AMERICAN 60 DAY CLAUSE**

This Policy not transferable unless countersigned by an authorized representative of this Company or the Assured.
Countersigned:

IN WITNESS WHEREOF, this Company has executed and attested these presents.

_____

Secretary   *President*

Form 80-340 Printed and Sold by UNZCO 190 Baldwin Ave.. Jersey City, NJ 07306 • (800) 631-3098 • (201) 795-5400

CERTIFICATE OF ORIGIN

The undersigned _____
_____
(Owner or Agent, or &c)

for _____ declares
(Name and Address of Shipper)

that the following mentioned goods shipped on S/S _____
(Name of Ship)

on the date of _____ consigned to _____
_____

_____ are the product of the United States of America.

MARKS AND NUMBERS	NO. OF PKGS., BOXES OR CASES	WEIGHT IN KILOS		DESCRIPTION
		GROSS	NET	

Sworn to before me

Dated at _____ on the _____ day of _____ 19 _____

this _____ day of _____ 19 _____

_____   _____
                                          (Signature of Owner or Agent)

The _____ , a recognized Chamber of Commerce under the laws of the State of

_____ , has examined the manufacturer's invoice or shipper's affidavit concerning the
origin of the merchandise and, according to the best of its knowledge and belief, finds that the products named originated in the
United States of North America.

Secretary _____

Form 10-900 ©, 1986 UNZCO 190 Baldwin Ave., Jersey City, NJ 07306 • (800) 631-3098 • (201) 795-5400

LETTER OF CREDIT INSTRUCTIONS

Date

Name

Company (exporter)

To (buyer)

Address

Telephone   FAX   Telex

Gentlemen:

Following are the particular details we wish to have included in your documentary Letter of Credit, issued in reply to our pro forma invoice number _____, dated _____.

Please instruct your bank to open and issue this credit in accordance with the folliwng terms and subject to the Uniform Customs and Practices (UCP) for Documentary Credits, International Chamber of Commerce Publication 400 (the internationally recognized set of rules and regulations that govern most letters of credit).

We have made every effort in these instructions to provide you with terms that can be easily accommodated. If you or your bank cannot comply with these terms and conditions, please consult with our offices prior to the issuance of the credit to avoid delay or nonshipment. Thank you for your cooperation.

1. The letter of credit shall be irrevocable (meaning that all parties must agree to any changes terms and conditions).

2. The credit shall be
( ) advised by (U.S. bank name & address)
( ) confirmed by

3. The credit shall be payable at

(name and address of exporter's bank or of the issuing bank's branch)

4. The credit shall show the beneficiary as
(identical name and address as shown on the L/C)

5. The credit shall be payable in _____, in the
amount _____ (currency)

6. The credit shall be payable
( ) at sight
( ) _____days from sight
( ) _____days from _____
upon presentation at the
counters of the bank named in item 3 above
(Note: "Payable at" spells out the timing and location
of payment. "At sight" means when the paying bank "sees"
the documents and completes its examination process,
generally 72 hours after presentation. The other options
allow you to set a specific number of days after sight,
invoice date, shipment or bill of lading date, or a
specific date.)

7. The credit shall show that all banking charges
incurred
(   ) inside the beneficiary's country
(   ) outside the beneficiary's country
are for the account of the applicant.
(Traditionally, each party pays "local" bank charges,
although this is subject to negotiation.)

8. The credit shall show that all charges for amendments
to the credit, including related communications
expenses, are for the acount of
(   ) applicant
(   ) beneficiary
(This stipulates which party is responsible for changes,
amendments, to the L/C. If you require the applicant to
pay the cost of amendments, it may encourage compliance
with your letter of credit instruction.)

9. Patial shipments
(   ) shall be allowed
(   ) shall not be allowed
(If it is necessary for you to make partial shipments,
this must be expressly stated in the letter of credit.)

10. Transshipments
( ) shall be allowed
( ) shall not be allowed
(Transshipment describes a situation in which your goods
are off-loaded from one carrier and placed on another
carrier, vessel or conveyance. If your shipment is
scheduled to be made to a port not serviced by shipping
lines sailing from the port of embarkation stated in the
L/C, you should allow transshipment. If transshipment is
not specified in a L/C, it assumed to be allowed.)

11. The credit shall allow for required transport
documents dated no later than _____.
(This allows you to stipulate the latest date that can
appear on the required transport documents.)

12. The credit shall allow for a minimum of _____ days
after receipt of required transport documents at the
counters of the bank stated in item 3 above.

(This timing may be important to assure that no undue
delays occur in the buyer's receipt of documents so that
the shipment may be cleared through customs. UCP 400
establishes this minimum at 21 days.)

13. If designated, the forwarder shall be shown as

14. If designated, the carrier shall be shown as

15. Special instructions:
(for any special conditions you wish to include)

Glossary of International Trade Terms and Expressions

Air Waybill Bill of lading that is a contract between the exporter and the airline for delivery of goods to a specified location. It is non-negotiable and serves as a receipt for the exporter, indicating that the air carrier has received the goods to be shipped. See also **Bill of Lading, Through.**

Balance of Trade The difference between a country's total exports and its total imports. A favorable balance exists if exports exceed imports; an unfavorable balance exists if imports exceed exports.

Bank, Advising Bank in the exporter's country that handles the letter of credit.

Bank, Correspondent The foreign buyer's bank.

Bank, Remitting Bank that sends a draft to the overseas bank for collection.

Barter Exchanging merchandise for merchandise rather than for cash.

Beneficiary The person in whose favor a letter of credit is issued or a draft is drawn.

Bill of Lading Contract between the owner of the goods and the carrier to move the goods to a specified destination.

Bill of Lading, Clean A receipt for goods that indicates that they were received in good condition (without visual damage or defect). It is usually issued by carrier who receives goods.

Bill of Lading, Inland A bill of lading used in transporting goods overland to the exporter's international carrier. Although a through bill of lading can be used in some situations, it is usually necessary to prepare both an inland bill of lading and an ocean bill of lading for export shipments.

Bill of Lading, Ocean Contract between the exporter and the ocean carrier to deliver the merchandise to a specified location. It is also proof that the cargo has been actually loaded on the vessel. These bills of lading may be purchased, sold, or traded while the shipment is in transit.

Bill of Lading, Through A single bill of lading covering both the domestic and international carriage of an export shipment. An air waybill is a through bill of lading. However, ocean shipments usually require two documents, an inland bill of lading for domestic carriage and an ocean bill of lading for international carriage.

Bonded Warehouse A warehouse authorized by customs officials for the storage of goods on which payment of duties is deferred until the goods are removed.

Booking An arrangement with a steamship company to load and carry a shipment.

C&F (Cost & Freight)   A price quoted C&F foreign port means that the exporter is responsible for all shipping charges until the merchandise reaches the foreign port (the buyer is responsible for insurance coverage).

C&I (Cost & Insurance)   A price quoted C&I means that the costs of the product and insurance are included in the quoted price. The buyer is responsible for freight to the named port of destination.

Carnet   A customs document which permits you to send or carry merchandise into a country duty- and tax-free (for a limited period of time, i.e., visit or trade show).

Cash in Advance   The foreign buyer pays for the merchandise *before* it is shipped. (This payment option offers the least amount of risk to the exporter.)

Certificate of Inspection   Certifies that the goods were in good condition immediately prior to shipment.

Certificate of Origin   A document that certifies the country of origin of the goods being shipped. Required by some countries for tariff purposes.

CIF (Cost Insurance Freight)   Same as C&F with insurance provided by the exporter.

Collection Papers   Documents such as the commercial invoice and bill of lading submitted to a buyer for the purpose of receiving payment for a shipment.

Commercial Attaché   Commerce expert on the diplomatic staff of his or her's country embassy or consulate.

Consignment   The exporter turns over goods to an agent and does not receive payment until they are sold.

Consular Declaration   A formal statement to the consul of a foreign country describing the goods to be shipped.

Convertible Currency   A currency that can be bought and sold for other currencies at will.

Credit, Deferred Payment   A type of letter of credit providing for payment some time after presentation of shipping documents by the exporter.

Credit, Documentary   An arrangement by banks for settling international commercial transactions. It is a written undertaking by a bank (issuing bank) given to the seller (beneficiary) at the request, and on the instructions, of the buyer (applicant) to pay at sight or at a determinable future date up to a stated sum of money, within a prescribed time limit and against stipulated documents such as a commercial invoice, certificate of origin, insurance certificate and a transport document of a type appropriate to the mode of transport used.

Customhouse Broker   An individual or firm licensed to enter and clear goods through customs.

Customs   The authorities who collect duties levied by a country on imports and exports. The term is also used to describe the procedures involved in duties collection.

Devaluation　Lowering the value of a country's currency on the international currency market (it is worth less in relation to foreign currencies than before).

Discrepancy　Documents presented do not conform to the letter of credit.

Dock Receipt　Issued by the ocean carrier acknowledging receipt of the goods to be shipped.

Draft　Contract between the buyer and seller that the buyer will pay the exporter a certain amount of money, within a prescribed time limit, for the goods specified in the commercial invoice.

Draft, Date　A payment option draft that matures in a specified number of days after the date it is issued (expiration does not depend on date of acceptance).

Draft, Demand or Sight　A draft which is payable upon presentation to the drawee. It is used when the exporter wishes to retain control of the shipment for credit reasons or for title retention. This instrument requires the buyer to pay the bank before receiving the documents to claim the goods (similar to a domestic COD transaction).

Draft, Time　Once a buyer has accepted the draft in writing, he must pay within a certain amount of time from the date of acceptance. (The exporter is really extending credit to the buyer because payment may be made after the goods are received.)

Drawee　Buyer in draft document.

Dumping　Exporting merchandise into a country at a price below the cost of production and shipment.

Duty　A tax imposed on imports by the customs authority of a country.

EC (European Community)　European Common Market—Belgium, Denmark, West Germany, France, Greece, Ireland, Italy, Luxembourg, the Netherlands, Portugal, Spain and the United Kingdom—the world's largest trading bloc.

EMC (Export Management Company)　A private firm that serves as the export department of several noncompetitive manufacturers for commission, salary, or retainer plus commission.

ETC (Export Trading Company)　A private firm that usually takes title to goods and offers a broad range of services to its manufacturing clients. The distinction between an EMC and an ETC is becoming blurred.

Eurodollars　U.S. dollars placed on deposit in banks outside the United States.

Ex　A price quoted "Ex Factory" or "Ex Dock" means the quoted price applies only at the point of origin, e.g., from the factory or the dock. In practice this quotation indicates that the seller agrees to place the goods at the disposal of the buyer at the specified place within a fixed period of time.

Eximbank (Export-Import Bank of the U.S.)　Agency that facilitates and aids in financing exports of U.S. products.

Export Broker　Brings foreign buyers and sellers together for a fee.

Export Declaration　Part of shipper's export documentation to be completed by exporter.

Export License   Required by law in order to export products, may be general (no paperwork necessary) or validated (must apply for special permission to export).

Export License, General   Any of various export licenses covering export commodities for which validated licenses are not required. A broad grant of authority by the government to U.S. exporters. No formal application or written authorization is needed to ship exports under a general export license.

Export License, Validated   A specific grant of authority to a particular exporter to export a particular product to a certain destination. The license is for a specific transaction or time period in which the exporting is to take place. An application must be made to the DOC's Office of Export Licensing.

Factoring Houses   Financial companies that purchase an exporter's accounts receivable at a discount.

FAS (Free Alongside)   A pricing term which means that the price quoted includes the cost of delivering goods alongside a designated vessel. A shipment delivered "alongside" is placed on the dock so that it can be loaded aboard the ship.

FCIA (Foreign Credit Insurance Association)   An Eximbank program that offers credit insurance which covers 100% of a company's losses from political conflict (war, currency inconvertibility) and up to 95% of commercial losses (buyer insolvency, default).

FOB (Free on Board)   A price quoted FOB at some location means that the buyer will be responsible for all charges incurred from that location on.

Foreign Sales Agent or Representative   Equivalent of a manufacturer's rep in the U.S. The agent or rep works on a commission and uses product literature and samples to present the product to potential buyers.

Free Trade Zone   A port designated by the government of a country for duty-free entry of goods. Products may be stored, displayed, used for manufacturing, serviced or repaired, repackaged without duties being paid. Duties are imposed only when the goods pass from the zone into an area of the country subject to customs jurisdiction.

Freight Forwarder   A freight forwarder arranges for transportation of your merchandise from a specified shipping point in the U.S. to a foreign port or to your customer's location overseas.

GATT (General Agreement on Tariffs and Trade)   Multilateral treaty whose object is to help reduce trade barriers between the signatory countries. GATT agreements establish general guidelines for the conduct of international trade, especially reductions in tariffs and other barriers. Its member nations account for about 80% of all international trade.

Gross Weight   The full weight of the shipment, including goods and packaging.

Harmonized System   Classification system for goods in international trade. Exporter puts the harmonized code for their product on the Shipper's Export Declaration.

Invoice, Commercial Document that is used for international transactions. It states the exporting company's name and address, buyer's name and address, contents of shipment, amount charged, name of carrying vessel, order number, and payment terms.

Invoice, Consular A document required by some countries describing the shipment.

Invoice, Pro Forma The exporter sends this invoice to the buyer to outline the terms of sale (description of merchandise, quantity, price, shipment requirements, date of shipment, conditions of payment).

Letter of Credit Document which is a promise that the buyer's bank will pay the exporter or the exporter's bank a specified amount of money upon receipt of certain documents. This payment method provides the exporter some protection in that the buyer must have a line of credit or collateral in order to get credit from the bank.

Letter of Credit, Confirmed The U.S. bank will guarantee payment if buyer's bank defaults when a letter of credit is confirmed.

Letter of Credit, Irrevocable Payment is guaranteed by the bank if all terms and conditions stated in the letter of credit are met.

Letter of Credit, Revocable A letter of credit that can be cancelled or altered by the buyer after is has been issued by the drawee's bank.

Marine Insurance Insurance for goods transported via ocean carrier.

Open Account A non-guaranteed payment arrangement whereby the exporter ships the merchandise, sends the necessary documents to the buyer and waits for payment.

Packing List A list showing the number and kinds of items being shipped, including weight, package dimensions, quantity of goods in each package and contents of shipment. It serves as a checklist that the correct cargo has been received and helps the buyer inventory the shipment.

SED (Shipper's Export Declaration) A form required by the U.S. Treasury Department indicating the value, weight, destination and other information about an export shipment.

SIC (Standard Industrial Classification) A standard numerical code system used by the U.S. Government to classify products and services.

SITC (Standard International Trade Classification) A standard numerical code system developed by the U.N. to classify commodities shipped in international trade.

Steamship Conference A group of steamship companies that uses mutually agreed freight rates.

Tare Weight The weight of the container and packing materials without the weight of the goods it contains.

Tariff A country's tax on imports. The term also refers to the rate at which a category of goods is taxed.

Tariff, Ad Valorem A tariff determined as a percentage of the value of goods clearing customs.

Warehouse Receipt A listing issued by a warehouse indicating goods have been received for storage.

280 EXPORT PROFITS

Foreign Economic Trends (FETs), 28
Foreign exchange risk, 128–129
Foreign sales corporations (FSCs), 3–4
Foreign trade organizations (FTOs), 64–65
Foreign Traders Index (FTI), 90
Franchising, 66
Free Alongside Ship (FAS), 115
Free Carrier, 115
Freight forwarders, 7, 31, cost of, 105, information needed by, 107, selection of, 106–107, services of, 104–105
FTA (Free Trade Agreement), 15
Funding, sources of, 13–14

GATT (General Agreement on Tariffs and Trade), 16, intellectual property rights, 55, Uruguay Round, 55
GATT Inquiry Point, 17
Global Translations, 86
GLOBAL Vantage, 38
Goods classification, 22
Government regulations, 52–53
Growth, 8
Guide to Agencies Providing Foreign Credit Information, 127
Guide to Canadian Manufacturers, 33–34
Guide to Drafting International Distributorship Agreements, 78
Guide to Incoterms, 115

Hazardous materials, 114
Hedging, 129
How to Find Information on Foreign Firms, 72
HS (Harmonized System of Tariff Classification), 15, 22, 97

Incoterms, 115
Incoterms 1990, 115
Indirect export vs. direct export, 57–58

Information, government sources of, 25–29, nongovernment sources of, 30–35, publications, 32–35. *See also* Appendix, Published Sources of Information
Insurance, 127–128
Intellectual property, 55–56
Intermediaries, 69–72
International Directory of Corporate Affiliations, 34
International Marketing Handbook, 34
International Trade Administration (ITA), 5, 6, 17, 52, publications, 28–29
Invoice, pro forma, 97–98, sample, 99

Japan External Trade Organization (JETRO), 32, 71
Japan Trade Directory, 34
Jobbers, 69
Joint business ventures, 67–68
Journal of Commerce, 43, 76

Key Officers in Foreign Service Posts, 74
Korean Trade Promotion Center (KOTRA), 71

Legal conditions, 37, 52–53
Letter of credit, 121–123, payment sequence, 122, variations of, 122–123
Licensing, 65–66

Mailing lists, 90–91
Mail List, 91
Major Companies of the Far East, 34
Marine insurance, 128
Market entry channels, 65–66
Marketing channels, 57–58, types of, 59–60
Market presence channels, 67–68
Markets and marketing, channels: selection, 57–58, climate, 36,

Notes

Notes

Notes

Notes

Notes

Notes

Notes

Notes